AF560062

REDLINES REDRAWN

REDLINES REDRAWN

OPERATION SINDOOR AND INDIA'S NEW NORMAL

MAJ GEN BIPIN BAKSHI | AIR MSHL RAJESH KUMAR
AMB ANIL TRIGUNAYAT | BRIG AKHELESH BHARGAVA

Konark Publishers Pvt. Ltd
206, First Floor
Peacock Lane, Shahpur Jat
New Delhi - 110 049
+91-11-4105 5065
india@konarkpublishers.com, us@konarkpublishers.com
www.konarkpublishers.com

Copyright © Bipin Bakshi, Rajesh Kumar, Anil Trigunayat, and Akhelesh Bhargava, 2026

All rights reserved. No part of this book may be reproduced or utilised in any form or by any means, electronic or mechanical, including photocopying, recording, or by any information storage and retrieval system, without prior written permission from the authors or the publisher. The views and opinions expressed in this book are solely those of the authors. While the accuracy of the facts, as reported by the authors, has been verified to the fullest extent possible, the publisher is not liable in any way for the content.

Disclaimer: This publication is an account based on the data collected from various sources including open domain. Attributability for the contents lies purely with the authors.

ISBN: 978-81-993018-2-5

Edited by Preeta Priyamvada

Jacket design by Sourish Mitra

Typeset by Saanvi Graphics, Noida

Printed and bound in India by Thomson Press India Private Limited

Endorsements

"An essential and detailed chronicle of India's emphatic response to Pakistan's terror machine. This is a story that needs to be told and retold. The book is fact based and clinical in documenting Operation Sindoor, and the planning that went into it. It also brings out details of platforms used and the efficacy of Indian military planning in meeting the political objectives set for them by the Indian leadership. A commendable effort."

—Amb Pankaj Saran
Convenor NatStrat, Member NSAB and former Deputy NSA

"An extremely timely analysis on a subject that has touched an emotional chord in the hearts of all citizens of our country. India has shown firm resolve in tackling the scourge of terrorism and as the book highlights, we will not shy away from hitting where it hurts, something that had been advocated for long, but put into effect only now, as a part of Op Sindoor."

—Gen (Dr) M.M. Naravane PVSM, AVSM, VSM, SM, Retd
Former Chief of Army Staff

"This book has to be listed as part of essential reading for anyone who wants to understand not just the backdrop or the details of Operation Sindoor, but also the trajectory of our future policy. The book brings out why the Operation is one of those rare watershed moments that shape history, and offers some very grounded recommendations on the way forward. That in particular makes it a remarkable book, written with considerable acumen."

—Ms Tara Kartha
Director (R&A) CLAWS and former Director, NSCS

"An anatomical account of a very critical event in the country's recent history. Written in an inimitable style that will pull in readers from the word 'go'."

—Sudeep Lakhtakia
Former Director General, National Security Guard

"I strongly commend this book on Op SINDOOR. It draws viewpoints from various domains, yet fuses and integrates them into a wholesome policy piece. The insights are unique as are the nuances deep. A veritable strategy document for the Post-Sindoor era."

—Lt Gen Raj Shukla PVSM, YSM, SM, Retd
Member UPSC and former Army Commander

"A timely, comprehensive and fact-based study that dissects the pattern of Pakistan's proxy war and substantiates it with ample data. The study uniquely takes you through the chilling journey of the Pahalgam attack and the multi-pronged myriad nuances of Operation Sindoor. The book provides an in-depth assessment of India's resolve and military preparedness to respond to Pakistan's acts of terror and future conflicts. A commendable effort, which is a must-read for all."

—Dr Shalini Chawla
Distinguished Fellow Centre for Aerospace Power and Strategic Studies, New Delhi

---

"A comprehensive yet concise narrative of Operation Sindoor based on detailed research and facts. Demonstrates India's Strategic Resolve to raise the costs and consequences for Pakistan sponsored and perpetuated terror war. A must read book for all."

—Lt Gen Vinod Bhatia, PVSM, AVSM, SM, Retd
Former DGMO and Director, Centre for Joint Warfare Studies

"The authors, with decades of experience, share a remarkable step-by-step analysis of the events pre and post Op Sindoor. With masterful insights, this timely, data driven narration of events from varied sources is indeed valuable. I recommend this simplistic narration to the younger generation for a better grasp and understanding."

—Vice Admiral A.B. Singh, PVSM, AVSM, VSM
Former Commander-in-Chief, Western Naval Command and Eastern Naval Command

---

"The book contains deep insights and perspectives on multiple dimensions of Op Sindoor. It provides a lucid overview of the operational construct and application of Indian military power against an adversary that holds modern weapon systems as a testbed for China.

A must read for all students of contemporary military studies."

—Lt Gen Amardeep Singh Bhinder
Ex General Officer Commanding-in-Chief,
Southwest Command

Contents

Tables, Figures, and Photographs

Tables

Figures

Photographs

Preface

India's Operation Sindoor, carried out with the fierceness of a lion's roar in the Indian subcontinent in May 2025, saw the country shoot into prominence, once again, as an emerging superpower on the global stage. I was reminded of the cover page of *The Time* magazine in the wake of the Maldives Operation of November 1988 by the Indian Armed Forces. Titled "India, The Awakening of an Asian Power", the cover story mentioned that the operation was but the latest indicator that the "sleepy giant of the subcontinent" is determinedly transforming itself into a "regional superpower". Being on the staff of the Parachute Brigade in 1989–93, I assisted our commander, Brigadier FFC Bulsara, in documenting and presenting the details, giving me an insight into the international intervention operation. Well, "the Lion" has awakened, I thought to myself, remembering that operation and its subsequent discussions.

The Indian response to the grave provocation by Pakistan's deep state, which carried out a dastardly terrorist attack at Pahalgam, Kashmir, on 22 April 2025, has been widely acclaimed as proportionate, measured, and effective. However, the discussion on whether this will result in a permanent or temporary setback to the terror factory in Pakistan, universally recognised as the global epicentre of terror, commenced in strategic circles even before the operations were paused on 10 May 2025.

Operation Sindoor may well turn out to be a defining moment in history. Just as the defeat of the Mughals in the Battle of Saraighat in 1671 became their culmination point, when the Ahom General, Lachit Borphukan, halted the Mughals' further Eastward expansion into Assam, Op Sindoor could become a similar tipping point, with India writing a new playbook on the security paradigm in the Indo-Pacific region in general and the Indian subcontinent in particular.

The parallel with the Battle of Saraighat came rapidly to my mind as Operation Sindoor progressed, due to my close personal connect with sailing in that region, for which my NCC Directorate earned a mention in the Limca Book of Records 2020. The Ahoms and Mughals had fought a naval battle, where sailing vessels of the Ahom Navy, launching from Biswanath Chairali, defeated the Mughal Navy in 1671. Our sailing expedition, in 2019, named Lachit-I, mirrored the same route, commencing from the same base, Biswanath Chairali, and terminating at Saraighat, next to Guwahati, where it was flagged in by Shri Sarbananda Sonowal, the then Chief Minister of Assam, on 28 October 2019, after completing 220 km sailing on the mighty Brahmaputra over 10 days from 20 October 2019 onwards. Correlating Operation Sindoor to the Battle of Saraighat, therefore, came naturally to my mind.

Even as the guns fell silent on both sides of the India–Pakistan border, I was approached by Mr KPR Nair, Founder and Managing Director of Konark Publishers Pvt. Ltd, to explore the possibility of writing a book on Operation Sindoor. Our conversation was invigorating, and it became clear that this would be a project fuelled as much by passion as by academic inquiry. From the outset, we agreed that the book must bring in the views of recognised domain experts who could illuminate critical dimensions of the conflict, including diplomacy, escalation dynamics, narrative warfare, aviation, and air defence. I was fortunate to receive the generous support of Air Marshal Rajesh Kumar, Ambassador Anil Trigunayat, and Brigadier Akhelesh Bhargava, each of whom brought invaluable depth from their respective fields. I remain deeply grateful to them, as well as to Konark Publishers, for embracing this endeavour in its entirety and ensuring its timely completion.

This book meticulously documents **Operation Sindoor,** offering a comprehensive record of the events that led to the conflict, the execution of military operations, and its profound future impact on regional security. The study also makes some recommendations relating to our preparedness and security apparatus for handling future conflict situations.

The book begins with an elucidation of the background, in Chapter 1, that establishes the crucial context: Pakistan's long-standing proxy war against India, with a specific focus on Kashmir. This backdrop sets the stage for Chapter 2, which details the Pahalgam attack of April 2025 and the initial investigations following the incident. Following this, Chapter 3 provides an operational narrative of Operation Sindoor, outlining India's diplomatic and military actions taken in the aftermath of the Pahalgam attack. Here the authors also chronicle the maritime and cyber dimensions of the conflict.

The subsequent two chapters, Chapters 4 and 5, delve into the specifics of military operations. They cover land and air operations, including critical aspects of logistics, technological advancements, maintenance, and self-reliance. Chapter 4 also explores how hostilities teetered on the brink of escalation and, ultimately, how the cessation of hostilities was announced. It further addresses the pivotal role of space-based assets and the nuclear dimension of Operation Sindoor. Chapter 5 elaborates how seven terror camps were destroyed by the Indian Army on 7 May 2025 and explains the mechanics of the Air Defence Battle over the Indian skies in considerable detail. It also covers the intense action in the Rajauri-

Baramulla sectors where heavy degradation of Pakistani positions was carried out by the Indian Army.

Chapter 6 expands on the conflict's broader implications, examining its diplomatic and information dimensions. It also details India's actions concerning the Indus Waters Treaty. The involvement of USA, Türkiye, Azerbaijan, and China, alongside the pervasive misinformation campaigns and the apparent bias of some media outlets in favouring Pakistan's narrative over India's, is also examined there.

Chapter 7 assesses the overarching impact of Operation Sindoor, the "New Normal" in India's strategy calculus with inputs pertaining to the escalatory ladder, and implications for national security. Finally, in the last chapter, while summarising the conclusions and recommendations, the impact of Operation Sindoor on Pakistan's approach to their India policy is explored and the evolution of India's military doctrine, Cold Start to Dynamic Response, is outlined.

While some of the facts in the book have been obtained through interaction with serving military officials, the opinions and analysis expressed are those of the authors and do not reflect the official positions or views of the government. None of the ideas expressed in this volume should be construed as representing the individual views of any of the individual authors. The collection is a collaborative effort, and the authors have attempted to present the issues as objectively as possible, without introducing the subjective opinions of any agency about them.

Our team of authors acknowledge the encouragement we have received from the Government and Armed Forces representatives who met us or gave us answers to our questions about the operations to the extent they could provide. These include General Anil Chauhan, Chief of Defence Staff, Indian Armed Forces; Ambassador Pankaj Saran, Convenor NatStrat, and member, National Security Advisory Board; Major General Sandeep S Sharda, ADG Strategic Communication, Indian Army; Army Air

Defence Directorate, Media and Public Information Cell, Indian Navy; and officials from the Indian Air Force.

My gratitude also extends to Ms Preeta Priyamvada, our meticulous editor, whose sharp eye and thoughtful suggestions greatly enhanced both the clarity and precision of the text. I also wish to acknowledge Ms Rekha Dixit and Ms Vranda Sharma, whose contributions in curating the content were of great assistance, as well as many other friends who supported this journey in various ways. Above all, I owe a special debt to my wife, Anita, whose inspiration and unwavering encouragement sustained me throughout this challenging endeavour.

The co-authors of this book join me in saluting the armed forces personnel, political leadership, diplomats, scientists, government officers, and the defence industry for their resolute efforts made towards securing our nation in this recent conflict with Pakistan. We are conscious of the increasing challenges we face as our proud nation takes great strides in progress on multiple fronts, and we recognize the need for collective effort and informed dialogue to navigate them effectively. We hope this book provides our readers with both information about Operation Sindoor and food for thought for the future.

Jai Hind!

Maj Gen (Dr) Bipin Bakshi, AVSM, VSM, Retd
Distinguished Fellow
Centre for Land Warfare Studies
New Delhi

Foreword

It is a privilege to pen this foreword for an outstanding collaborative work authored by Major General Bipin Bakshi (Retd), Brigadier Akhelesh Bhargava (Retd), Air Marshal Rajesh Kumar (Retd) and Ambassador Anil Trigunayat. This volume stands as a testament to the spirit of jointness and **'Whole of Nation Approach'** that underpins Indian Army's architecture in this **Decade of Transformation.**

Operation SINDOOR captures a defining chapter in India's strategic evolution. It reflects the confluence of military precision, diplomatic foresight and technological innovation. As the Indian Army advances confidently through the **Decade of Transformation,** the themes explored in this book resonate deeply with our ongoing efforts to harness information, technology and strategy as instruments of comprehensive national power.

The authors, each bringing a unique professional expertise, have woven a compelling narrative that highlights not only operational acumen but also the evolving philosophy of **integrated national security**. Their work underscores the importance of **aligning military capability, technological advancement and diplomatic outreach** to safeguard India's sovereignty and promote stability in the region.

I commend the authors for their clarity, depth and vision. Their work is a timely contribution to India's growing body of strategic thought and a reminder that transformation, when guided by purpose and unity, is our greatest strength.

May this book contribute to a broader understanding of India's contemporary security challenges and future trajectory of its defence preparedness. Let it also stand as a tribute to the courage, sacrifice and professionalism of the Indian Armed Forces, who serve and protect our beloved nation with unwavering dedication.

'Jai Hind'

(Upendra Dwivedi)
General
Chief of the Army Staff

1

State-Sponsored Terror

A Prelude

MAJOR GENERAL BIPIN BAKSHI

> *"The ISI was quite convinced that what they had done to the Soviets in Afghanistan, they could do to India in Kashmir, using the same instruments—Islamic Militants, recruited from Pakistan as well as the larger Muslim World."*
>
> —ANATOL LIEVEN[1]

On 22 April 2025, Pakistan-based terrorist organisations orchestrated a devastating terrorist attack at Pahalgam in Kashmir, resulting in the tragic loss of 26 innocent tourists. India responded decisively, launching Operation Sindoor on 7 May 2025, targeting nine terrorist strongholds in Pakistan and Pakistan-occupied Jammu and Kashmir (POJK). India's strikes meticulously avoided civilian and military targets, focusing solely on terrorist infrastructure. In retaliation, Pakistan launched attacks on Indian civilian and military targets over the next three days, prompting India to escalate its attack by striking Pakistani military targets until 10 May 2025, when Pakistan's Director General of Military Operations (DGMO) called his counterpart in India, at 15:35 hours Indian Standard Time (IST), and it was "agreed between them that both sides would stop all firing and military action on land and in the air and sea" with effect from 17:00 hours IST, the same day.

On 12 May 2025, in another DGMO level interaction, it was further clarified that "as far as the continuation of the break in hostilities are concerned, there is no expiry date to it" and both sides "reiterated their commitment to avoid aggressive and inimical actions, including refraining from firing a single shot at each other", thus considering "immediate steps to reduce troop deployments in border and forward areas". This reflected a broader attempt to de-escalate tensions and implying a longer-term commitment to peace.

As the dust settled on this operation, the authors undertook the project to pen down this volume. The Pahalgam attack is not the first proxy war terrorist action against India from across the border. This introduction thus seeks to set the context for the study, as also, to analyse the motivations behind Pakistan's actions, providing a backdrop for understanding India's response and the broader implications of the conflict.

Background: Terrorism and the Proxy War in Kashmir

Terrorism in Jammu and Kashmir (J&K) was initiated by Pakistan in the late 1980s leveraging the armed Jihad (1979–1989) waged against Soviet forces in Afghanistan[2] not only by Afghan mujahideen but also radical Islamists drawn from countries around the world. Following the Soviet withdrawal in 1989, these mercenaries, comprising the battle-hardened fighters from Afghanistan, Sudan, Chechnya, and different parts of Pakistan, were redirected to Kashmir, a fact that was noted in the BBC report (refer Endnote 2), which mentions "the arrival in the valley of Kashmir of large numbers of Islamic 'Jihadi' fighters who had fought in Afghanistan against the Soviet Union in the 1980s". The absence of a border fence at that time, along the Line of Control (LC), facilitated large-scale infiltration, with groups carrying substantial arms, ammunition, and explosives. Data from the South Asia Terrorism Portal (SATP) indicates a sharp rise in terrorist incidents from 1989 to 1994.

Figure 1.1: Decline of terrorist incidents in J&K

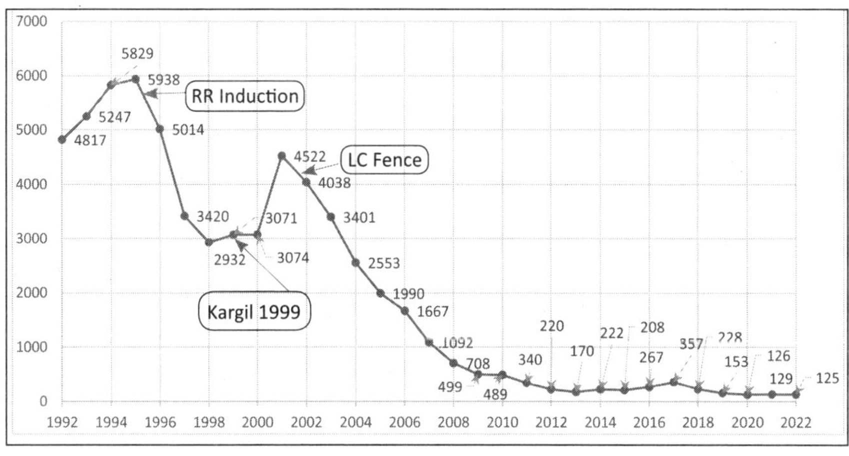

Source: Data from MHA Annual Reports.

The Indian response was robust, with the deployment of an additional Army division in the early 1990s and the establishment of the Rashtriya Rifles from 1995, which significantly curbed this surge. By 1998, terrorist incidents had declined to 614 annually, a 47% reduction from the peak. The combined efforts of the Indian Army, Rashtriya Rifles, and local police disrupted the operations of foreign militants, who were found in large numbers during this period (see Table 1A.1). These foreign militants were originally trained for fighting the Soviets in Afghanistan, having arrived in Pakistan from places as far away as Sudan and Chechenya. This phenomenon of inducting global mercenaries into Kashmir could not have been perpetrated without active logistic and material support by Pakistan. They were extremely well trained and highly radicalised, notoriously ferocious fighters who never surrendered even when outnumbered, fighting to the end, last man, last bullet. Indian forces combatting these terrorists found a marked difference in their operational tactics compared to the local terrorists who were fewer in number and not prone to such fanatic fighting. The figures detailed in Table 1A.1 tell us that there were 1252 foreign fighters killed and 110 arrested between 1990 and 1999, giving a clear picture that terrorism in Kashmir remained an externally driven phenomenon, contrary to Pakistan's narrative of an indigenous uprising.

Against this backdrop, Pakistan was desperate to destabilise Kashmir, which was clearly visible during the 1999 Kargil intrusions. That was a calculated move by Pakistan to divert the Indian forces from counter-terrorist operations in J&K and scotch India's peace initiative, the famous Lahore Bus Journey by Prime Minister Atal Bihari Vajpayee in February 1999. The Kargil conflict temporarily increased terrorist incidents; Indian troops were redeployed to Ladakh. However, with a swift victory in Kargil, India renewed the focus on operations in Kashmir, and it was at this time that the need for a formidable fence along the Indian defensive line was felt.

The construction of the LC fence, initiated in 2002 and operationalised by 2003, marked a significant turning point. Infiltration of foreign terrorists dropped significantly, with South Asia Terrorism Portal (SATP) data showing a 68% reduction in terrorist-related fatalities between 2002 (2,014 deaths) and 2007 (777 deaths). This fence, coupled with concerted efforts to restore normalcy through elections and governance reforms, further eroded the terror momentum. By 2010, terrorist incidents had plummeted to 489, reflecting a 90% decline from the peak. Pakistan's attempts to revive militancy through tactics like kidnapping foreign tourists (see Table 1B.1) failed to regain the intensity of the early 1990s, as local populations increasingly distanced themselves from externally sponsored violence.

The 1999 IC 814 hijacking had already exposed Pakistan's role in terrorism. The Indian Airlines flight, from Kathmandu to Delhi, was hijacked by Harkat-ul-Mujahideen. It had 190 occupants: 179 passengers and 11 crew members. After tense in-flight moments and diversions, it was made to land at Kandahar in Afghanistan, where the Taliban facilitated the release of three high-profile terrorists, including Masood Azhar, who later founded Jaish-e-Mohammed (JeM). Little wonder then that the hijackers as well as the released terrorists got a free pass by Taliban up to the Pakistan border. This incident, coupled with the 2001 Parliament attack (when terrorists attempted to enter the Indian Parliament building with weapons to kill the parliamentarians) attributed to JeM and Lashkar-e-Taiba (LeT), underscored Pakistan's use of terrorism as a state policy. The global spotlight on Pakistan's duplicity intensified post-9/11, with a 2004 Congressional Research Service report highlighting links between Pakistani extremist groups and Kashmiri militancy: "President Musharraf has taken steps to crack down on indigenous Pakistani extremist groups. Many of these groups have links not only to individuals and organizations actively fighting in Afghanistan and Pakistan, but also with groups that continue to pursue a violent separatist campaign in the disputed Kashmir region along Pakistan's northeast frontier".[3] Former Pakistani President Pervez Musharraf admitted in a 2010 Spiegel Online International interview to fostering militant groups to pressure India on Kashmir, stating, "They were indeed formed. The government turned a blind eye because they wanted India to discuss Kashmir".[4] Excerpts from the interview:

> SPIEGEL: Why did you form militant underground groups to fight India in Kashmir?
>
> Musharraf: They were indeed formed. The government turned a blind eye because they wanted India to discuss Kashmir.

> SPIEGEL: It was the Pakistani security forces that trained them.
>
> Musharraf: The West was ignoring the resolution of the Kashmir issue, which is the core issue of Pakistan. We expected the West—especially the United States and important countries like Germany—to resolve the Kashmir issue. Has Germany done that?

As seen above, with the swift Indian victory in Kargil and the subsequent construction of the LC fence, there was a significant downward trend in violence by 2007. The drop in violence levels was due to external factors inhibiting Pakistan's open support to terrorism, reduction in the Afghanistan-returned foreign terrorists, as well as the concerted efforts by Indian forces to restore normalcy. In the first decade of this century, we thus saw a marked decline in the terrorism markers, with the consistent normalisation of the internal democratic process through holding of regular elections, and a lack of local support, which prevented a revival of the militancy.

Despite the marked fall in terrorist successes in Kashmir, the Pakistan Army and the ISI have continued their efforts to reverse the falling trends, and consistently failed in their attempt. They are obsessed with their unreasonable goal of wresting Kashmir from India to avenge their failure in East Pakistan in 1971, the creation of Bangladesh, and the humiliating military defeat that they suffered. The Pakistan Army's motivations are thus rooted in their thousand cuts doctrine to bleed India, and the rallying of nationalistic fervour against India as the single unifying force.

Pakistan's infamous "a thousand cuts" military doctrine is credited to its former President, General Zia-ul-Haq.[5] It entails bleeding India with multiple minor strikes. Pakistan's crushing defeat in the 1971 war made it realise that instead of engaging in a conventional war with India, where its chances of victory were slim, it could instead destabilise its foe with repeated militant strikes, and rustle up unrest in India by trying to create a communal rift. Zia's implementation of this doctrine has its genesis in Zulfiqar Ali Bhutto's announcement of launching a 1,000-year war against India. Bhutto made this statement on the floor of the United Nations Security Council on 22 September 1965 as the Foreign Minister in Ayub Khan's cabinet, when he said, "We will wage a war for 1,000 years"[6] in the context of the Kashmir issue.

Although Muslims in India have also been victims of Pakistan's attacks, the communal fingerprint is visible in most of the Pakistani strikes. In Pahalgam, it was underlined in an unprecedented manner, with the victims being identified on the basis of religion.

The Inter-Services Intelligence (ISI) and Pakistan Army view Kashmir as a means to maintain domestic political dominance. It is a well-known fact that the Pakistan Army has usurped all major power and controls various facets of both governance and economy, sidelining the civilian officials. US President Donald Trump's recent lunch invite to Pakistan's Army Chief Asim Munir only confirms this fact. Therefore, the voices raised in Pakistan calling for secession of Kashmir gain greater stridency whenever there are internal problems faced by the Pakistan Army. Despite declining militancy, Pakistan persists in sponsoring terrorism to keep the Kashmir issue alive. Accordingly, they have tried to up the ante by orchestrating a few isolated incidents in the last 10 years, namely, the Pathankot and Uri attacks in 2016 and the Pulwama attack in 2019, all of which were specifically targeted against Indian security forces.

The most recent major marker after the LC fencing and the elections in Jammu and Kashmir was the amendment of Article 370 in August 2019, a few months after the Pulwama terror attack. Following this, Kashmir made unprecedented progress on all parameters of the economy, tourism, employment, and overall development, while incidents of terrorism and stone-pelting went down drastically. The data for stone-pelting incidents is as under:[7]

Table 1.1: Decline in stone-pelting incidents since 2010

Year/Period	Stone-pelting Incidents
2010	2,654
2016	2,653
2017	1,412
2018	1,458
2019	1,811
2020	222
2021	76
2022	20
2023	0

Source: Data from MHA Annual Reports.

The graph for the last seven years is as under:

Figure 1.2: Stone-pelting incidents in the past seven years

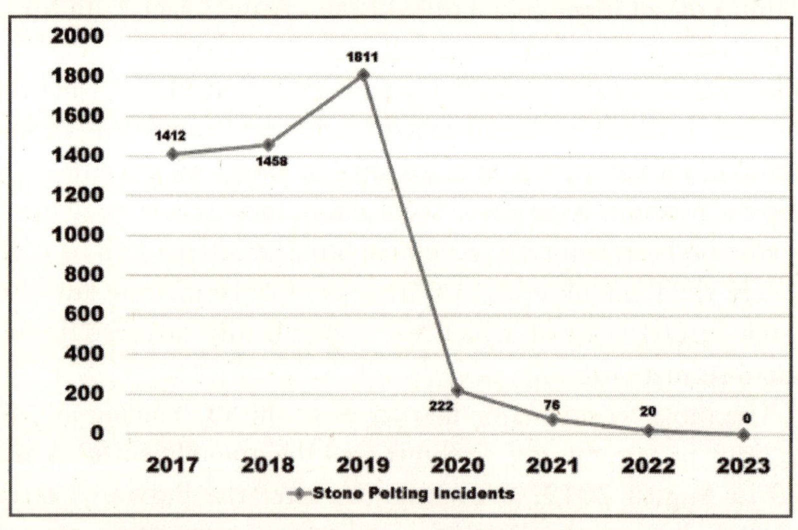

Source: Data from MHA Annual Reports.

After a gap of six years, however, Pakistan has now tried to upscale terror in J&K by orchestrating the Pahalgam attack. It is useful to take a look at the major terror incidents in J&K from the year 2000 onwards to put this attack in context.

Previous Terror Incidents

Pakistan's proxy war has manifested in a series of meticulously planned attacks, often timed to coincide with significant diplomatic events to maximise international attention. An expanded chronology of major incidents, with additional analysis and data, to highlight Pakistan's strategy since the valley-wide genocide of Kashmiri Pandits in 1989-90 is given below:

Table 1.2: Major terror incidents in J&K (2000–2024)

Year	Incident	Location	Description	Fatalities	Attribution/ Response
2000	Sikh Village Massacre	Chittisinghpura, Anantnag (J&K)	Militants killed 35 Sikh residents during the visit of US President Bill Clinton	35	Attributed to Lashkar-e-Taiba
2001	J&K Assembly Car Bombing	Srinagar	Jaish-e-Mohammed suicide attack targeting governance	38	Jaish-e-Mohammed
2001	Parliament Attack	Delhi	Attack on India's Parliament House	9	Jaish-e-Mohammed and Lashkar-e-Taiba

Year	Incident	Location	Description	Fatalities	Attribution/ Response
2002	Kaluchak Massacre	Jammu	Attack on a tourist bus and army camp	31	Lashkar-e-Taiba
2002	Akshardham Attack	Gandhinagar, Gujarat	Attack on Akshardham Temple; NSG responded overnight	31 (plus 3 responders)	Two terrorists killed; NSG response led by Gujarat CM Narendra Modi and Dy PM Advani
2008	Mumbai Attack (26/11)	Mumbai	Coordinated attacks by sea on hotels, stations, civilians; largest urban counter-terror operation	164	Lashkar-e-Taiba; Operation Black Tornado by NSG
2016	Pathankot Attack	Pathankot, Punjab	JeM terrorists stormed airbase; prolonged "search and destroy" mission	Lt Col Niranjan + others	Jaish-e-Mohammed; NSG's Dhangu Suraksha operation by NSG with Indian Air Force and Indian Army assistance

Year	Incident	Location	Description	Fatalities	Attribution/ Response
2016	Pampore Attack	Pampore (J&K)	Ambush on CRPF convoy	8	Lashkar-e-Taiba
2016	Uri Attack	Uri (J&K)	Attack on Army base; retaliated with surgical strikes	20	Indian Special Forces response by Surgical Strikes in POJK
2018	Sunjuwan Attack	Jammu	Terrorists attacked military camp	11	Lashkar-e-Taiba
2019	Pulwama Suicide Bombing	Pulwama (J&K)	Suicide bombing on CRPF convoy; deadliest attack on security forces in recent years	40	Retaliatory Balakot Air Strikes by India
2024	Reasi Attack	Reasi District (J&K)	Pilgrim bus targeted; attackers fired at survivors post-crash	9	Attribution not detailed; severe civilian casualties

Source: Author's compilation.

A comprehensive description of the aforementioned incidents is presented below:

- **2000 Sikh Village Massacre:** In a heinous attack, militants killed 35 Sikh residents of a Sikh village, Chittisinghpura, in Anantnag District. The atrocity was attributed to Lashkar-e-

Taiba, wherein they mercilessly killed all residents including women and children, and the timing was connected to the visit of Mr Bill Clinton, the then US President. This was the only incident against the vibrant Sikh community of Kashmir who live in harmony with all other communities in Kashmir.

- **2001 J&K Assembly Car Bombing:** A suicide attack by Jaish-e-Mohammed terrorists targeting regional governance, the car bomb at Srinagar claimed 38 lives.
- **2001 Parliament Attack:** An audacious assault on India's democratic heart, the Parliament House at Delhi, resulting in nine fatalities. This was attributed to Jaish-e-Mohammed and Lashkar-e-Taiba, both Pakistan-based terrorist groups.
- **2002 Kaluchak Massacre:** Thirty-one lives were lost in an attack by Lashkar-e-Taiba terrorists on a tourist bus and Army camp at Kaluchak in J&K.
- **2002 Akshardham Attack:** On 24 September 2002, two terrorists attacked the Akshardham Temple in Gandhinagar, Gujarat, a cultural landmark, killing 31 devotees. The then Gujarat Chief Minister Shri Narendra Modi called the Deputy Prime Minister Shri L K Advani and asked for NSG to manage the situation. The NSG commandos reached Akshardham by 22:10 hours and began their operations by 23:30 hours, neutralising the terrorists by 06:45 hours the next day. Two NSG Commandos and one state police officer were martyred in this attack.[8]
- **2008 Mumbai Attack:** In a horrific attack, 164 civilians were killed in a wanton bloodbath that sent shockwaves through the world. The Lashkar-e-Taiba (LeT) terrorists came from Pakistan, by sea, landed in Mumbai and attacked civilians at hotels, railway stations, and houses on the night of 26 November 2008. The National Security Guard (NSG) elite counter terrorist unit, 51 Special Action Group (51 SAG) was

flown in from Manesar, near Delhi, and the unit commenced operations to neutralise the terrorists around 08:00 hours on the following day. Operation Black Tornado, as it came to be known, was one of the largest and most complex urban counter-terrorism operations that the NSG had undertaken. The NSG commandos had to engage multiple venues simultaneously,[9] including slithering down at one location using helicopters of the Indian Air Force. Pakistan continued to deny any involvement in the attack till irrefutable proof was provided through multiple means, conclusively linking the attack to Pakistan.

- **2016 Pathankot Attack:** On 2 January 2016, heavily armed men of Pakistan-based Jaish-e-Mohammed (JeM) stormed the Pathankot airbase and opened indiscriminate fire at the security personnel.[10] The NSG had been mobilised by air to Pathankot based on intelligence inputs of an impending attack in the vicinity of Pathankot. The commandos immediately launched a "search and destroy" operation codenamed *Dhangu Suraksha*.[11] The operation was extended till late night on 4 January 2016 due to the thick foliage, vastness of the area and lack of cover. All the terrorists who carried out the attack were neutralised by the NSG, and one braveheart Lt Col Niranjan EK[12] laid down his life in the operation.[13] A graphic novel by the author of this chapter has illustrated this operation.[14] Pakistan again denied any involvement in the attack and when an impartial joint investigation was suggested, they refused to respond.
- **2016 Pampore Attack:** Eight CRPF personnel were killed during an ambush on a CRPF convoy by Lashkar-e-Taiba militants.
- **2016 Uri Attack:** A brazen strike on an Indian Army base, this caused 20 fatalities. This was responded to by the

ground assault on terrorist launch pads, using Indian Special Forces, causing large loss of life and destruction of terrorist locations in POJK.

- **2018 Sunjuwan Attack:** This was an assault on a military camp, which led to 11 fatalities.
- **2019 Pulwama Suicide Bombing:** One of the deadliest attacks on Indian security forces, which claimed 40 lives. Balakot Air Strikes was India's response to this attack.
- **2024 Reasi Attack:** A tragic terrorist attack struck Reasi district in Jammu and Kashmir, India, targeting a bus carrying Hindu pilgrims from the Shiv Khori cave to Katra. The driver, hit by gunfire, lost control, causing the bus to plunge into a deep gorge. The attackers continued shooting at the wreckage for about 20 minutes, killing nine people, including a two-year-old and a 14-year-old, and injuring 41 others.

Correlation with International Visits

The pattern of timing the attacks with high-profile diplomatic events is a deliberate Pakistani strategy to amplify global attention and pressure India. Examples include:

- **2000 Chittisinghpura Massacre:** US President Bill Clinton's visit (21–25 March 2000).
- **2002 Kaluchak Massacre:** US Assistant Secretary of State Christina B. Rocca's visit (14 May 2002).
- **2016 Pathankot Air Base Attack:** PM Shri Narendra Modi had visited Afghanistan on 25 December 2015 to inaugurate the new Afghan Parliament building. He stopped over for a friendly visit in Pakistan on return, and a few days later the Pathankot attack took place.

- **2018 Sunjuwan Attack (10–11 February 2018):** PM Modi was visiting Palestine, UAE, and Oman (9–12 February 2018). The attack was possibly specially planned as these were all Middle East nations who were earlier sympathetic to Pakistan, but Indian diplomacy was causing a shift in perception across the world.
- **2024 Reasi Attack:** Connected to the presence of foreign dignitaries during PM Modi's oath-taking ceremony (9 June 2024).
- **2025 Pahalgam Attack:** Visit of foreign dignitaries, including Mr Vance (22 April 2025).

The staggering human cost of Pakistan's proxy war in Jammu and Kashmir, as reported by India's Ministry of Home Affairs from 1990 to 2025, underscores the scale and persistence of this conflict. Over 19,000 civilians and 6,500 security personnel have lost their lives, while the Indian forces have neutralised more than 29,000 terrorists during this period. These figures reflect not only the tragic toll of sustained violence but also Pakistan's continued use of terrorism as a strategic tool against India—a low-cost tactic that has exacted an immeasurable cost on Indian society.

Table 1.3: Trends of terrorist violence

S.N.	Year	Civilians Killed	Security Forces Personnel Killed	Terrorists Killed
1	1990 – 2005	15206	4784	21459
2	2005 – 2014	2342	903	4207
3	2014 – 2019	780	524	2192
4	2019 – 2025	691	315	1493
5	**Total**	**19019**	**6526**	**29351**

Source: Data from MHA Annual Reports.

For decades, the perpetrators of these attacks operated with impunity, facing no significant punitive consequences. This status quo held until 2016, when India initiated the Surgical Strikes—its first direct kinetic response—marking a decisive shift in the country's posture toward cross-border terrorism and redefining its approach to deterrence.

It is noteworthy that every significant dip in terrorist activity in Jammu and Kashmir has been followed by a conspicuous spike in high-profile attacks, seemingly orchestrated to reignite instability and international attention. Pakistan, perceiving a steady normalisation in the region, has recurrently resorted to brutal spectacles of violence as a means to sustain the relevance of the conflict and to undermine India's stabilising efforts.

This cycle of desperation and disruption has punctuated India's counterterrorism trajectory, with each act marked by increasing brazenness. The pattern continued until the 2025 Pahalgam attack, yet another grim reminder of the extent to which Pakistan is willing to escalate in order to prolong a proxy war that India has persistently worked to contain.

Recent Developments Preceding the Pahalgam Attack

Kashmir's trajectory toward stability has been remarkable. The revocation of Article 370 in 2019, coupled with governance reforms under the Union Territory administration, has spurred economic growth. The J&K Economic Survey 2024-25 reports[15] investments of Rs 5,319 crore between 2019 and 2024, with tourism surging from 1,650 foreign visitors in 2021 to a much higher figure of 65,452 in 2024.[16] Infrastructure projects, including the Katra-Srinagar rail link and all-weather roads, have integrated J&K with India, boosting economic and social cohesion. Several initiatives have been taken to enhance investments in various industries like handlooms, handicrafts, wool processing and other industries, resulting in substantial increase of investments.

Kashmir is steadily progressing to regain its former glory as a multicultural, secular haven. Governance has improved under the Union Territory administration leading to rail connectivity across the Pir Panjal Ranges and stable security environment, accelerating economic development and drawing larger number of tourists to J&K, as indicated by the figures above.

Table 1.4: Rising tourism and investment figures in Kashmir in the past five years

Year	Tourists Visiting Kashmir Valley
2021	6,65,777
2022	26,73,442
2023	31,55,835
2024	34,98,702
Total 2021-2024	**99,93,756**

Year	Amount of Investment (in Rs Crore)
2019-20	296.64
2020-21	412.74
2021-22	376.76
2022-23	2153.00
2023-2024 up to October 2023	2079.76

Source: Data from MHA Annual Reports.

With the completion of the Katra–Srinagar rail link and the development of new roads and tunnels providing all-weather, year-round connectivity between Kashmir, Ladakh, and the Indian heartland, the region is becoming more deeply and irreversibly integrated with India. These infrastructure advances, along with marked improvements across multiple indicators, have reinforced this trajectory of progress. Predictably, this has provoked alarm within Pakistan's deep state and activated the ISI and Pakistan-based terrorist outfits, having deep nexus between them. The Army in Pakistan, the institution wielding real power in the country, has long viewed such development as a threat to its strategic objectives.

Their reactions, often manifesting as acts of desperation, follow a familiar and recurring pattern.

While India, and Kashmir in particular, continue to make steady strides in governance, connectivity, and development, Pakistan remains mired in persistent economic and political turmoil. The debt burden from the China-Pakistan Economic Corridor (CPEC) has grown unsustainably, even as revenue shortfalls widen. Recurring IMF bailouts have become indispensable, and Pakistan's financial apparatus remains under intense scrutiny, especially following its inclusion on the Financial Action Task Force (FATF) Grey List from 2018 to 2022 due to concerns over terror financing. Even earlier Pakistan was on the Grey List several times. The first listing in February 2008, lasted 848 days; the second, in February 2012, ran for 1,106 days; and the third, beginning June 2018, dragged on for 1,576 days. While Pakistan managed to escape the scrutiny each time with all kinds of assurances, their terror finance machinery survived and morphed into new areas like dark web and crypto currency. UNODC, accordingly, recognised this threat and conducted a workshop in Karachi on 9-10 October 2023, which served as "An Eye Opener"[17] for the world, as mentioned in the UN report published on 13 October 2023.[18]

At the internal level, Pakistan continues to grapple with entrenched challenges—chief among them the unrest in Balochistan. Since its contested accession to Pakistan in 1947,[19] the province has remained a locus of resistance, with the Balochistan Liberation Army (BLA) spearheading a protracted insurgency. In the year preceding the high-profile Jaffar Express attack in March 2025, the BLA executed over 150 violent operations against the Pakistan Army, signalling both organisational resilience and growing tactical sophistication.

One of the most dramatic incidents occurred on 11 March 2025, when the BLA hijacked the Jaffar Express, in what became the deadliest such event in Pakistan's history. According to the Inter-Services Public Relations (ISPR), 21 soldiers and 10 civilians were killed.[20] However, Baloch fighters claimed a higher toll, asserting that they had allowed women and children to exit safely while executing over 100 Pakistani male hostages during a two-day standoff—figures significantly exceeding official accounts. Apart from this, Tehreek-e-Taliban Pakistan (TTP), an Islamist militant group, has intensified its attacks on security forces since the return of the Taliban government in Afghanistan in a bid to install a Taliban-like government in Pakistan. There is simmering discontent in Sindh and Khyber Pakhtunkhwa threatening internal security as well.

In the face of all this, quite expectedly, Pakistan quickly blamed India for orchestrating the hijack and further alleged Afghan complicity in supporting the BLA. Both India and Afghanistan have categorically denied[21] these accusations, and called them as baseless. Nevertheless, Pakistan's military leadership issued strongly worded statements, explicitly naming India and vowing retaliatory measures.

General Asim Munir reaffirmed Islamabad's uncompromising stance on Kashmir, declaring it Pakistan's "jugular vein"[22] and vowing that it would never be forgotten, during a globally telecast address from Islamabad. The timing of this statement delivered on 15 April 2025 was notable, closely following the Jaffar Express train hijack.[23] This has prompted speculation among observers that the subsequent Pahalgam attack may have been an ill-conceived attempt at deflecting domestic embarrassment through external provocation, ostensibly to avenge the loss of life inflicted by Balochi separatist fighters on the non-Balochi males aboard the Jaffar Express. In fact, some experts like Indrani Bagchi of Aspen Centre have surmised that his anti-Hindu tirade in this rabble-rousing speech may have directly resulted in the Pahalgam Attack.[24] Further, even Pakistani media felt that the address carried a political, divisive, and troubling message—one that reinforced the military's ideological monopoly, suppressed democratic dissent, and distorted the foundational principles of Pakistan. Marvi Sirmed, in an episode of UNRAVELLED, discusses the military's long-standing manipulation of the Baloch insurgency, the mythmaking around the two-nation theory and Pakistan's secular foundations, among other issues.[25]

Figure 1.3: Pakistan Chief of Army Staff, General Asim Munir delivering what he called a Motivational Speech at a conclave of Overseas Pakistanis on 15 April 2025

Source: *APNLive.com*, 17 April 2025 and New Wave Global, *Friday Times*, 5 May 2025.

General Munir's rhetoric notably tried to revive the ideological underpinnings of the "Two-Nation Theory", emphasising the purportedly irreconcilable differences between Hindus and Muslims that led to the subcontinent's partition in 1947 and the creation of Pakistan. This invocation seemed aimed at reinforcing Pakistan's historical narrative and justifying its continued claims over Kashmir.

Meanwhile, Pakistan's internal security landscape remains deeply volatile. In addition to ongoing insurgent violence in Balochistan, the Pakistan Army faces mounting attacks in Khyber Pakhtunkhwa from the Tehreek-i-Taliban Pakistan (TTP). Simultaneously, the country is reeling from the political fallout of the ouster of former Prime Minister Imran Khan and grappling with a rapidly deteriorating economy. Against this canvas of huge unrest and instability, Kashmir's trajectory stands in stark contrast—marked by growing stability and developmental progress.

The Context and Contents of this Book

It is in the context of this complex backdrop, that the Pahalgam terrorist attack of April 2025, and India's calibrated response, must be examined, not as an isolated event but as part of a larger shift in the region's security architecture. The Indian Armed Forces' execution of Op Sindoor, marked by precise strikes on carefully chosen targets, signalled a decisive evolution in India's military doctrine and its response framework to cross-border terrorism.

As the conflict unfolded, Pakistan resorted, predictably, to nuclear sabre-rattling, briefly casting a shadow of escalation over the region. However, the swift cessation of hostilities was followed by a firm and unequivocal message from Prime Minister Modi emphasising that Pakistan must desist from future provocations or be prepared to face severe consequences. He explicitly warned against the use of terrorism under the cover of nuclear blackmail, signalling a fundamental redrawing of the deterrence threshold.

It is now clear that the regional security paradigm—extending beyond South Asia into the broader Indo-Pacific—has been significantly reshaped. India's posture in the aftermath of the Pahalgam attack reflects a new strategic template, one grounded in resolve, precision, and deterrence-by-punishment. The cumulative cost imposed on Pakistan for its sponsorship of cross-border terrorism, from the Uri strikes in 2016 to Op Sindoor in 2025, has reached an unprecedented level.

As strategic analysts and policymakers assess the contours of this "new playbook", a critical question emerges: How will Pakistan recalibrate its proxy war strategy in response to this evolving Indian doctrine? The answer may well define the trajectory of South Asian stability in the years to come.

Annexure 1A
Extract of Government of India Press Release

8 December 1999

Terrorism by Foreign Mercenaries in J&K

As per the information received from the State Government, a total of 110 foreign mercenaries has been arrested and 1252 killed in J&K during the period between 1 January 1990 to 31 October 1999 as per the country wise break up indicated in Table 1A.1.

Table 1A.1: Number of foreign mercenaries killed or arrested

S. No.	Name of Country	Number of Foreign Mercenaries Killed	Number of Foreign Mercenaries Arrested
1.	Pakistan/POJK	349	93
2.	Afghanistan	162	14
3.	Egypt	1	–
4.	Sudan	7	–
5.	Yemen	4	–
6.	Lebanon	–	1
7.	Bahrain	2	–
8.	Chechnya	1	–

S. No.	Name of Country	Number of Foreign Mercenaries Killed	Number of Foreign Mercenaries Arrested
9.	Bosnia	1	–
10.	England	–	1
11.	Tajikistan	–	1
12.	Others	725	–
	Total	**1252**	**110**

Note: This information was given by Shri Ch. Vidyasagar Rao, Minister of State for Home Affairs, in reply to a written question in Rajya Sabha by Shri Krishna Kumar Birla.

Pakistan actively redirected battle-hardened and highly radicalised foreign terrorists—originally indoctrinated as Mujahideen to fight the Soviets in Afghanistan—into Kashmir. With no war left to fight after the Russian withdrawal, these individuals became a potent, new weapon in Pakistan's proxy war against India. Yet, despite their ferocity and absolute refusal to surrender (as the figures attest, they fought to the last, avoiding capture unless critically wounded), India systematically eliminated them. By 1999-2000, their infiltration into Kashmir had effectively ceased.

There can be no doubt that these mercenary fighters were brought in from far-away places with considerable effort, finances, and logistics that would be needed for such an influx. Once the Soviet forces left Afghanistan, this potent irregular force needed a new direction, which was provided to them by Pakistan, inducting them into Kashmir. However, once the news about the robust counter-terror operations by the Indian Army reached back to the launch pads, and the funding for creating the mujahideen stopped, it was not possible to continue such recruitment for the battle in Kashmir.

Source: Press release by Press Information Bureau, Government of India, from archives available at https://archive.pib.gov.in/archive/releases98/lyr99/l1299/r081299.html

Annexure 1B

Atrocities on Foreign Nationals in J&K

Table 1B.1: Data of atrocities on foreign nationals recorded by South Asia Terrorism Portal

Date	Place	Incident
11 July 2000	Rangdum, Kargil District in Ladakh	A German tourist was abducted and later killed on 12 July by unidentified terrorists.
July 1995	Pahalgam, Anantnag district	Six foreign tourists, including two American nationals, were kidnapped. One of the hostages, John Childs (a citizen of the USA) escaped, another (a Norwegian national) was beheaded by the Harakat, and four others, including an American national, remained missing.
9 July 1995	Pahalgam, Anantnag district	John Childs, one of the three abducted US citizens, escaped and was rescued by a helicopter.
8 July 1995	Anantnag	German tourist Dirk Hassert was abducted by Al Faran terrorists.

Date	Place	Incident
4 July 1995	Pahalgam, Anantnag district	Al Faran terrorists abducted four British and three US citizens to demand the release of three HuA cadres.
20 October 1994	Delhi	HuA terrorists abducted Bela Josef Nuss, a US national, to demand the release of three detained Harkat-ul-Ansar (HuA) leaders and seven other terrorists of different groups.
16 October 1994	Delhi	HuA terrorists, under the name of 'Al Hadid', abduct British nationals Christopher Miles Crocton and Paul Benjamin, to demand the release of three detained HuA leaders and seven other terrorists of different groups.
29 September 1994	Delhi	British national Rhys Curget Partiridge was abducted by HuA to apply pressure on the Union government for the release of three detained HuA leaders and seven other terrorists of different groups.
2 November 1994	New Delhi	A California man was held hostage by Kashmiri separatists for 12 days as his captors aimed to draw international attention to terrorism in Jammu and Kashmir. He was rescued along with three British tourists in two raids by the Indian police after the kidnappers demanded the release of 10 jailed Kashmiris and threatened to behead their captives.
19 July 1994	Safakadal, Srinagar	US national Stephen Paul was abducted and later killed by Ikhwan-ul-Muslimeen terrorists.

Date	Place	Incident
6 June 1994	Pahalgam, Anantnag	Two British nationals—including Kim Housego, South Asia correspondent of Financial Times—were abducted by the HuA to demand the release of three detained Pakistani terrorists—Maulana Masood Azhar, Sajjad Afghani and Nasarullah Langaryal. However, the abductors set them free on 23 June 1994, following international pressure.
14 October 1991	Kishtwar, Doda district	A French engineer working with Dul Hasti Project in Kishtwar was abducted by Al Fatah and released after three months.
25 July 1991	Srinagar	A Japanese tourist was abducted by unidentified terrorists and set free after two days in captivity.
26 June 1991	Srinagar	Seven Israelis and a Dutch citizen were abducted by the Pasdaran-e-lnquillabi Islam group from a houseboat at Dal Lake. In the ensuing scuffle, an Israeli and two terrorists were killed, while others escaped from captivity.
31 March 1991	Tangmarg Road, Baramulla	Two Swedish engineers working with Uri Hydel Project were abducted by a group of seven terrorists affiliated to the Muslim Janbaz Force (MJF). Later, on 6 July they were set free following prolonged negotiations held between Pakistan-based MJF leaders and the relatives of the Swedes in Pakistan.

Source: https://www.satp.org/datasheet-terrorist-attack/india-jammukashmir/India-JammuandKashmir-Atrocities.

Following the exit of foreign mercenaries (as noted in Table 1A.1), tourist abductions in Kashmir sharply decreased after 1999–2000. These acts of terror, falsely framed as a "freedom struggle", severely damaged the local tourism industry, a primary source of income for residents who never saw such violence as a viable alternative to their livelihoods.

This welcome shift, avoiding all attacks on pilgrims and tourists persisted for years, in deference to local sentiments, until the significant assaults on Amarnath yatris in 2017 and pilgrims at Reasi in 2024. However, the Pahalgam attack of April 2025 was the first case of a terrorist attack on Indian tourists.

Notes

1. Anatol Lieven, *Pakistan: A Hard Country* (London: Penguin Books, 2011), 189.
2. BBC News, UK, India Pakistan Relations. http://news.bbc.co.uk/hi/english/static/in_depth/south_asia/2002/india_pakistan/timeline/1989.stm
3. Congressional Research Service Report for Congress, *International Terrorism in South Asia*, Serial RL32259 dated 13 December 2004, 17. https://www.everycrsreport.com/files/20040809_RL32259_b7296fdc69f3e0f3500450cf0702feae3a3552f4.pdf
4. SPIEGEL International, 4 Oct 2010, Pakistan is Always Seen as the Rogue, SPIEGEL Interview with Pervez Musharraf. accessed on 21 June 2012; also published in *Express Tribune*, 06 October 2010. https://www.spiegel.de/international/world/spiegel-interview-with-pervez-musharraf-pakistan-is-always-seen-as-the-rogue-a-721110.html
5. The Print, 6 April 2023, Khalistan – Pakistan's 'Bleed India with a thousand cuts' doctrine at work. https://theprint.in/world/khalistan-pakistans-bleed-india-with-a-thousand-cuts-doctrine-at-work/1502307/
6. Bhutto website, Speech delivered at the UN Security Council on 22 September 1965 on Kashmir Issue, available at https://bhutto.org/index.php/speeches/speeches-from-1948-1965/speech-delivered-at-the-un-security-council-on-september-22-1965-on-kashmir-issue/
7. News 18, 12 December 2023, How Stone-pelting Incidents Fell in Kashmir Post Abrogation of Article 370. https://www.news18.com/explainers/how-incidents-of-stone-pelting-fell-in-kashmir-post-abrogation-of-article-370-explained-8700202.html
8. *OpIndia*, 24 September 2020, Akshardham Temple Attack: 18 years ago, on this day, two terrorists laid siege on our faith., https://www.opindia.com/2020/09/18-years-since-akshardham-temple-attack-2002-baps-swaminarayan-nsg-commando-lashkar-terrorists/
9. *Times Now Digital*, 26 November 2020, Operations Black Tornado: How NSG Commandos Ended the Siege of Mumbai. https://www.

timesnownews.com/india/article/operation-black-tornado-how-nsg-commandoes-ended-the-siege-of-mumbai/687044.

10. Vijaita Singh, 17 November 2021, 20 NSG Commandos were Injured in Pathankot: NIA *The Hindu*. https://www.thehindu.com/news/national//article60628723.ece.
11. NSG, Ministry of Home Affairs, Government of India, Operation Dhangu Suraksha, Pathankot. Retrieved on 9 September 2022, from https://nsg.gov.in/sites/default/files/ops_dhangu.pdf.
12. Rekha Dixit, 7 February 2021, Scars and Sketches, Indian War Heroes are Being Resurrected in Graphic Novels, *The Week*. Retrieved from https://www.theweek.in/theweek/leisure/2021/01/28/scars-and-sketches.html
13. Bipin Bakshi and Rishi Kumar, *Niranjan*, *The Bomb Buster*, Warrior Series (New Delhi: AAN Comics, 2020).
14. Ibid.
15. PIB Delhi, Press Release, 6 December 2023, Development in Jammu and Kashmir. https://www.pib.gov.in/PressReleasePage.aspx?PRID=1983101
16. Daily Excelsior, 8 March 2025, Kashmir Received 13% of Total Tourist Footfall in J&K from 2021 to 2024, *Daily Excelsior.com*. https://www.dailyexcelsior.com/kashmir-received-13-of-total-tourist-footfall-in-jk-from-2021-24/
17. United Nations,13 October 2023, Sensitization Workshop for TF Stakeholders on Use of Cryptocurrencies & Darkweb, UNODC Pakistan. https://www.unodc.org/copak/en/Stories/SP4/sensitization-workshop-for-tf-stakeholders-on-use-of-cryptocurrencies-and-darkweb.html
18. Ibid.
19. Abid Hussain, 12 March 2025, Who are the BLA, the group behind Pakistan's deadly train hijack? EXPLAINER, *Al Jazeera*. https://www.aljazeera.com/news/2025/3/12/who-are-the-bla-the-group-behind-pakistans-deadly-train-hijack
20. Saadullah Akhtar, 3 April 2025, Dead or alive? Surviving Pakistan's 28-hour train hijack in an engine, *Al Jazeera*. https://www.aljazeera.

com/features/2025/4/3/dead-or-alive-surviving-pakistans-28-hour-train-hijack-in-an-engine

21. Dr Farzana Shaikh, 18 April 2025, The hijacking of a train marks a watershed in the Balochistan insurgency, *Chatham House*. https://www.chathamhouse.org/2025/03/hijacking-train-marks-watershed-balochistan-insurgency

22. Amit@apnlive.com, 17 April 2025, General Asim Munir reaffirms Pakistan's hardline stance on Kashmir and Balochistan, *APNLive.com*. https://apnlive.com/world-news/general-munir-kashmir-balochistan-remarks/

    Note: The above site—Endnote 22—was found blocked in London on 29 June 2025 when access was attempted by the author.

23. Neena Gopal, 23 Apr 2025, End of the Kashmir Summer: Is Pahalgam the payback for the Jaffar Express hijacking? *The New Indian Express*. https://www.newindianexpress.com/web-only/2025/Apr/23/end-of-the-kashmiri-summer-is-pahalgam-the-payback-for-the-jaffar-express-hijacking

24. Indrani Bagchi, 27 June 2025, US backs Pakistan, China arms it—why India must rethink its Strategy. https://timesofindia.indiatimes.com/toi-plus/international/us-backs-pakistan-china-arms-it-why-india-must-rethink-its-strategy/articleshow/122110128.cms

25. Marvi Sidmed, 5 May 2025, Pakistan Military Chief Addresses Overseas Pakistanis Convention, on #Unravelled, New Wave Global, *Friday Times*. https://thefridaytimes.com/05-May-2025/pakistan-military-chief-addresses-overseas-pakistanis-convention

2

Pahalgam

A Paradise Disrupted

MAJOR GENERAL BIPIN BAKSHI

> "*Agar firdaus bar roo zameen ast, hamin asto, hamin asto, hamin ast.*"
>
> "If there is paradise on earth, it is here, it is here, it is here."
>
> —A famous couplet[1]

"They told me, 'Go tell Modi'."[2] Ms Pallavi Rao recounts the response of the murderous group of terrorists who shot her 46-year-old husband, Mr Manjunath Rao, when she begged them to shoot her and her son too. The family trio were on their first-ever trip outside Karnataka, to celebrate the success of their son, Abhijaya, in his second PUC (Class XII) exam, with a score of 97%.[3]

Pahalgam Valley of Kashmir, often called the "Mini Switzerland", had been alive with the laughter of tourists on that fateful morning of April 2025. Families from across India had come to experience the breathtaking meadows, ride ponies through pine forests, and feel the crisp mountain air. Among them were newly-weds, retirees, children on their first mountain trip, and seasoned travellers seeking solace in Kashmir's famed beauty. Little did they know that danger lurked in the pine forests on the higher mountain ranges above Baisaran Valley, which extends from the main Pahalgam axis, climbing up towards the misty Himalayan Range that separates Kashmir from Ladakh.

Baisaran Valley: A Remote Scenic Location

Baisaran valley is located 45 km to the Southeast of Srinagar as the crow flies. It is a remote area with no motorable roads, no habitation; hence there is no security forces presence and it is not even visited by tourists or locals in winter months. The remoteness of the area made it approachable for terrorists coming on foot through the jungles on the Pir Panjal Range to the Warwan Valley to the East of Pahalgam, to execute the terror attack without encountering any posts of the security forces. As most of the other tourist spots in Srinagar and Gulmarg were well covered by security forces, it appears that the remoteness of Baisaran Valley was the main reason for its selection as the point of strike.[4] Moreover, the entire Pahalgam Valley is a peaceful area, and these areas have no habitation and no history of terrorism, and are thus largely outside the routine security envelope provided to the inhabited areas, except during the Amarnath Yatra period of June/July every year.

Pahalgam Valley itself is an offshoot of the main Kashmir Valley, forming the connection from the valley floor to the Himalayan Range massif, and is the main route to the Holy Amarnath Shrine. The other route to Amarnath cave takes you through Srinagar, skirting around the famous Dal Lake, towards Sonamarg, from where the pony route emanates along the mighty Himalayas towards the holy cave.

Figure 2.1: Map of Baisaran and Pahalgam Valley

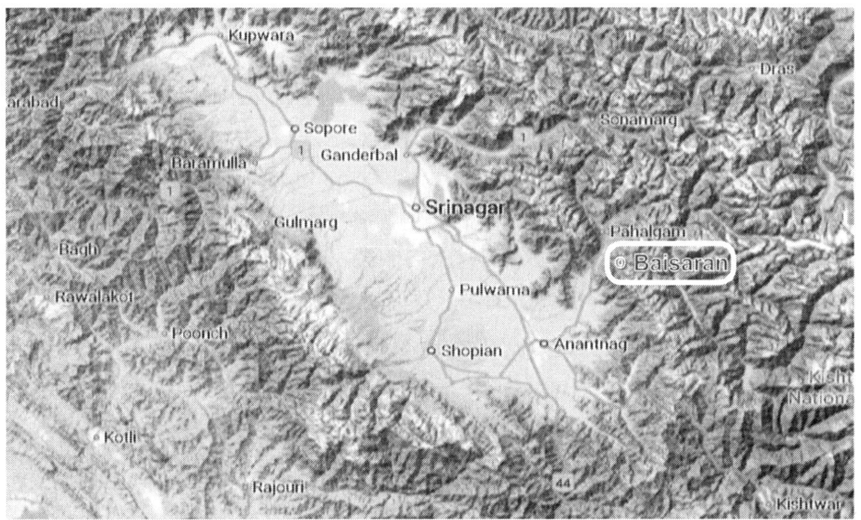

Source: Google Map.

Baisaran is about 3 km northwest of Pahalgam, accessible via a 45-minute hike or pony ride through pine forests. This is one of the many picturesque spots on the slopes rising towards the Himalayas, all of which are unoccupied and only visited by tourists in the summer months. No one imagined that in the afternoon of 22 April 2025, this paradise would be transformed into a scene of terror and tragedy—the deadliest and most deplorable attack on civilians in India since 2008.

For many, the trip to Pahalgam was a long-awaited dream. Shubham Dwivedi, a 31-year-old newly-wed from Kanpur, had arrived with his wife and extended family, eager to explore the valley's famed horse trails. Lieutenant Vinay Narwal, an Indian Navy officer from Haryana, was on his honeymoon, his wife Himanshi glowing with post-wedding joy. Prasant Kumar Satpathy, an accountant from Odisha, travelled with his wife and nine-year-old son, savouring every moment of their holiday.

Tourists from Karnataka, Maharashtra, Gujarat, Bengal, and Andhra Pradesh mingled in the meadows. Children played, couples posed for photos, and local pony operators guided groups up the gentle slopes.

The attack took place when the tourists were far from habitation in this remote meadow, which was fenced on all sides with a single gate for entry and exit. As mentioned earlier, the area was reachable only on foot or horseback, as there was no motorable road to the meadow. The terrain peculiarity slowed down responders from the Security Forces[5] on the one hand while lending proximity to the remote mountain region for an easy escape for terrorists on the other hand. The terrorists deliberately attacked only non-Muslim men, leaving women and children traumatized. To identify non-Muslims, the attackers ordered the victims to recite verses (*kalima)* of the Quran, and killed those who refused or were unable to recite the verses correctly. It was evidently an attempt to provoke the Indian nation while trying to draw a schism between different religious communities in India.

During the attack, an officer from Intelligence Bureau, Shri Manish Ranjan, and an Indian Navy Officer, Lt. Vinay Narwal, were also killed and there were some men who were injured and hospitalised in critical condition.[6] Among the survivors who escaped was Col Bhat, a serving Indian Army officer, who showed great presence of mind by guiding his group of tourists and his family away from the terrorists, finding an exit from the meadow through the side fence and ensuring safety of the group till the security forces arrived.

The Resistance Front (TRF), an open proxy of the Pakistan-based militant group of Lashkar-e-Taiba, initially took responsibility for the attack and repeated the claim after a few hours. However, they subsequently changed their stance, saying that the claim was on account of a cyber glitch! This attack was the first large-scale attack on tourists over a considerable period of time. In earlier instances, terrorists had kidnapped tourists to negotiate terms with the Indian Government.[7]

Brutality, Eyewitnesses, and the Chaos

The attackers, dressed in military-style uniforms, moved swiftly and deliberately. Witnesses described how they singled out victims based on religion:

- Tourists were asked to recite the Islamic *kalima.*
- Hindu men were forced to remove their trousers to check for circumcision.
- Those unable to recite Islamic verses or prove Muslim identity were shot at close range.

As the gunfire intensified, crowds fled in all directions. Some ran toward the main gate, only to find militants waiting. Others, like Prasanna Bhat and his family, scrambled for cover. He was among the few who evaded fate and survived, with the help of his brother, a serving Army officer. Bhat shared:

> We could see a terrorist approaching in our direction, so we decided to run the other way. Fortunately, we found a narrow opening under the fence, and most of the people hiding slid through the fence and started running the other way.[8]

Bhat's brother, an Army officer, Colonel Prashang Bhat, quickly assessed the situation and led 35-40 people down a slippery, muddy slope toward a water stream that offered some protection from gunfire. Many slipped and fell but managed to escape. Prasanna relates their experience:

> We managed to take cover in a narrow pit under the trees a few hundred metres from the location, desperately praying for our lives. The sound of gunshots continued to echo through the valley for half an hour until 3 pm.[9]

A local pony operator, Syed Adil Hussain Shah, tried to wrestle a gun from one of the attackers to protect the tourists. He was shot and killed—a rare moment of heroism amid chaos.

Photo 2.1: A photo of four attackers at Baisaran Valley

Source: *India TV News*, 23 April 2025.

Witness Accounts: Terrorists' Appearance and Behaviour

Witnesses provided several consistent details about the terrorists involved in the Pahalgam attack:

- Military-style uniforms: The attackers were described as wearing military-style uniforms, which contributed to the initial confusion among tourists and locals, as some mistook them for security personnel.
- Armed and organised: They carried automatic weapons and moved in a coordinated manner, suggesting prior planning and familiarity with the terrain.
- Concealed identities: Their faces were either partially covered or obscured, making identification difficult for survivors during the chaos.

Eyewitnesses described the terrorists' actions and demeanour as follows:

- Deliberate targeting: The attackers singled out victims based on religious identity. Those unable to prove Muslim identity were shot at close range.
- Calm and ruthless: Witnesses noted that the terrorists acted with chilling calmness, showing no hesitation or remorse as they moved from group to group. Their actions were methodical, and they appeared unmoved by pleas for mercy.
- Aggression against resisters: When a local pony operator, Syed Adil Hussain Shah, attempted to intervene and protect tourists, he was shot and killed on the spot, demonstrating their intolerance for any resistance.
- Verbal threats and taunts: Survivors recalled the attackers making statements like "Go tell Modi", after sparing some victims, using threats and taunts to instil fear and send a political message.

The violence of the assault was unprecedented and unpredictable. As mentioned by eyewitness, the attackers were carrying M4 carbines and AK-47s and they escaped into the nearby forests before security personnel arrived.[10] After the first gunshots were fired at the Baisaran meadow that day, two terrorists who had earlier mingled with the tourists, herded the startled crowd towards two other armed terrorists, who then segregated and killed the people based on religion, a senior government official said[11] about the incident.

Besides the extremely brutal nature of the killing, the terrorists evidently wanted to traumatise the women and children who would be haunted by the gruesome sights of murder. At the same time, the terrorists sought to perpetrate a chilling religious divide—trying to sow seeds of communal disharmony in India's diverse population.

Victims and Survivors: Some Individual Stories

Terrorists turned the vibrant Baisaran Valley into a killing field, leaving behind not just bodies, but unforgettable wounds on dozens of families spread across India. The stories of the victims of Pahalgam attack are not only about grief—they are about memory, witness, and the stubborn human urge to find meaning even amidst devastation. This is the story of those families—of love, laughter lost, anguish inherited, and the dreary road to healing. Their voices, fractured but unyielding, remind the world that behind every headline there are real lives—imperfect, precious, and forever changed.

The Jagdale family: A daughter's silent courage

"My father's last hug."

Santosh Jagdale, a businessman from Nagpur, Maharashtra, was the very embodiment of kindness, say his friends. On 21 April, he arrived in Pahalgam with his teen daughter, Avari, and brother-in-law. The Jagdales had delayed their trip to Kashmir for years, always promising to visit "someday". This year, after his daughter scored well in her board exams, Santosh finally decided to take her to Kashmir.

Avari recalls their last morning together:

> Papa woke me up early. He said the air here would make all the years of waiting worth it. I remember he put his arm around my shoulders at breakfast and joked about the spicy Maggi… that hug, I still feel it.

At Baisaran meadow, as the attackers opened fire into the crowd, Santosh pushed Avari down and shielded her with his own body.

> There were shouts, gunfire everywhere. I saw Papa tug at my hand, then let go. When I looked up, he was on the ground.

> Blood on his shirt. My uncle was also shot, and I screamed their names, but the men shouted at me in a language I didn't understand.

Avari survived, running until a local guide pulled her to safety. She returned home to Nagpur in the same blood-drenched clothes for her father's funeral. At the cremation, she stood grim-faced, clutching a photograph. "I want everyone to remember him as a father who didn't hesitate to give everything for his daughter", she told local reporters, her voice eerily calm, from trauma and exhaustion. "I remember everything. I don't want to forget. Someone must answer for this."

Her mother, Ritu, displays a faded family photo on their living room wall: "His absence fills this house. I keep replaying the last call, his laughter, how he promised to bring our daughter home safe. Why us?"

The Rao family: "Tell Modi what you saw"

Manjunatha Rao, a 47-year-old real estate agent from Shivamogga, Karnataka, had never left his home state until the Pahalgam trip; a reward for years of frugal living. The Raos—Manjunath, Pallavi, and their 17-year-old son—were thrilled by what Kashmir had to offer—snow-capped mountains, green meadows, and pony rides. Then, the terrorists appeared. Pallavi recalls:

> They told the men to remove their trousers. They said vile things... My husband did what they said, but it didn't matter. They shot him, once, twice, three times. Our boy was screaming. I couldn't do anything.

Manjunath died in front of his family. Pallavi begged the attackers to kill her and their son too. Instead, they sneered, "Go tell Modi". The chilling taunt would haunt her nightmares. "We lost our pillar", says her brother-in-law, Prakash. "He was a good man—devout, generous, one who never spoke harshly. They were ordinary people. What did they do to deserve this?" Social workers say, "She wants justice, but there's no justice for her loss. She wants the world to remember Manjunath as a loving husband and gentle father, not as a statistic".

The Dwivedi family: Newly-weds torn apart

"He made me laugh till the last moment."

Shubham Dwivedi, a 31-year-old from Kanpur, Uttar Pradesh, radiated optimism. His wedding, held just three months before, was a joyous affair. His wife, Shaniya, barely speaks of 22 April without tears: "We went horse-riding that morning. I was nervous, but he kept joking, trying to distract me because he knew I was scared. It was such a beautiful day..."

As the shooting began, all she remembers is Shubham trying to shield her, shouting at her to run.

> I heard him gasp. I turned and saw him slide off the pony. His face—he was looking for me. There was so much blood. Everything is a blur after that.

Shaniya was rescued by locals and security forces. She called her husband's family, sobbing, to break the news. At Shubham's family home, his parents sit in silence. His sister keeps his wedding photograph on her mantel. "He was too young. We are angry, but there is only so much shouting you can do", says his father, clasping trembling hands. "Our boy is gone. Married for just a few months. That's all."

Prasanna Kumar Bhat and family, a few lives saved

Bhat's account captures the terror and resilience of survivors:

> We stayed put in the pit for an hour, petrified, hopeless, and praying for safety. We didn't know if we had to stay put or

run in some random direction hoping to escape the death trap. All the while we kept thinking about our little children and parents who we had left behind home and not knowing when this would end.[12]

Photo 2.2: Troops move to the scene

Source: The Indian Express, 25 April 2025.[13]

By 3:40 pm, the sound of a helicopter signalled the arrival of security forces. By 4 pm, the Army had secured the area and escorted survivors to safety. Prasanna shares:

> The gunshots still echo in our ears, and the terror still makes my gut wrench. This will leave a permanent scar, a memory that cannot be erased of what Kashmir's beauty hides underneath.[14]

The Satpathy family: A son's first taste of loss

"Baba loved us deeply."

Prasant Kumar Satpathy, an accountant from Odisha, planned the Kashmir trip as a lesson in joy for his nine-year-old son, Arun. His wife, Priyadarshini, recalls the peaceful moments just before violence struck:

> We'd finished the ropeway ride. Arun wanted a picture by the stream. Prasant went ahead while I took out the camera. Then a bang—a loud, sharp noise. I saw my husband fall. Blood pouring from his head. In a second, our world ended.

Arun, badly shaken, kept asking about his father weeks after returning to Odisha. "Baba loved us deeply", he tells visitors. He fiddles with a toy his father bought before the trip—a memory he clings to. Priyadarshini struggles to explain the loss to Arun. "He asks if heaven has internet, if his father can still see him draw pictures. I have no words", she says, voice breaking. "How do I answer that?"

The Narwal family: Eight days of happiness

"I can't forget his smile."

Lieutenant Vinay Narwal, an Indian Navy officer from Haryana, married his college sweetheart Himanshi in early April. For their honeymoon, they chose Kashmir, hoping for "a slice of paradise".

Just eight days into their marriage, tragedy struck. Himanshi describes the nightmare:

He was trying to keep me calm. When they separated us, he looked at me and smiled, that mischievous smile he always had. One of the terrorists asked him his name, and then… he shot him, three times, in the neck, in the chest, and thigh.

Himanshi was left alone in the meadow, shaking and numb. "Everything that was good in my life ended in a moment. I can't forget his smile, his voice, how proud he was to wear his uniform."

At Narwal's ancestral home, his parents grieve quietly. "He wanted to make the world a safer place, and now this… I miss hearing him call me", his mother whispers. "Himanshi is our daughter now. She keeps saying she can't sleep. We all just want

Photo 1: An artist's painting of Kashmir Valley annotated by the author, showing Baisaran location

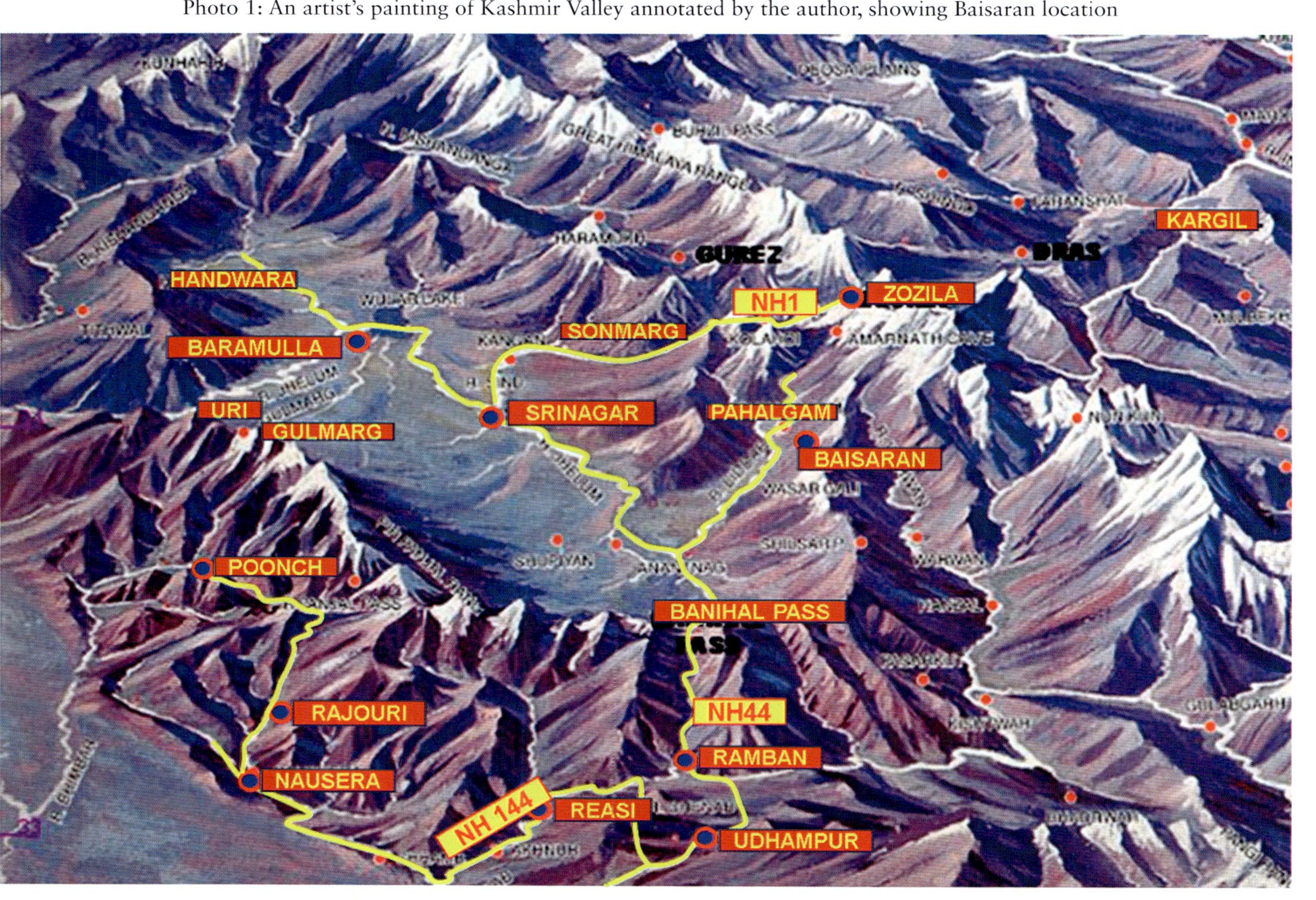

Photo 2: Baisaran, the arena for unspeakable terror

Source: Internet, 4 December 2018.

Photo 3: Himanshi Narwal with late Lt. Vinay Narwal

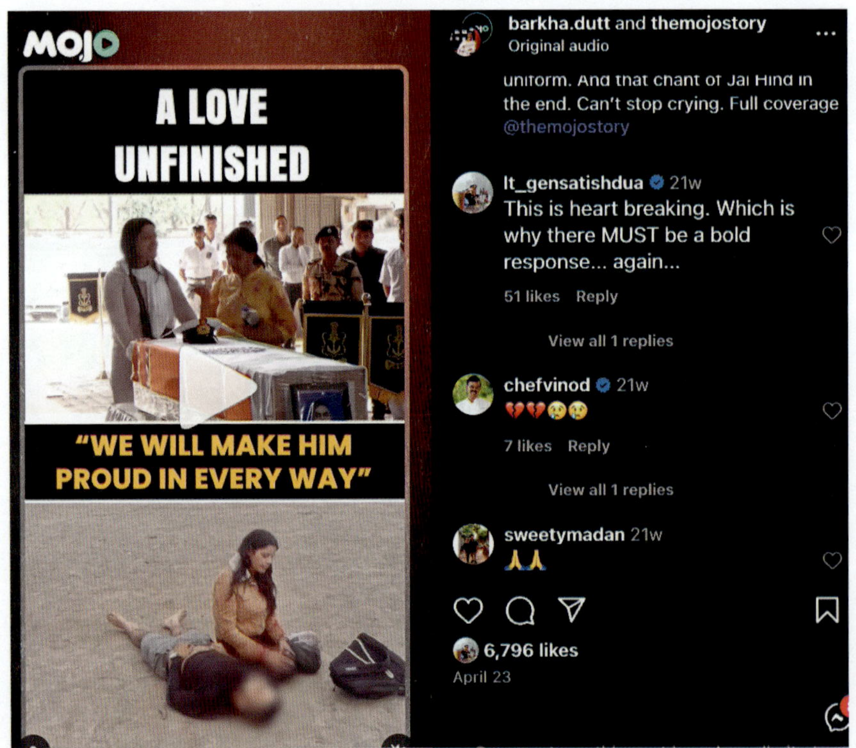

Source: Mojo Story (@themojostory), 23 April 2025.

Photo 4: A grieving relative at Pahalgam

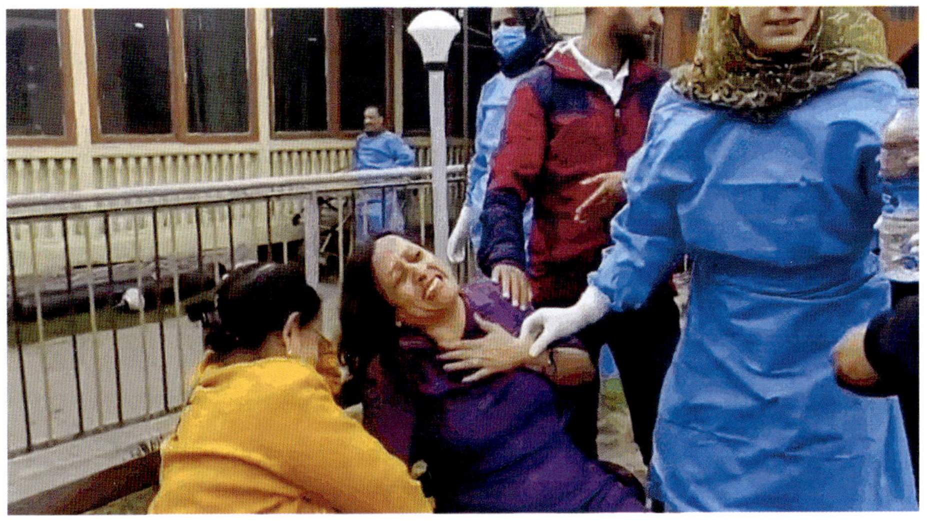

Photo 5: Injured being rushed to the hospital

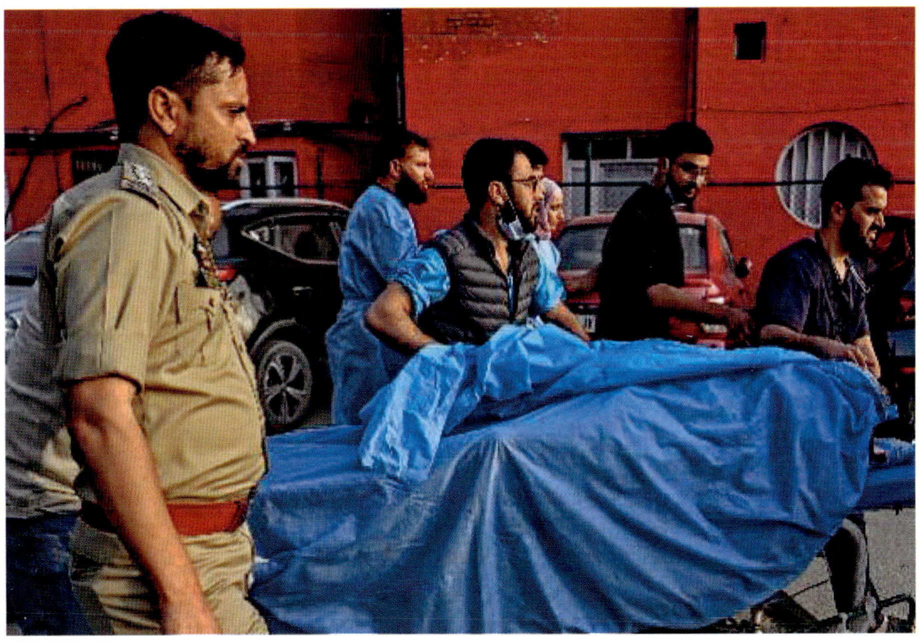

Source: KNO.

Photo 6: Bhubaneswar MP Aparajita Sarangi consoling a grieving family at Srinagar

Source: *ETV Bharat*, 23 April 2025.

Photo 7: Troops at the Pahalgam Attack site on 26 April 25

Source: KNO.

Photo 8: Chairs lying outside makeshift shops at Baisaran

Source: KNO.

Photo 9: Tour guide Nazakat Ahmad Ali Shah (left) who saved 11 tourists, and Syed Adil Hussain Shah, a pony operator, who was himself killed while defending others

Source: *Kashmir News Observer*, 24 April 2025.

Photo 10: Grieving families of Pahalgam attack victims

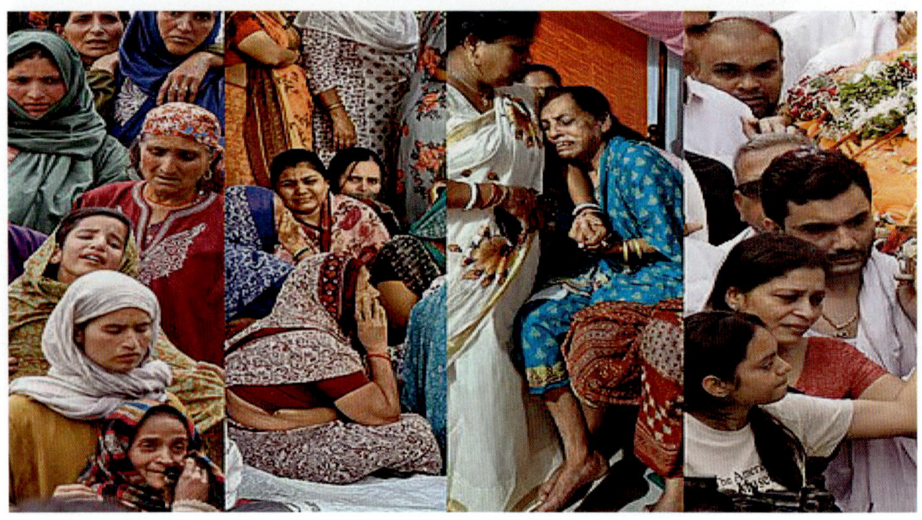

Photo 11: Home Minister Amit Shah paying tribute to people who died in Pahalgam attack

Source: PIB press release 23 April 2025.

Photo 12: Home Minister Amit Shah at Baisaran Valley on 23 April 2025

Source: KNO.

Photo 13: Army Chief Gen Upendra Dwivedi being briefed by commanders in Srinagar, 25 April 2025

Source: Indian Army.

Photo 14: Funeral of killed terrorists in Muridke carried out by Abdul Rauf (Specially Designated Global Terrorist), LeT Commander. Top brass of Pakistan Army and Police attended

Source: Media briefing on 8 May 2025.

him back." Vinay's father says the Navy and government officials were supportive, but nothing can fill the void. "We're proud of our boy, but pride does not take away the pain."

The Ranjan family: A father's journey interrupted

"He told us to be strong."

Manish Ranjan, an Intelligence Bureau officer originally from Bihar, was visiting Kashmir with his wife and children. The family describes Manish as stoic, fiercely protective, and someone who lived for his children's happiness. "He was always taking pictures, playing jokes on us", recalls his son, Kabir, aged 11. "He made everything fun."

Manish was killed in front of his family. His wife Anju became the anchor, guiding her children to safety amidst the chaos. In the aftermath, Anju tries to help her children recover:

> He told me, 'Whatever happens, keep the kids safe'. I keep replaying that moment. At night, Kabir cries out for his papa; our daughter won't let go of his last handwritten note. I have to be strong, for their sake.

Friends and neighbours in Hyderabad visit regularly, offering prayers and financial help. "He was devoted to his work, devoted to his family. Now, we're just trying to survive each day", says his brother.

The Kalathiya family: A birthday uncelebrated

"He remembered everyone else's happiness."

Bank officer Shailesh Kalathiya from Surat, Gujarat, took special pride in family occasions. The Kashmir trip was meant to celebrate his own upcoming birthday, a rare chance for the usually hardworking banker to relax with his wife and two children. "He insisted we go, even though I was worried", recalls his wife Alka.

"He said, 'Let's make memories for the kids.' Now the memories are all pain."

Shailesh was killed just a day before his birthday, while protecting his child. His wife Alka and his children sustained minor injuries but survived. At their home, birthday cards and party decorations ordered before the trip remain unopened. "He remembered everyone else's happiness, never his own. Every time I try to celebrate anything now, thinking he'd want us to, but I just can't," Alka says, weeping.

The Adhikary family: Reunion turned tragedy

"He called us his lucky charms."

Bitan Adhikary, a techie from Kolkata working in Florida, made annual trips home to India. This year, he convinced his family to vacation together in Kashmir. "He called us his lucky charms", says his wife, Suchismita, attempting a smile through tears.

> Bitan loved taking selfies. He was joking around right before it happened, pretending to 'interview' us with his phone. Then everything turned black. I remember being on the ground, our little girl crying. I saw him, but couldn't get to him.

Bitan died before help arrived. His wife and daughter spent days in hospital with minor injuries. "I keep replaying those happy moments before the attack. My daughter asks, 'When's Baba coming back from the mountain?' I don't know what to say."

The extended Adhikary family has since rallied; uncles and aunts visit to help with chores and support his widow. "He wanted us to experience the world. Now I'm afraid to take my daughter anywhere", Suchismita admits.

The Chandramouli family: Grandfather's final embrace

"He shielded us with his whole body."

J. Chandramouli, a retired bank employee from Visakhapatnam, Andhra Pradesh, was travelling with his wife and two grandchildren. As gunfire erupted, he wrapped himself around his family, taking fatal bullets while his wife and grandchildren survived with minor injuries.

His daughter, Lavanya, recounts: "My father always put us first. When the children were born, he spoiled them silly. He saved their lives with his own." After returning to Andhra Pradesh, the family faced not just grief but hospital stays and therapy for the children. "They have nightmares", says Lavanya. "They cry for their grandpa, and so do I."

The Shah family: A Kashmiri's ultimate sacrifice

"I just wanted to save someone's child."

There were local heroes too throughout the crisis;[15] for example, tour guide Nazakat Ahmad Ali Shah saved 11 tourists by ushering them to safety by a hidden route, while putting his own life at risk, and his cousin Syed Adil Hussain Shah, a pony operator, was himself killed while defending others.[16] He saw the shooters and rushed towards the danger, trying to wrest a gun away from an attacker. He was gunned down in the attempt.

Shah's widow, Maimoona, said:

> He always said if you can help, you must. He died trying to keep that promise. Our children have lost their father, and all we can do is pray people remember him for his courage.

Locals arranged a funeral and some survivors returned to thank his family. "He gave his life for strangers", says his brother Bilal. "He was a son of Kashmir."

Across India: The Ripple of Grief and Collective Trauma

The violence sent families across states into mourning—Karnataka, Odisha, Maharashtra, West Bengal, Bihar, Andhra Pradesh, Gujarat, and more. In each house, rituals of grief mixed with media attention. "It was not just that some people have died", a community leader from Surat said, "but entire families are now condemned to live with ghosts".

Children, spouses, parents—all left behind, struggle with nightmares, survivor's guilt, financial worry, and an unfillable absence at the dinner table. "We try to smile for the children's sake", says Shailesh's widow Alka, "But the silence is everywhere".

Families formed informal support groups. "No one else understands", one mother said at a gathering in Nagpur, "unless they've also stood where we stand, waiting for someone who will never come back".

In April after the devastating attack, children lit candles before portraits of lost fathers, mothers traced the lines on faded photographs, newly-weds went to bed alone. Birthdays passed uncelebrated, festivals became quieter, and families are finding small ways to commemorate the love and heroism of those taken from them. "We survived," says Avari Jagdale quietly, "But every day is a struggle to remember the life before. My father's story is unfinished. I want to tell it, every year, until everyone remembers."

A Tragic Tale, Victims from Far and Wide

During the heinous attack, at final count, 26 civilians were killed (including a Nepali tourist), and 17 were wounded.[17] The victims were from different parts of India and even abroad. Table 2.1. and Table 2.2 list the names of the deceased and injured people.

Table 2.1: List of deceased people

S. No	Deceased	State of residence of the deceased
1	Atul Shrikant Moni	Maharashtra
2	Bitan Adhikary	West Bengal
3	Dilip Jayaram Desale	Maharashtra
4	Dinesh Agarwal	Chandigarh
5	Hemant Suhas Joshi	Maharashtra
6	Shailesh Kalathiya	Gujarat
7	J. Chandramouli	Vishakhapatnam
8	Kastuba Ganvotay	Maharashtra
9	Madhusudan Somishetty	Bangalore
10	Manish Ranjan	Bihar
11	Manjunatha Rao	Karnataka
12	N. Ramachandra	Kerala
13	Neeraj Udhawani	Uttarakhand
14	Prasant Kumar Satpathy	Odissa
15	Sameer Guhar	West Bengal
16	Sanjay Lakshman Lali	Maharashtra
17	Santosh Jagdale	Maharashtra
18	Lt Shubham Dwivedi	Uttar Pradesh
19	Sumit Parmar	Gujarat
20	Sundip Nevpane	Nepal
21	Sushil Nathanyal	Madhya Pradesh
22	Syed Adil Hussain Shah	Jammu and Kashmir
23	Tagehalying	Arunachal Pradesh
24	Udhwani Rradeep Kumar	UAE
26	Vinay Narwal	Haryana
27	Yatesh Parmar	Gujarat

Source: Author's compilation from government sources.

Table 2.2: List of injured people

S. No.	Injured	Residence
1	Abhaya M. Rao	Karnataka
2	Akansha	Madhya Pradesh
3	Balachandru	Maharashtra
4	Dobhi Vino Bah	Gujarat
5	Dr. A Parmeshwar	Tamil Nadu
6	Harsha Jain	Maharashtra
7	Jaya Mishra	Telangana
8	Jennifer	Madhya Pradesh
9	Lakshita Dass	Chhattisgarh
10	Manik Patel Panwel	Maharashtra
11	Nikita Jain	Maharashtra
12	Renu Panday	Nepal
13	Santano	Tamil Nadu
14	Shabariguha	West Bengal
15	Shashi Kumari Naik	Karnataka
16	Sobede Patil	Maharashtra
17	Vinay Bai	Gujarat

Source: Author's compilation from government sources.

Investigations in the Aftermath of the Attack

Union Home Minister Amit Shah flew in from Saudi Arabia, where he had to cut short an important visit. After conducting an emergency security meeting at Srinagar, he briefed the Prime Minster at Delhi.

PM Modi condemned the attack on X (formerly Twitter), stating, "Those behind this heinous act will be brought to justice… Their evil agenda will never succeed". Consequent to this attack, several high-level meetings were held including one organised by the Home Minister, Shri Amit Shah, to identify vulnerable points in and around Pahalgam, which need to be manned continuously by security personnel to enable round-the-clock surveillance and prompt response mechanisms.[18] Security officials ramped up search and seizure operations in the Pahalgam sector to identify and apprehend the perpetrators of the attack as well as their local informants and sympathisers. One of the identified suspects was Ahmed Bilal, who was arrested on 6 May 2025.[19]

Indian intelligence services who have been investigating these terrorist attacks have been assiduously working to identify other perpetrators. Two of them were identified as Pakistanis and the other two were locals,[20] who had gone out to Pakistan 10 years ago for training, and clearly were sent back for this mission.

The investigators also corroborated the testimonies of the witness and the harbourers, successfully identifying the terrorists, the sources said, adding that one of them was believed to be a former Pakistan army regular.[21] This group is also suspected to be the mastermind behind the Sonamarg Z-Morh tunnel attack in July 2024, which resulted in the death of six labourers and a doctor. "The Kashmiri duo who have been identified have no previous records and appear to have infiltrated recently for the Pahalgam attack", an intelligence official said.

Finally, after a massive manhunt, three of the four terrorists involved in the Pahalgam attack were tracked down and eliminated on 28 July 2025.[22] Home Minister Amit Shah announced this news in the Lok Sabha on 29 July. In a joint operation, titled Operation Mahadev,[23] the soldiers of 4 PARA (Special Forces unit) of the Indian Army, CRPF and Jammu and Kashmir Police, succeeded in tracking down and neutralising Suleiman Shah (LeT commander), Hamza Afghani, and Jibran. Their weapons were forensically matched with the bullets fired at Pahalgam. Shri Amit Shah told the House that the National Investigation Agency (NIA) had arrested the people who had given shelter to these three terrorists. He shared that when the bodies of these three terrorists were brought to Srinagar, four witnesses identified them and confirmed that these were the three terrorists who had carried out the terrorist attack in Pahalgam. Shah added that the forensic report of the cartridges found at the site of the Pahalgam terrorist attack were matched with the three rifles recovered from these three terrorists in Dachigam. He said that these three rifles were transported to Chandigarh by a special plane and their empty shells were generated by firing, and they were found to match with the shells from the Pahalgam attack site. Hence, it was confirmed that these three rifles were used to kill our innocent citizens in Pahalgam on 22 April 2025.

Investigations have shown that there were only two overground workers (OGWs) who facilitated the logistics for the conduct of the attack. Agencies have found no prior records for these two harbourers, Parvaiz Ahmed and Bashir Ahmad, and suspect that this was a deliberate strategy by Pakistan state actors to create a new module with minimal involvement of local OGWs. They believe that the involvement of locals was kept to a bare minimum to maintain secrecy, and the entire module was moved recently from their bases in Pakistan. The OGWs would have facilitated logistics, such as arranging for accommodations, leading the attackers through the terrain, and potentially assisting in the provision of arms and ammunition. Electronic intelligence revealed communication between the OGWs and the attackers during the planning stage, to guide and assist the Pakistani terrorists in this heinous attack.[24] Radicalisation of such individuals was probably carried out using online platforms, where extremist content was spread to indoctrinate and recruit operatives.[25] Organisations such as the TRF are reported to have used encryption messaging applications and online communities to spread radical ideologies, recruit new members, and organise attacks. This internet strategy has helped them access more people and facilitate their operations.

Jyoti Malhotra, a YouTuber, the owner of the YouTube channel "Travel with Jo", and a travel influencer from Hisar, Haryana, was arrested on 16 May spying for Inter-Services Intelligence (ISI) and Pakistan. It is believed that she had visited Kashmir and Baisaran Valley before the attack. She had reportedly been sharing several critical items of information with her handlers of ISI.[26]

Two other persons, Palak Sher Masih and Suraj Masih, were arrested in Amritsar on 03 May 2025, for espionage, passing information about Indian Army and Indian Air Force to Pakistani operatives.[27] These two were among the 11 individuals identified and apprehended from several locations across India.

Evidence Against Pakistan

The most recent acknowledgement by third parties about Pakistan's role in fomenting trouble all over the globe and particularly in India comes from the statement of the Secretary of State, USA, who designated The Resistance Front (TRF) as a Foreign Terrorist Organisation (FTO) and as a Specially Designated Global Terrorist (SDGT). He also clarified in the statement that it was TRF which had claimed responsibility for the Pahalgam attack. India acknowledged and appreciated the leadership of Secretary of State Mr Marco Rubio in this regard, in the press release of 18 July 2025.[28] The text of the Indian press release reiterates that TRF took responsibility for the Pahalgam massacre and also conveyed that the subject designation of TRF is a timely and important step reflecting the deep cooperation between India and the United States on counter-terrorism. Evidently this confirms to the world that Indian investigative agencies, as well as the intelligence agencies of USA, have been able to collect adequate evidence and intelligence about the culpability of Pakistan-based terrorist groups in this deplorable attack on tourists in Kashmir.

Figure 2.2: Pakistan Minister admits training and funding terror camps on 25 April 2025, "Doing the dirty work of the United States for three decades"

We have been doing the dirty work of the United States for three decades".

Pakistan's Defence Minister Khawaja Asif spoke to me last night in a remarkable and wide ranging interview about the escalating situation in Kashmir. India is blaming Pakistan who says there is no evidence for this.

He also told me that Pakistan is "already prepared" for strikes from India. #India #Pakistan #PahalgamTerroristAttack #Kashmir

Source: Sky News interview posted on X, 25 April 2025.[29]

Pakistan Defence Minister Khawaja Asif in an interview with Sky News, UK, announced to the world about his country's history of supporting, training, and funding terrorist organisations, terming this as the "dirty work for the West",[30] and commenting that this was a mistake for which Pakistan had suffered. During the interview on 25 April 2025, the news presenter Yalda Hakim had asked Asif about Pakistan's stance on terrorism in the aftermath of the terrorist attack in Pahalgam.

"You do admit, sir, that Pakistan has had a long history of backing and supporting and training and funding these terrorist organisations", asked Hakim.

"Well, we have been doing this dirty work for the United States for about three decades, you know, and the West, including Britain", replied Asif.

"That was a mistake, and we suffered from that, and that is why you are saying this to me. If we had not joined the war against the Soviet Union and later on (joined) the war after 9/11, Pakistan's track record, was an unimpeachable track record", he said.

Prior to this incident too, questions had often been raised by international media about the evidence that would connect Pakistan to terror attacks, as Pakistan has always been in a denial mode despite irrefutable evidence provided on several occasions. On this occasion too, there was a huge perception management exercise launched by Pakistan in various Western nations to swing an anti-India narrative on Op Sindoor. Recently, in a publicly available video of a press conference in Washington, Shashi Tharoor's son, Ishaan Tharoor, from the *Washington Post*, had asked him about the evidence linking Pakistan to the attack.

Here the gist of the answer given by Shashi Tharoor.

- **9/11 attack in New York:** India had a 37-year pattern of repeated terror attacks from Pakistan accompanied by repeated denials. Americans haven't forgotten that Pakistan didn't know allegedly where Osama bin Laden was until he was found in a Pakistani safe house right next to an army camp in a Cantonment city in Pakistan.

Photo 2.3: 9/11 Attack on World Trade Center by Osama bin Laden

- **Mumbai attack 2008:** Pakistan denied having anything to do with it. One of the terrorists was captured alive, his name, his identity, his address in Pakistan, everything was revealed on interrogation. He confessed where he was trained, and how the attack was carried out. The US intelligence, as well as ours, recorded the chilling voice of the Pakistani handler, giving minute-by-minute instructions to the killers in Mumbai, telling them where to go, and informing them that there were people hiding on the third floor of that hotel and they should go find them there.

Photo 2.4: Mumbai terrorist attack 26/11

- **Pahalgam attack:** Within 45 minutes or so of the Pahalgam attack, a group called the Resistance Front claimed credit. The Resistance Front of the Lashkar-e-Taiba (LeT), a banned organisation listed by the United Nations, enjoys safe havens in the town of Muridke Pakistan. The evidence about the Resistance Front and its doings was presented by India to the UN Committee on Terrorism in December 2023 and repeatedly again in 2024. However, as Pakistan too is a member of that committee, the Resistance Front was not listed by the UN, although its identity was known and publicised. The Resistance Front repeated that claim 24 hours later; then their handlers must have woken up to the gravity of the situation and told them to take it off their site. However, the credit claim was on record and the world has seen it. When India retaliated with strikes by the Indian Army and the Indian Air Force on Pakistani terrorist camps, funerals were conducted for the deceased terrorists of some key organisations, including the Jaish-e-Mohammed, in particular, and the LeT. These funerals were attended by Pakistani generals and police officers in uniform, as can be seen in the photographs of the funeral shared on the social media.

As per information released by India[31] during the media briefings, there were several key figures among the LeT terrorists who were killed in the 7 May strikes at Muridke. The list included Khalid Abu Akasha, an LeT operative who facilitated arms smuggling from Afghanistan. He was a member of LeT's Central Committee and closely linked to leaders such as Yahya Mujahid and Qari Yakub Sheikh. Another key figure killed was Mudassir Khadian Khas, who oversaw the Muridke camp as security-in-charge for Al-Khidmat Committee, and was a son-in-law of the militant ideologue Hafiz Saeed. Besides them, Mohammad Hassan Khan, son of Jaish-e-Mohammed (JeM) PoJK commander Mufti

Asghar Khan Kashmiri; and Maulana Masood Azhar's brother-in-law Hafiz Muhammad Jameel, a Bahawalpur-based JeM Shura member, were also neutralised.

According to the reports, the funeral in Muridke saw the presence of Lieutenant General Fayyaz Hussain, Major General Rao Imran, and Brigadier Mohammad Furqan of the Pakistan Army, alongside Punjab Inspector General of Police Usman Anwar, Legislator Malik Sohaib Ahmed, and other senior officials. Their attendance, it was noted by India, "highlights the complicity of state actors in sheltering and celebrating global terrorists".

While briefing the media on 8 May 2025, Foreign Secretary Vikram Misri referred to the photograph of Abdur Rauf,[32] leading the funeral prayers (see photo 14 from the page inserts of this chapter) at Muridke, and to the photographs of several other slain terrorists, whose coffins were draped in the Pakistan national flag. "If only civilians were killed in these attacks, I wonder what message this picture actually sends to all of you", Mr Misri said. "As far as we are concerned, the individuals eliminated at these facilities were terrorists. Giving terrorists state funerals may be a practice in Pakistan. It doesn't seem to make much sense to us", he added.

Even PM Modi referred to this funeral in his address to the nation on 12 May 2025. "Top Pakistani army officers came to bid farewell to the slain terrorists. This is strong evidence of state-sponsored terrorism", he said.[33]

Correlation between Pahalgam and Previous Attacks

As recounted above, the Pahalgam terror attack of April 2025 was one of the most brutal and targeted assaults on tourists in the history of Jammu and Kashmir. This incident in the Kashmir division came after a considerable gap since 2019, the more recent terrorist incidents being in Jammu Division, to include Rajouri (2023), Reasi (2024), and Kathua Ambush (2025).

Attacks against tourists have been extremely rare, as brought out in detail in the Introduction Chapter of this book. The last significant attack was against pilgrims at Reasi, near Katra, which coincided with the swearing-in ceremony of the Modi Government on 9 June 2024 in the presence of foreign dignitaries. Just an hour before the oath ceremony was to take place at the forecourt of the Rashtrapati Bhavan, 9 pilgrims were killed and 41 injured as their bus was fired upon by terrorists when they were returning from Shiv Khori Temple towards Mata Vaishno Devi shrine. They were religious pilgrims in the Jammu Division, not normal tourists visiting Kashmir Division, who had never been attacked in this manner earlier.

A discernible pattern can be observed while considering big terrorist attacks in Jammu and Kashmir during the past few years. Many of those incidents were synchronised with major national events or times when Prime Minister Narendra Modi was busily involved in important governmental activities or foreign visits. The timing has generated debate regarding whether such attacks are strategically designed to achieve maximum psychological and political impacts. On this occasion, it was US Vice President J D Vance who was in India at the time of the attack in Pahalgam. In case of the previous incidents, PM Narendra Modi was on foreign visits.

The previous history of attacks has been recounted in Introduction. However, in the last two years preceding the Pahalgam attack, some issues are of note, namely, the series of incidents in South of Pir Panjal during the last three years, since the move of a division strength of Rashtriya Rifles, a Uniform Force, from Reasi to Ladakh after the Galwan Crisis 2020. None of these attacks generated the kind of international attention the perpetrators of these attacks desired and, in the meanwhile, normalcy was rapidly returning to Kashmir after the abrogation of

Article 370. The train service to Kashmir was just about to start, and therefore secession of Kashmir from India was becoming a rapidly fading dream for the Pakistan Army. If we now correlate the venomous speech of the Pakistan Army Chief on 15 April 2025 (see Figure 1.3), and the number of Pakistani Sunni Muslims killed in the Jaffar Express hijack incident of March 2025, the motivations for the Pahalgam attack become starkly evident.

In the Jaffar Express incident, 21 civilians and 4 paramilitary soldiers were killed as reported to *Al Jazeera* by Pakistan security forces,[34] a total of ***25 Pakistani citizens.*** Nearly 70 passengers, the women, children, and elderly hostages, were released by the Balochi hijackers, evidently after some kind of ethnic and religious profiling which could be expected in any hijack situation. We may now correlate that the tourists were killed at Pahalgam after carrying out a specific religious profiling. Among the people killed there were ***25 non-Muslim Indian citizens*** and one Muslim. The attackers left after killing 25 non-Muslims, while they had the opportunity to inflict more casualties before the arrival of Indian security forces.

The evidences pieced together by India's NIA, and other security agencies, was presented to the world in the aftermath of the attack, and a majority of the nations expressed solidarity with India, while condemning the heinous terrorist atrocity. The stage was set for India's response, it was probably not about whether there would be retribution, but about when would the hammer strike.

Notes

1. Good reads quotes, https://www.goodreads.com/quotes/7386585-farsi-couplet-agar-firdaus-bar-roo-e-zameen-ast-hameen-ast-o
2. NDTV, 23 April 2025, “Won’t Kill You. Go, Tell Modi”: Terrorist To Woman During Pahalgam Attack. available at https://www.ndtv.com/india-news/pahalgam-terror-attack-survivor-recalls-nightmare-go-tell-modi-8229491
3. eTV Bharat, 23 April 2025, From Celebratory Trip To Tragedy: Pahalgam Terror Attack Shatters Karnataka Realtor's Family. available at https://www.etvbharat.com/en/!state/from-celebratory-trip-to-tragedy-pahalgam-terror-attack-upends-karnataka-realtor-family-enn25042303644
4. Subham Tiwari, 23 April 2025, *India Today*, Rough terrain, no security: Why attackers chose Pahalgam's Baisaran. https://www.indiatoday.in/india/story/pahalgam-terrorist-attack-rough-terrain-no-security-attackers-pahalgams-baisaran-osint-2713520-2025-04-23
5. Dalip Singh, 8 May 2025, *Businessline*, M4 rifles used in Pahalgam attack may have been procured by JeM de-facto chief Mufti Abdul Rauf Asghar. https://www.thehindubusinessline.com/news/m4-rifles-used-in-pahalgam-attack-may-have-been-procured-by-jem-de-facto-chief-mufti-abdul-rauf-asghar/article69552371.ece
6. Abhinav Gupta, 22 April 2025, *Money Control*, Pahalgam terror attack: Newly-married UP man among 26 killed; ‘terrorists confirmed religious identity before shooting’. https://www.moneycontrol.com/news/india/pahalgam-terror-attack-newly-married-up-man-among-26-killed-terrorists-confirmed-religious-identity-before-shooting-13001307.html/amp
7. SD Pradhan, 7 May 2025, *The Times of India*, Pahalgam terror attack investigations: Inputs confirm Pak Army’s role. https://timesofindia.indiatimes.com/blogs/ChanakyaCode/pahalgam-terror-attack-investigations-inputs-confirm-pak-armys-role/
8. Aparna Vats, 27 April 2025, *India Today*, https://www.indiatoday.in/india/story/pahalgam-attack-army-officer-guides-35-40-people-to-safety-jammu-and-kashmir-2715950-2025-04-27

9. Ibid.
10. Nazir Masoodi, 24 April, 2025, NDTV, J&K's 'Mini Switzerland' Is In Nature's Lap. Its Remoteness Became A Curse. https://www.ndtv.com/india-news/pahalgam-terror-attack-explained-how-rough-terrain-delayed-rescue-after-pahalgam-terror-attack-8245382
11. Vijaita Singh, 4 May 2025, *The Hindu*, Pahalgam terrorist attack: Terrorists mingled with crowd. https://www.thehindu.com/news/national/pahalgam-attack-terrorists-mingled-with-crowd-herded-them-towards-armed-members-who-killed-toursists-at-baisaran/article69534814.ece
12. *The Hindustan Times*. 27 April 2025, https://www.hindustantimes.com/india-news/hid-in-narrow-pit-karnataka-man-reveals-how-he-survived-pahalgam-terror-attack-101745727635774.html
13. *The Indian Express*, 25 April 2025, Congress sharpens Pahalgam stand, available at https://indianexpress.com/article/political-pulse/pahalgam-terror-attack-congress-cwc-meeting-resolution-bjp-9963331/
14. Ibid.
15. *The Times*, 10 May 2025, How the Kashmir massacre unfolded, according to those who witnessed it. https://www.thetimes.com/world/asia/article/what-happened-kashmir-phalagam-attack-india-pakistan-nzh6z8xmt
16. Ilhaq Tantray and Umer Farooq, 28 April 2025, *Kashmir Times*, I could not save Adil, but I saved 11 tourists: A story of courage from Pahalgam, *Kashmir Times*, Apr 28, 2025. https://kashmirtimes.com/news/a-story-of-courage-from-pahalgam
17. *Indo-Asian News Service*, 23 April 2025, NDTV, 32-Year-Old Jaipur Resident Among 26 Killed In Pahalgam Terror Attack. https://www.ndtv.com/india-news/32-year-old-neeraj-udhwani-jaipur-resident-among-26-killed-in-pahalgam-terror-attack-8236233
18. ANI, 22 April 2025, *Rising Kashmir*, Pahalgam terror attack: Amit Shah chairs high-level security meeting with all agencies. https://risingkashmir.com/pahalgam-terror-attack-amit-shah-chairs-high-level-security-meeting-with-all-agencies/

19. Vinay Mishra, 6 May 2025, *Free Press Journal*, Big Breaking: Terror Attack Suspect Arrested Near Carnage Site In Pahalgam. https://www.freepressjournal.in/india/big-breaking-terror-attack-suspect-arrested-near-carnage-site-in-pahalgam
20. Bharti Jain, 29 April 2025, *The Times of India*, Pahalgam massacre: Pakistani terrorist former para commando, says probe. http://timesofindia.indiatimes.com/articleshow/120709449.cms?utm_source=contentofinterest&utm_medium=text&utm_campaign=cppst
21. Mukesh Ranjan, 17 July 2025, *New Indian Express*, Pahalgam terrorists fired shots in air to celebrate massacre. https://www.newindianexpress.com/nation/2025/Jul/17/pahalgam-terrorists-fired-shots-in-air-to-celebrate-massacre-witness-to-nia
22. PIB, 29 July 2025, https://www.pib.gov.in/PressReleasePage.aspx?PRID=2149811
23. Pradip R Sagar, 1 August 2025, *India Today*, Operation Mahadev Nailing the Pahalgam perpetrators. https://www.indiatoday.in/magazine/up-front/story/20250811-nailing-the-pahalgam-perpetra tors-2764689-2025-08-01
24. Bharti Jain, 27 April 2025, *The Times of India*, 15 local cadre helped Pahalgam attackers. https://timesofindia.indiatimes.com/india/15-local-cadres-helped-pahalgam-attackers-probe/articleshow/120655474.cms
25. Ibid.
26. Bikash Kumar Singh, 20 May 2025, *India Today*, Honeytraps and high treason: The faces behind India's spy scandals.https://www.indiatoday.in/india/story/honeytraps-and-high-treason-the-faces-behind-indias-spy-scandals-2727654-2025-05-20?
27. Man Amar Singh Chhina, 5 May 2025, *The Indian Express*, 2 arrested in Amritsar for spying for Pakistan, sharing sensitive information about Army and Air Force bases to ISI. https://indianexpress.com/article/cities/chandigarh/punjab-police-bust-pakistani-spy-network-amritsar-2-arrested-9981788/
28. Media Center, MEA, Govt of India, 18 July 25, Designation of The Resistance Front (TRF) by the United States Department of State. https://www.mea.gov.in/press-releases.htm?dtl/39810

29. Sky News interview posted on X, 25 April 2025, available at, https://x.com/SkyYaldaHakim/status/1915682394985709595

30. *The Hindu* (London), 25 April 2025, Pakistan doing West's dirty work for decades: Pakistan Defence Minister. https://www.thehindu.com/news/international/pakistan-doing-wests-dirty-work-for-decades-pakistan-defence-minister/article69490687.ece

31. *Pratidin Time*, 12 May 2025, India Names Pakistani Generals at LeT Funeral After Op Sindoor. https://www.pratidintime.com/world/india-names-pakistani-generals-at-let-funeral-after-op-sindoor-9059435

32. Suhasini Haidar, 9 May 2025, *The Hindu*, 'State funeral for terrorists in Pakistan': Foreign Secretary slams Pakistan's links to TRF, LeT, and JeM leaders. https://www.thehindu.com/news/national/state-funeral-for-terrorists-in-pakistan-foreign-secy-slams-pakistans-links-to-trf-let-and-jem-leaders/article69554240.ece

33. PIB Delhi, 12 May 2025, English rendering of PM's address to the Nation. https://www.pib.gov.in/PressReleasePage.aspx?PRID=2128268

34. Abid Hussain, 11 March 2025, *Al Jazeera*, EXPLAINER, Deadly Pakistan train hijack: What happened, who was rescued, what's next? https://www.aljazeera.com/news/2025/3/11/deadly-pakistan-train-hijack-what-happened-and-whats-next

3

Multidomain Responses

A Chronicle of Operation Sindoor

MAJOR GENERAL BIPIN BAKSHI

India took various measures in response to the dastardly attack on tourists at Pahalgam, which concluded in cross-border strikes during Operation Sindoor from 7 to 10 May 2025. Pakistan also took various actions and issued various statements during this period. This chapter provides a detailed account of the actions taken up to 10 May 2025, based on officially released information, interaction with the concerned authorities, and media reports.

The terror attack in Pahalgam, India, on 22 April 2025, marked the start of a rapid escalation. The Indian government accused a Pakistan-based terror group of masterminding the incident. Pakistan's Ministry of Foreign Affairs responded within hours, issuing an official written denial through a press release. The spokesperson rejected any involvement, calling Indian allegations "baseless" and stating that Pakistan would only agree to a neutral, international probe. This was echoed by the Inter-Services Public Relations (ISPR), which delivered an evening briefing confirming that the Army was already on heightened alert along the Line of Control (LC). In a significant statement aired on television that night, Pakistani Army Chief, General Syed Asim Munir, declared that the Pakistan Army "is monitoring the situation with utmost seriousness", and assured, "No provocation will go unanswered". This multipronged response was apparently aimed at signalling vigilance to India, reassuring their domestic population, and presenting Pakistan's version to the international community.

When the unbearable weight of systematic external aggression stretches restraint beyond limits, a nation moves towards a decisive, meticulously planned response. What would this look like in the context of Pakistan's long-standing proxy war actions against India? Step into India's recent strategic symphony that redefined the bilateral rules of engagement. From 23 April to 10 May 2025, India executed a series of synchronised actions that seamlessly blended military precision, unwavering political resolve, and astute geo-political leverage. The operation, named "Sindoor"—vermilion, a symbol of strength, commitment, and auspiciousness in Indian culture—embodied a collective national spirit uniting the government, armed forces, and citizens in a singular, resolute response. This was not just a military action; it was a carefully composed masterpiece of retaliation and deterrence. Launched as a response to the Pahalgam attack, Op Sindoor was a multi-dimensional, meticulously coordinated campaign, designed to degrade Pakistan's terror infrastructure while simultaneously maintaining strict escalation control.

Deliberations, Messaging, Posturing, and Diplomatic Actions

Across a series of National Security Council meetings, India mapped out its political, diplomatic, and military strategies—including outreach to foreign partners and the mobilisation of air and ground forces close to the Line of Control (LC) from 23 April to 06 May 2025.

Figure 3.1: Sequence of actions on the Indian side from 22 April to 6 May 2025

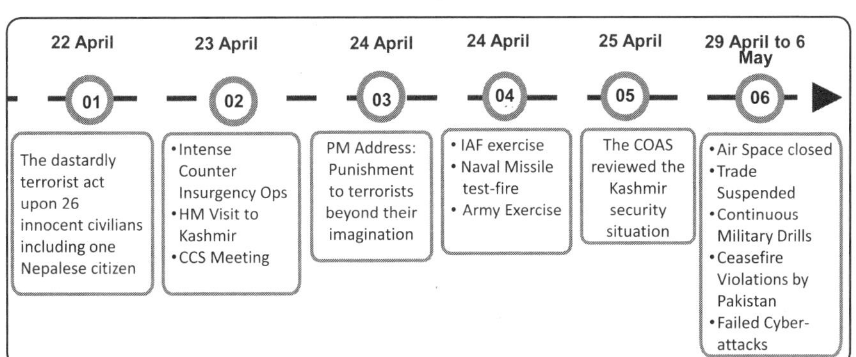

Source: Compiled by the author with inputs from the Indian Army.

23 April 2025

- The Indian Prime Minister convened an emergency meeting of the Cabinet Committee on Security (CCS) in New Delhi. A press release from the Prime Minister's Office (PMO) stated that the CCS reviewed the security situation in Jammu and Kashmir and "authorized a comprehensive and decisive response to the terror attack in Pahalgam". The PMO release emphasised the government's "zero-tolerance policy towards terrorism" and its unwavering commitment to protecting India's sovereignty and its citizens.[1] A slew of measures were announced which included the following:
    - India declared that the Indus Waters Treaty with Pakistan will be held in abeyance, until Pakistan credibly and irrevocably abjures its support for cross-border terrorism.
    - Expulsion of all Pakistani defence attaches from New Delhi and withdrawal of Indian attaches from Islamabad was ordered within a week.
    - Both high commissions were directed to reduce staff from 55 to 30 by 01 May 2025.

  - All SAARC Visa Exemption Scheme (SVES) visas for Pakistani nationals were cancelled and affected individuals were given 48 hours to leave India.
  - Attari Integrated Check Post, the only operational land border crossing with Pakistan, was ordered to be closed, with only limited exceptions for returnees until 01 May 2025.[2]

- The Indian Union Home Minister visited Pahalgam to assess the ground situation and offer condolences to the victims' families. A PIB release highlighted the Home Minister's assurance that "the perpetrators of this heinous act will be brought to justice, and India's response will be swift and impactful". This visit underscored the government's direct engagement and empathy. Simultaneously, the Chiefs of Staff Committee (COSC) met to finalise operational plans, leveraging real-time intelligence from satellites, drones, and human sources to pinpoint targets with extreme precision.

- In the meanwhile, Pakistan intensified its diplomatic and defensive posture. On 23 April, the Pakistani Ministry of Foreign Affairs (MOFA) again publicly denied any involvement, offering full cooperation with a third-party investigation. The Foreign Office's statements portrayed India's response as "premature" and called for restraint. Militarily, the Inter-Services Public Relations (ISPR) reported that all forward posts were on high alert, and the Army was closely monitoring developments over the LC. That day included the first of a series of operational readiness reviews, as General Munir held secure video conferences with regional commanders. The dual-track approach aimed to balance the government's diplomatic denials with a clear message of military preparedness.

24 April 2025

- The IAF conducted extensive air exercises across various sectors "Exercise Aakraman", described by the Ministry of Defence (MoD) in a press briefing as "demonstrations of capability beyond conventional imagination". These exercises involved a wide array of combat aircraft, including Rafale multi-role fighters, Sukhoi-30 MKI air superiority jets, and Apache attack helicopters, simulating deep penetration strikes and high-precision targeting.[3] The MoD spokesperson stated, "These exercises underscore the IAF's readiness to respond to any contingency and project India's air power across the region".
- Pakistan announced similar diplomatic actions mirroring India's steps and also threatened to suspend the Simla Agreement with the following statement:

  Pakistan shall exercise the right to hold all bilateral agreements with India, including but not limited to, Simla Agreement, in abeyance, till India desists from its manifested behaviour of fomenting terrorism inside Pakistan.[4]
- Pakistan also closed its air space to Indian-owned or operated airlines. The other steps announced included closing of Wagah Border with return allowed till 30 April only, declaring Indian defence attaches *persona non grata*, for exit of SVES visa holders except Sikh pilgrims within 48 hours.
- The ISPR issued a bulletin noting that no "cross-LC" violations or abnormal activity had been detected, signalling an intention to avoid escalation. Meanwhile, in the Parliament, General Munir briefed a closed-door session, providing lawmakers with an assessment of security conditions. He reiterated the Army's readiness to meet any challenge, declaring, "The Army stands ready for all contingencies".

25–26 April 2025

The Pakistan Army undertook various preparatory measures at the highest levels. ISPR publicly referenced a "tabletop exercise" at General Headquarters (GHQ), where senior military leadership simulated likely Indian steps, potential escalation triggers, and the operational impact of possible airspace closures. The Army Chief participated directly, hearing briefings and discussing hypothetical scenarios, though no active military posture was altered at this stage. This proactive war-gaming underscored how seriously the Pakistan Army was anticipating possible confrontations, a fact shared with the public through official briefings to deter miscalculation. The ISPR continued regular updates, noting a continued absence of cross-LC exchanges and claiming that maximum restraint was being maintained. Army units were tasked to keep regional civilian officials informed, ensuring local authorities were kept abreast of military directives and protocols. These steps were paired with further MOFA statements urging India not to escalate the situation and reiterating Pakistan's preference for international mediation over direct confrontation.

27 April 2025

The Indian Navy successfully conducted a test-fire of the BrahMos supersonic cruise missile from a frontline warship in the Arabian Sea.[5] A press release from the Ministry of Defence (Navy) confirmed the successful engagement of a designated target with "pinpoint accuracy", reiterating the missile's formidable range (400 km) and speed. The release emphasised that this test-fire "reaffirms India's credible deterrence capabilities in the maritime domain and its ability to project power far beyond its shores".

27–29 April 2025

As the weekend progressed, Pakistan's primary focus was on diplomatic signalling. MOFA releases repeatedly condemned any

Indian hint of reprisal and warned against "war hysteria". The MOFA spokesperson stated, "Pakistan remains committed to peace based on mutual respect and sovereign equality. However, any threat to its security or territorial integrity will be met with firm and proportionate measures, in accordance with Article 51 of the UN Charter".[6] Behind the scenes, Army and intelligence branches increased surveillance of forward areas. The military command chain issued standby orders to rapidly deploy units if required; however, no changes to the visible military posture were announced. ISPR stated, "Contingency units placed on standby". The Pakistan Army Chief at a Corps Commanders' Conference, emphasised, "Pakistan's strategic restraint should not be seen as weakness". This marked a rhetorical and operational escalation, designed both to reassure a tense domestic audience and to deter Indian action, which was evidently being quietly planned across the border.

Photo 3.1: Prime Minister Narendra Modi meets Defence Minister Rajnath Singh, NSA Ajit Doval, CDS Gen Anil Chauhan, Army Chief Gen Upendra Dwivedi, Navy Chief Admiral Dinesh K. Tripathi, and IAF Chief Air Chief Marshal Amar Preet Singh in New Delhi

Prime Minister Narendra Modi chaired a meeting with Defence Minister Rajnath Singh, National Security Advisor Ajit Doval, Chief of Defence Staff General Anil Chauhan, and the chiefs of the three services on 29 April to consider various options for the Indian countermeasures. As per reports, PM Modi affirmed India's "national resolve to deal a crushing blow to terrorism", and said that the Indian armed forces have his full confidence and "complete operational freedom to decide on the mode, targets and timing"[7] of India's response in the aftermath of the previous week's terror attack at Pahalgam.

30 April 2025

India's Ministry of Civil Aviation announced temporary restrictions on Pakistani overflights through Indian airspace, citing "security concerns following recent terrorist activities".[8] Concurrently, the Ministry of Commerce and Industry announced the imposition of enhanced trade restrictions on certain goods originating from Pakistan, stating that these measures were "a direct consequence of Pakistan's continued support for cross-border terrorism and its failure to dismantle terror infrastructure on its soil". These economic measures were explicitly aimed at further pressuring Pakistan's already "fragile economy", with its persistent reliance on international financial assistance. Subsequently, over the next two days, Pakistan's Civil Aviation Authority (CAA) began issuing internal advisories to commercial airlines, alerting them to the risk of possible disruptions in Pakistani airspace. These warnings were not yet made public and no restrictions were imposed but they reflected the government's awareness of the situation's potential to spill over into civil aviation. Meanwhile, the Army Chief continued to receive intelligence briefings, underscoring that all forces should maintain "highest alert" across sensitive sectors.

30 April 2025, midnight panic attack victim in Pakistan

Meanwhile, amid fear of being attacked Federal Minister for Information and Broadcasting, Attaullah Tarar held an emergency press meeting at 2 am on 30th April, stating "credible intelligence-based information has warned of an Indian military action".[9]

Photo 3.2: Attaullah Tarar, Pakistani Minister in an emergency press briefing on 30 April 2025

Source: The Statesman, 30 April 2025.

1–6 May 2025: Diplomatic activities

US Secretary of Defense Mr Pete Hegseth reiterated full support of the US government in India's fight against terrorism.[10] The Ministry of External Affairs (MEA) initiated an intensive diplomatic outreach campaign. Foreign Secretary-level briefings were held in Delhi with ambassadors and high commissioners of key international partners, including the P5 nations and major regional powers. MEA spokesperson briefings consistently apprised the international community of "irrefutable evidence of Pakistan's direct complicity in the Pahalgam attack and its long-standing policy of using terrorism as an instrument of state policy". These diplomatic efforts aimed to build international consensus against Pakistan's actions justify India's robust response as an act of self-defence, and further isolate Pakistan on the global stage.

During this period, ISPR confirmed through daily briefings that all major command headquarters were in direct contact with the Pakistan General Headquarters (GHQ), maintaining round-the-clock surveillance of the situation. The Pakistani Army Chief again presided over briefings, giving instructions on positioning rapid response teams near the LC and vital infrastructure facilities.

On 5 May, India announced a national-level civil defence rehearsal to be held across 244 officially designated Civil Defence districts on 7 May 2025.

7 May 2025: Operation Sindoor begins

The core of India's Op Sindoor was the execution of highly precise strikes aimed at dismantling Pakistan's entrenched terror ecosystem. These strikes, conducted by specialised units of the Indian Army and the Indian Air Force, targeted nine critical terrorist camps and staging areas located in Pakistan-occupied Jammu and Kashmir (POJK) and Punjab.[11]

Figure 3.2: Post by Indian Army on X at 01:51 hours, 7 May 2025

Source: Indian Army.

The Indian Army social media message highlighted India's response by saying, "Justice is Served", at 01:51 hours immediately after the strikes. India had initiated a focussed wave of precision strikes, targeting key terrorist facilities in POJK on the night of 6/ 7 May.

Figure 3.3: Terror targets struck on 7 May 2025

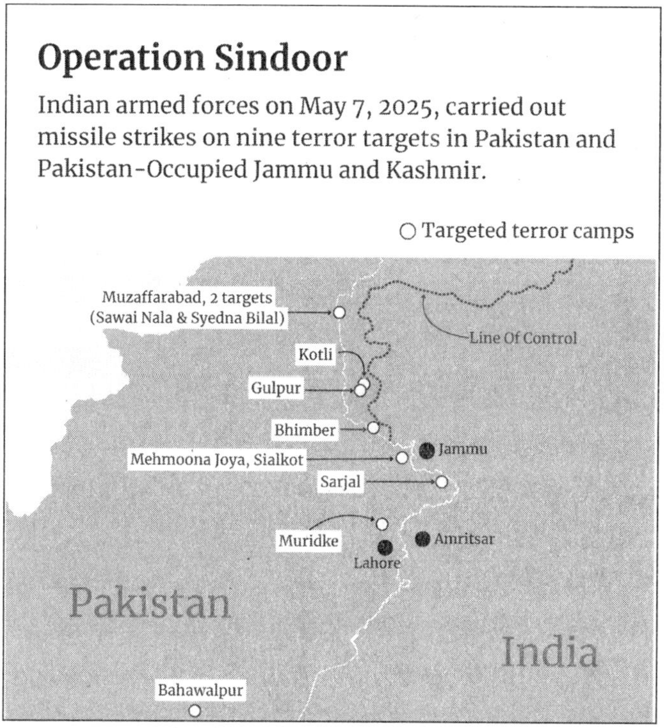

Source: *The Hindu*, 14 May 2025.[12]

The terrorist facilities included seven locations assigned to the Indian Army and two locations assigned to the Indian Air Force. The targets destroyed by the Indian Army were at Sawai Nala (Muzaffarabad), Syedna Bilal (Muzaffarabad), Abbas (Kotli), Gulpur (Kotli), Bhimber, Mehmoona Joya, Sialkot, and Sarjal,

Sialkot. The targets destroyed by IAF were the Markaz Taiba at Muridke and the Markaz Subhan Allah, Bahawalpur.

The General Officer Commanding (GOC) of Rising Star Corps, in a video interview with Gaurav Sawant, clarified that seven of the nine targets were assigned to the Indian Army and of these seven Army targets, two were hit by the Rising Star Corps.[13]

The Indian Ministry of Information and Broadcasting asked over-the-top (OTT) and media-streaming platforms, as well as intermediary services, to discontinue Pakistani web series, films, songs, podcasts, and other media content with immediate effect.[14] Concurrently, 16 Pakistani YouTube channels were banned, as a counter to the information war.

7 May 2025, activities during the day

A joint press briefing by the Indian spokespersons on 7 May 2025, at 10:30 hours in the morning confirmed the successful obliteration of the nine selected targets. Col Sofiya Qureshi, the Indian Army spokesperson, said that the strikes were "intelligence-driven, executed with surgical precision, and specifically designed to avoid civilian casualties or collateral damage to civilian infrastructure, in strict adherence to India's ethical warfare principles".[15]

Photo 3.3: Foreign Secretary Vikram Misri, Colonel Sofiya Qureshi, and Wing Commander Vyomika Singh

Source: DD News.[16]

Pakistan's Prime Minister convened the National Security Committee (NSC), with the Army Chief delivering a key military briefing and assessment of the strikes. In his first public address post-strike, General Munir stated, "Pakistan reserves the right to respond at a time and place of its choosing. No aggression will be tolerated".[17] ISPR announced that forward troop deployments had been revised, air defence assets moved into position, and rapid reinforcement was underway. Army units in border regions were ordered to remain in constant contact with civil authorities for local coordination. Simultaneously, the Foreign Ministry lodged a formal protest at the United Nations.[18]

India's deployment of key naval assets, including the indigenous aircraft carrier INS Vikrant (with its complement of MiG-29K fighters), destroyers like INS Kolkata (armed with BrahMos and advanced anti-submarine systems), and nuclear-powered submarines like INS Arihant alongside Scorpène-class vessels, effectively established a dominant posture in the Arabian Sea.

Figure 3.4: Sketch showing sites of Pakistani attacks on the night of 7 May 2025

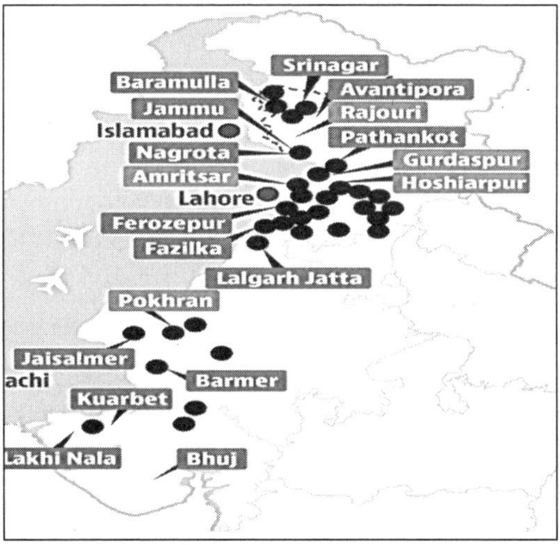

Source: Google Maps.

On the night of 7–8 May 2025, Pakistan attempted to engage 15 military stations in Northern and Western India including Awantipura, Srinagar, Jammu, Pathankot, Amritsar, Kapurthala, Jalandhar, Ludhiana, Adampur, Bhatinda, Chandigarh, Nal, Phalodi, Uttarlai, and Bhuj, using drones and missiles. These were neutralised by the Integrated Counter UAS Grid and Air Defence systems. The debris of these attacks was recovered from a number of locations that prove the Pakistani attacks.[19]

Pakistan also engaged several military locations and Indian towns near the LC with artillery fire, causing some damage and unnecessary civilian casualties. This was due to an increased intensity of unprovoked firing across the LC using mortars and heavy calibre Artillery in Kupwara, Baramulla, Uri, Poonch, Mendhar, and Rajouri sectors in Jammu and Kashmir. The PIB report the next day intimated:

> Sixteen innocent lives have been lost, including three women and five children, due to Pakistani firing. Here too, India was compelled to respond to bring Mortar and Artillery fire from Pakistan to a halt.[20]

In response to Pakistani actions of 7 May 2025, the Indian Army and Air Force executed proportional offensive operations, targeting Pakistani air defence radars at a number of locations, Pakistani artillery locations near the LC, and some additional LeT bases in POJK. The result, India assessed, was a "neutralised" air defence radar in Lahore. Abbas, Kotli (13 km from LC), a critical LeT base used for training suicide bombers (fidayeen) was neutralised, disrupting logistical support for cross-border attacks. Gulpur, Kotli (30 km from LC), an LeT camp involved in the Poonch attack of 20 April 2023 and the pilgrim assault on 9 June 2023, was decimated. To continue its clear signals of a non-escalatory intent, India emphasised[21] that its "response has been in the same domain, with the same intensity as Pakistan".

8 May 2025

Foreign Secretary Vikram Misri in his media briefing on 8 May, explicitly mentioned:

> India's response is non-escalatory, precise and measured. Our intention is not to escalate matters, and we are only responding to the escalation. No military targets have been selected. Only terror infrastructure has been hit.[22]

Pakistan's retaliatory military attacks, with several drone and missile attacks launched on Indian military targets, continued on the night of 8 May 2025. The Pakistan Army Chief publicly announced the launch as "a measured military response to safeguard sovereignty"—a statement broadcast for both international visibility and domestic morale. He also revealed the formation of a Joint Operational Command Cell in Rawalpindi to ensure unified coordination among the Army, Air Force, and Navy. Border-area civilians were urged to move to safe zones, and the National Disaster Management Authority (NDMA) was activated for logistics.

The Indian Border Security Force (BSF) Actions

BSF foiled a major infiltration attempt along the International Border in Samba district, Jammu and Kashmir, at around 23:00 hours on 8 May 2025. Acting on detected suspicious movement, BSF personnel swiftly engaged armed infiltrators in a fierce firefight, successfully preventing a significant breach. They also intercepted drones of various kinds across the Jammu and Punjab border areas and remained alert to thwart many infiltration attempts during Op Sindoor. Their relentless vigil and successful operations underscored the BSF's vigilance, operational preparedness, and its crucial role in maintaining border security during heightened tensions as mentioned in the government press brief of 18 May 2025.[23,24]

9 and 10 May 2025

The Airports Authority of India (AAI) and relevant aviation authorities issued a series of Notices to Airmen (NOTAMs) announcing the temporary closure of 32 airports across northern and western India for all civil flight operations, effective from 9 to 14 May 2025, due to operational reasons.[25] Surprisingly, Pakistan did not close civil airlines operations for domestic and international carriers other than India, except for a few hours during the day on 10 May, even when they were launching multiple missiles and armed drones through their air space in this period.

General Munir proclaimed, "Escalation control is being sought through strength, not submission", indicating to India and to Pakistanis that the government would respond forcefully but was also open to de-escalation through parity. He authorised the Army Public Relations Directorate to begin issuing standard, twice-daily situation updates. The CAA issued a further extension on airspace closure only to Indian carriers and worked directly with IATA to anticipate the impact on regional airlines.

In the early part of that last night of operations, Pakistan launched a huge wave of additional missile and drone attacks targeting Indian logistical nodes and air bases. This marked the scaled-up attack under Pakistan's "Operation Bunyan-un-Marsoos", an operationally expanded campaign.

While the previous two nights had seen a smaller number of military assets employed, this time there were around 500 drone intrusions at multiple locations from all along the border from Leh to Sir Creek. Intense artillery shelling was reported at seven locations in J&K. Drones were also used to attack the medicare centres and schools in Srinagar, Awantipora, and Udhampur military locations.

Figure 3.5: Indian locations subjected to intense drone and artillery attacks on 9 May 2025

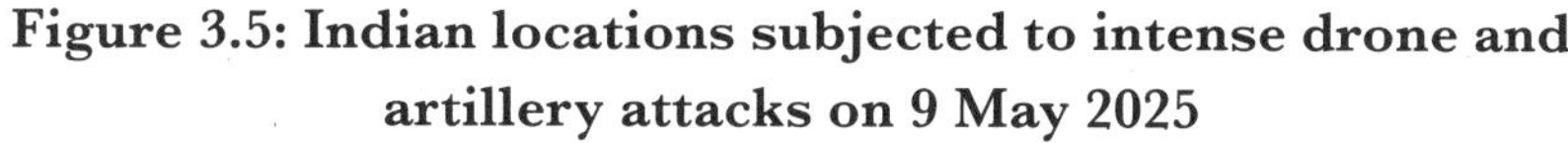

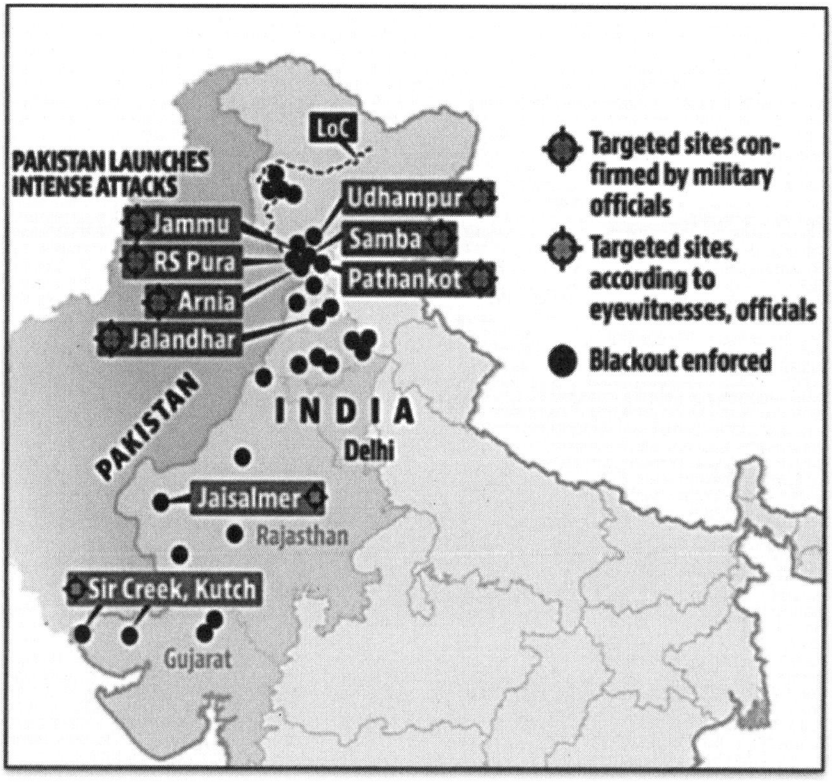

Source: Google Maps.

India's air defence systems intercepted a Pakistani Fatah-II missile over Sirsa, Haryana, averting disaster only 220 km from Delhi. The interception, part of broader escalatory actions including attacks on multiple targets across northern India, prompted decisive but measured Indian counter-strikes against military sites in Pakistan. Government and military briefings made clear that India's actions were focused on dismantling terror infrastructure while minimising civilian impact.

In response to Pakistan's continued belligerence, India launched a phase of precision strikes targeting Pakistani military assets.

The speed and ferocity of these attacks probably unsettled the further plans that Pakistan had made to upscale their attacks, by planning the use of a large number of air-launched missiles in the later part of the night and early hours of 10 May 2025. India struck multiple air bases and radar sites across the length and breadth of Pakistan, addressing areas that were not even struck at the height of hostilities in the 1971 war. These included command and control centres, their main UAV base at Sukkur, and many of their maintenance hangars on their main air bases, causing heavy damage to the PAF assets and capabilities.

Figure 3.6: Targets struck on 10 May 2025

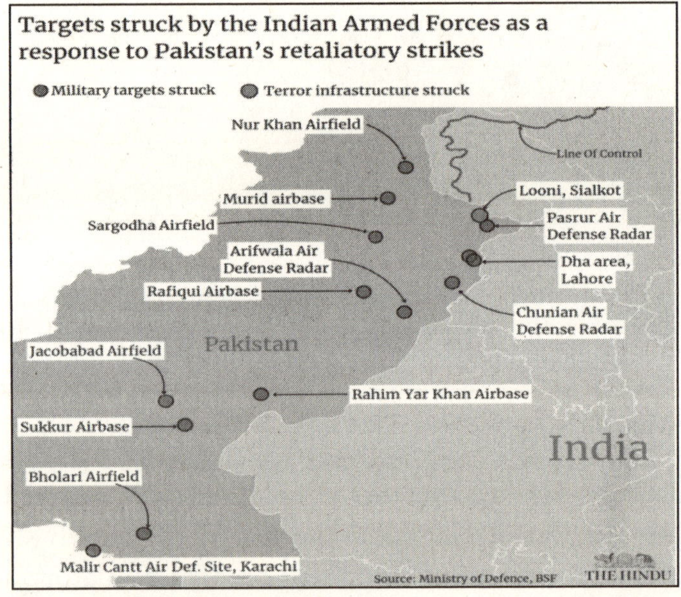

Source: *The Hindu*, 14 May 2025.[28]

At 03:53 hours on 10 May, minutes after the wide-ranging strikes, DG ISPR came on the air in a video message confirming India's strikes, claiming India had also bombed Afghanistan and Amritsar. "Now you just wait for our response" was his closing remark in an ominous tone. The video is available on the official handle X,[26] and the report is available on Radio Pakistan website.[27]

Figure 3.7: DG ISPR Gen Chowdhry makes an empty threat after India's strikes on 10 May 2025

Source: Accessed by VPN.[29]

The tremendous damage caused by these relentless Indian strikes evidently contributed towards forcing Pakistan into a defensive posture. On 9 and 10 May, there were a series of telephone calls between various dignitaries in India, USA, and Pakistan, culminating in the Pakistan Director General of Military Operations' (DGMO's) ceasefire proposal on May 10 at 15:35 hours (IST), the details of which will be elucidated further in the next chapters.

10 May 2025

Amid this heightened conflict, there were reports that Prime Minister Shehbaz Sharif had called for a meeting of the National Command Authority, the body that oversees Pakistan's nuclear arsenal. This move signalled Islamabad's readiness to make crucial security decisions at the highest level, reflecting both the seriousness of the ongoing crisis and international concerns about nuclear risks. The meeting followed Pakistan's initiation of major military operations against India, and both sides exchanged accusations of airspace violations, with at least 48 casualties reported in the escalating hostilities.[30, 31] However, the meeting did not take place and was apparently cancelled.

Diplomatic and military backchannels grew more active as Pakistan signalled openness to a ceasefire. Contradicting the earlier bravado, ISPR announced that defensive responses to the initial Indian strikes were complete, and that talks for a ceasefire were underway, facilitated through a direct hotline between Indian and Pakistani military commands. General Munir made a public statement at noon, committing to "uphold national security during negotiations, but matching any provocation with immediate response".

As reported subsequently in the day, it was at 15:35 hours (IST), that the DGMO of Pakistan initiated contact with his Indian counterpart, proposing that hostilities should be ceased. The exact conversation details were not announced; however, the following statement was made by the Indian Foreign Secretary about an hour after the call:

> The Director General of Military Operations of Pakistan called the Director General of Military Operations of India at 15:35 hours IST earlier today.
>
> It was agreed between them that both sides would stop all firing and military action on land and in the air and sea with effect from 17:00 hours Indian Standard Time today.
>
> Instructions have been given on both sides to give effect to the understanding.

Subsequently that evening, Pakistan violated its own proposal for cessation of hostile actions by several artillery and drone attacks in the Srinagar and Rajauri sectors. These offensive activities terminated in a few hours and the guns fell silent on both sides of the border by 11 May 2025.

11 May 2025

After the cessation of hostilities, there was a press briefing held by India wherein the DGMO, DG Air Ops, and Director General Naval Operations (DGNO) were present. During this briefing all aspects of the operation were briefed in detail and several achievements made were covered. In an extensive summary of actions taken by India and results achieved, India later also issued a press note on 14 May 2025.[32] As per the press note, and the DGMOs briefing on 11 May 2025, several significant results were achieved by India, some of these are listed below:

- Multiple high-profile terrorists on India's most wanted list were neutralised in a single night, crippling key operational modules. High-value targets eliminated include Yusuf Azhar, Abdul Malik Rauf, Mudassir Ahmad. These individuals were linked to the IC-814 hijack and Pulwama blast.
- Over 100 terrorists were killed when India successfully destroyed nine major terror launchpads while targeting Lashkar-e-Taiba, Jaish-e-Mohammed, and Hizbul Mujahideen facilities.
- India bombed Pakistan's Bholari Air Base, killing several armed forces personnel, including Pakistan's squadron leader Usman Yousuf, four airmen among others, as well as destroying Pakistan's fighter jets.
- Various ammunition depots and bases like Sargodha and Bholari that housed F-16s and JF-17 fighter jets were hit. This led to the destruction of 20% of the infrastructure of Pakistan's Air Force. Further details were announced by India's Chief of Air Staff on 9 August 2025, wherein he mentioned five fighter jets and one larger military aircraft were destroyed in the air besides the significant assets

destroyed during the strikes on the air bases and radar sites. Subsequent independent reports pitch the damage to PAF even higher.

Photo 3.4: Lt General Rajiv Ghai with Air Marshal A.K. Bharti, Vice Admiral A.N. Pramod, and Maj Gen S.S. Sharda, ADG Strategic Communications during a press conference on 11 May 2025

Source: Indian Army media cell.

At least 50 Pakistan armed forces personnel were killed by Indian strikes along the LC and the air strikes at multiple locations.

During this press briefing, Dinakar Peri from *The Hindu* asked about the Pakistani claim for having downed six Indian fighter jets. "I am happy that you have asked this question", Air Marshal Bharti the DGAO[33] said, and then gave his response:

> All I can say is that we have achieved the objectives that we selected and all our pilots are back home. We are in a combat scenario; losses are a part of combat. The question you must ask us is ... have we achieved our objective of decimating the terrorist camps? And the answer is a thumping yes. And the results are for the whole world to see. As for the details, what could have been … how many numbers … which platform did we lose … at this time I would not like to comment on that because we are still in a combat situation. If I comment on anything, it will only advantage the adversary. So, we don't want to give them any advantage at this stage.

The Naval Dimension: A Silent Chokehold and Strategic Pressure

Photo 3.5: Indian Navy Fleet deployed in the Arabian Sea

Source: Media briefings.

While the ground and air operations dominated immediate headlines, the Indian Navy played a pivotal and often understated role in Op Sindoor. The "naval missile test-fire beyond their imagination", as referenced in official briefings, was a crucial strategic signal. This test of the BrahMos supersonic cruise missile with its formidable 400-km range on 27 April 2025 unequivocally signalled India's overwhelming maritime dominance in the Arabian Sea and its ability to project power far beyond its territorial waters.

In a discussion with the authors on 24 July 2025, the CDS, Gen Anil Chauhan, conveyed his appreciation for the invaluable assistance provided by Indian Navy elements whose precision munitions were made available for employment alongside both Indian Army and Indian Air Force strikes during Op Sindoor.

The forward deployment of the Indian Navy in the Northern Arabian Sea created a de-facto maritime blockade, confining the Pakistan Navy to its harbours and crippling their operational agility. Karachi, responsible for around 60% of Pakistan's international trade, faced severe disruptions. India's naval presence, combined with economic and trade restrictions, intensified Pakistan's economic distress. Shipping companies issued advisories against Pakistani ports, contributing to a 10% drop in merchant traffic to Karachi and a 15-25% spike in additional war risk premiums and surcharges. Pakistani exporters struggled with export commitments and import backlogs—a direct outcome of India's maritime posture.

The Indian Navy deployment prompted Pakistan to issue navigational area (NAVAREA) warnings[34] amid fears of a possible naval strike. The heightened risk even led to international commercial vessels re-routing to avoid the tense waters around Karachi.

Photo 3.6: Indian Navy Ships deployed in the Arabian Sea

Source: Media briefings.

As mentioned in press brief "Operation SINDOOR: Forging One Force, The Synergy of India's Armed Forces" issued on 18 May 2025, the Indian Navy played a critical role in asserting maritime dominance during Op SINDOOR.[35] Operating as a composite networked force, the Navy deployed its Carrier Battle Group (CBG) equipped with MiG-29K fighter jets and airborne early warning helicopters. This ensured persistent surveillance and real-time identification of threats across the maritime domain. The CBG maintained a powerful air defence shield that prevented hostile aerial incursions, especially from the Makran coast. The Navy's presence created a strong deterrent, and effectively bottled up Pakistani air elements along their western seaboard, denying them any operational space. Naval pilots conducted round-the-clock sorties, further demonstrating India's readiness and strategic reach in the region. The Navy's ability to establish uncontested control over the seas also validated its anti-missile and anti-aircraft defence capabilities in a complex threat environment.

Responding to a questionnaire by the authors, the Indian Navy has provided the following inputs:[36]

- As the Indian Armed Forces undertook "Op Sindoor" as a response to the terrorist attack on innocent tourists at Pahalgam on 22 April 2025, abetted and supported by Pakistan, the preparatory activities immediately commenced, in the aftermath of the attack.
- Accelerated embarkation of war outfit on all operational platforms was undertaken and hundreds of missiles, including BrahMos, were embarked onboard frontline Indian Navy (IN) platforms in a very quick time. Thereafter, the Naval forces remained forward deployed in the Northern Arabian Sea in a deterrent posture, with full readiness and were poised to strike select targets at sea, and on land, when ordered.
- The operation was planned and seamlessly executed in a synergised manner by all three Services on the night of 6–7 May. Navy's Special Force elements (MARCOS) with precision munition were deployed with IA and IAF. The tri-service deep hinterland strikes on Pakistani terror infrastructure demonstrated the ability of our Defence Forces to undertake long-range precision strikes.
- The Navy's Western Fleet ships deployed in the Arabian Sea undertook multiple successful SSM and SAM firings on the Western Seaboard, within 96 hours of the terrorist attack,

thereby validating the combat readiness of the platforms, systems, and crew, to precisely deliver ordnance on target. These successful firings signalled intent and readiness of the IN to undertake long-range precision strikes against "the adversary targets".

- From 7 May onwards, the IN assets were forward deployed in a dissuasive deterrent posture in the Arabian Sea, to thwart any misadventure by the enemy at sea and to be ready to effectively respond to any such attempt. The Navy's surveillance assets developed credible Maritime Domain Awareness (MDA) in the Area of Operation (AOR), and movement of all Pakistan Naval units was closely monitored.

This operation marked one of the Indian Navy's largest real-time operational movements outside routine peacetime exercises. The deployment included destroyers equipped with SSM BrahMos cruise-missiles, MRSAM Barak-8, and Varunastra (heavyweight torpedoes), capable of engaging surface, aerial, and underwater threats. Also in position were stealth guided-missile frigates, including the newly inducted INS Tushil, forming a formidable naval wall, off the western coast. The operation also saw participation from submarines, fast attack crafts, and missile boats, bringing the total number of assets to around 36—outnumbering the Pakistan Navy, which currently fields fewer than 30 warships.[37]

Photo 3.7: Indian Navy Submarines deployed in the Arabian Sea

Source: Media briefings.

Strategic Effect of Tactical Actions

Even without direct military confrontation on the high seas, the Indian Navy's actions during Op Sindoor demonstrated the strategic impact of tactical manoeuvres. The Indian Navy's overwhelming presence and readiness not only neutralised potential maritime threats but also applied significant economic pressure on Pakistan, underscoring India's ability to leverage its maritime dominance to achieve broader strategic objectives.

As mentioned earlier, while the maritime dimension of the conflict remained away from media glare, it was no less significant in achieving the overall outcomes of India's strategic actions during Op Sindoor. The tactical manoeuvring by a formidable naval force, in possession of significant long-range weapons and aircraft, created the strategic effect of a highly potent force hovering on the horizon, ready to strike. The fact that the conflict was not expanded into the maritime dimension further signifies India's non-escalatory intent from the very beginning till the suspension of Op Sindoor.

The War in Cyber Space

Starting from 22 April, and continuing through Op Sindoor (7–10 May), India faced an unrelenting wave of cyber-attacks, primarily by Pakistani groups backed by Islamabad and Beijing, but also from hacker groups in Türkiye, Bangladesh, Malaysia, and West Asian countries.[38] According to Indian government sources, these groups launched over 1.5 million cyber-attacks targeting a wide swathe of India's critical infrastructure spanning defence, power, telecom, finance, and transportation during this period. In a cabinet meeting in early June, Prime Minister Narendra Modi put the number of attacks at 100 million.

Figure 3.8: Sources of cyber-attacks on India during Op Sindoor

A HACKERS' GALLERY

A few of the foreign hacking groups/ hacktivists who launched mayhem in the Indian cyberspace with their attacks

APT36 (Pakistan)
Also known as Transparent Tribe, it carried out phishing campaigns against armed forces personnel, but failed. Hacked websites of the Military Engineer Services, the Manohar Parrikar Institute and the DRDO

Team Insane Pakistan & HOAX1337 (Pakistan)
Hacked websites of Assam Rifles, Department of Atomic Energy, Armoured Vehicles Nigam Ltd

Turk Hack Team (Turkey)
Carried out unsuccessful DDoS attacks on Indian banking websites and media portals

Vulture (Iran)
Directed DDoS attacks on websites of CERT-In, National Testing Agency, PMO and the President's office

Mysterious Bangladesh
Tried to breach government portals like those of CBI, the Election Commission and BSNL

RipperSec (Malaysia)
Targeted the vice president of India's website but was repelled

R3VOX Anonymous (decentralised)
Launched abortive DDoS attacks on the Central Board of Indirect Taxes and Customs and Income Tax Department

APT41 & Mustang Panda (China)
Failed attempts to impair India's power grids, logistics chains and telecommunications networks

INDIA

Source: Author's compilation.[39]

Cyber-attacks have been seen to closely accompany kinetic operations in recent conflicts, targeting command-and-control systems, degrading civilian morale, and influencing international perception. With vital sectors like defence, finance, and communications dependent on sets of interconnected information systems on the internet, attacking these could grievously impair a nation's war-making capabilities.

Predictably, India's military-industrial infrastructure came in for special attention, while the power ministry confirmed that over 200,000 cyber-attacks on the Indian electricity grid were foiled between 7-10 May. The hackers resorted to acts like – website defacements, Denial of Service (DoS) and Distributed Denial of Service (DDoS) attacks (aiming to overwhelm and impair a target server/network), malware distribution (using viruses to infect systems and gain control) and phishing (use of deceptive emails to extract information). The sole aim was to steal defence information, particularly missile technology, and to undermine vital sectors.

Figure 3.9: The Defenders, Indian cyber-security agencies on the frontline

THE INDIAN DEFENDERS

Indian cyber-security agencies on the frontline

Indian Cyber Crime Coordination Centre (14C)

Operating under the Union home ministry, it provides a framework to deal with cyber crime. During the recent attacks, it spearheaded counter-hack operations. Under it, over 150 hostile command-and-control servers were taken down

Data Security Council of India

Set up by NASSCOM, it is an industry body on data protection. During the cyber attacks that erupted after April 22, it led a joint task force, coordinating with government, private and industry bodies. It red-flagged suspicious sites, blocked vulnerable Indian sites

CERT-In

Working under the ministry of information technology, the Indian Computer Emergency Response Team (CERT-In), is India's nodal agency dealing with cyber threats. It sent out alerts, emergency response procedures

NCIIPC

Functioning under the PMO, the National Critical Information Infrastructure Protection Centre (NCIIPC) safeguards vital assets like power grids. Along with CERT-In, it picked out threats in the telecom, energy, finance and transport sectors, led a swift response using its expert teams

Defence Cyber Agency

India took the attack to the hackers too. Elite cyber units of the Defence Cyber Agency, a tri-service command of the Indian military, carried out retaliatory digital strikes on critical assets of the enemy. Took down social media troll farms, disrupted servers

Source: India Today, 28 July 2025.

Indian cyber-security agencies, including the Indian Computer Emergency Response Team (CERT-In), the Defence Cyber Agency (DCA) and the National Critical Information Infrastructure Protection Centre (NCIIPC) successfully thwarted most attacks. However, India's victory in repulsing these attacks was not absolute. Websites of several Indian military, defence production, and defence research institutes, including the Defence Research and Development Organisation (DRDO), were successfully targeted. Approximately 150 out of the 1.5 million attempts succeeded. Clearly, more needs to be done to beef up India's cyber-security, as attacks on Indian cyber space continue. In retaliation, Indian hacking groups took the attack to Pakistan, targeting and breaching critical digital assets of its military and government.

Figure 3.10: Pakistanis' claim of hacking Indian Government sites. Operation Salaar, only 783 views as on 25 August 2025

Source: Accessed by VPN.[40]

Innefu Labs is an agency that works closely with the Ministry of Defence (MoD) in Cyber War. Its CEO Tarun Wig states, "These invasions are no longer just for ransom. They target critical infrastructures, steal sensitive data, and attempt to disrupt essential services".

Figure 3.11: Pakistan Air Force pseudo handle claims a hack

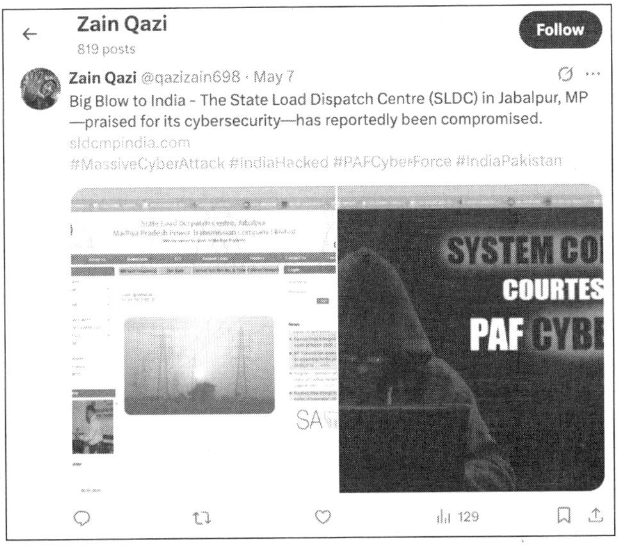

Zain Qazi
819 posts
Follow
Zain Qazi @qazizain698 · May 7
Big Blow to India - The State Load Dispatch Centre (SLDC) in Jabalpur, MP —praised for its cybersecurity—has reportedly been compromised.
sldcmpindia.com
#MassiveCyberAttack #IndiaHacked #PAFCyberForce #IndiaPakistan
SYSTEM CO
COURTES
PAF CYB
129

Source: Accessed by VPN.[41]

Figure 3.12: Pakistani Air Force Cyber Force handle claims to have hacked Indian servers and cameras, not substantiated

Zain Qazi @qazizain698 · May 9
Massive breach!
Indian Army, Navy, Air Force, Law Ministry — all mail servers down.
Govt office surveillance cameras also hacked.
#PAFCyberForce #OperationBunyanAlMarsous
HACKED
OPERATION BUNYAN AL-MARSOUS

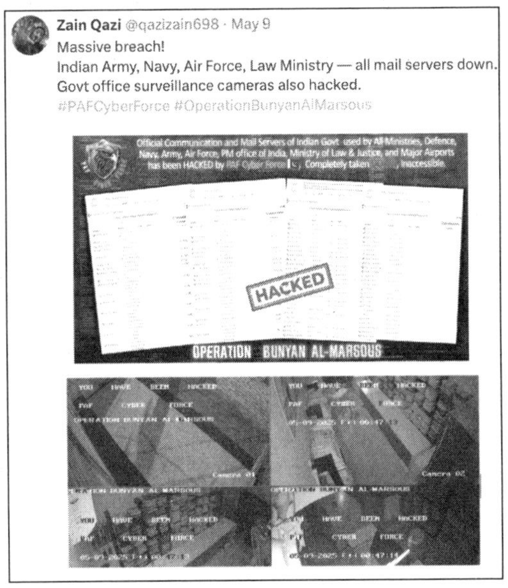

Source: Accessed by VPN.[42]

India's Response

Countering the cyber-attacks by pro-Pakistan hackers and hacktivist groups, India's cyber armies—independent and state-backed—launched thousands of attacks on Pakistan.[43] Indian hacking groups like "Indian Cyber Force", "Indian Cyber Defender", "White Horse", "echoOfGulmarg", "teamwhitelotus", and "Cyber Warriors India" claimed successful attacks on crucial Pakistani infrastructure. India's elite cyber unit under the DCA was mobilised and retaliatory digital strikes were carried out.

Indian cyber groups targeted Pakistan's critical infrastructure. The compromise of Pakistan Railways online ticketing and operational network was the most notable effect seen; it caused service interruptions.

Figure 3.13: Pakistan Rail reservation system disrupted

echoOfGulmarg
13 posts
Follow

echoOfGulmarg @echo0fGulmarg · May 11
OWNED by #echoOfGulmarg

PAKISTAN RAILWAYS DERAILED

Visit: pakrail.gov.pk

PAKISTAN RAIL DERAILED
CYBER STRIKE BY
ECHO OF GULM@RG
PAKISTAN RAIL NETWORK DESTROYED
0:07 / 0:30

Source: https://x.com/echo0fGulmarg/status/1921484117188780121

Figure 3.14: Pakistan Defence Housing Agency hacked by Indian hackers

Source: Internet Archive Wayback Machine, 9 May 2025.[44]

Figure 3.15: Pakistan's important bank hacked by Indian hackers

Source: echoOfGulmarg, 11 May 2025.[45]

Figure 3.16: Server level destructive attack by Indian hackers, video with control demonstration posted on X

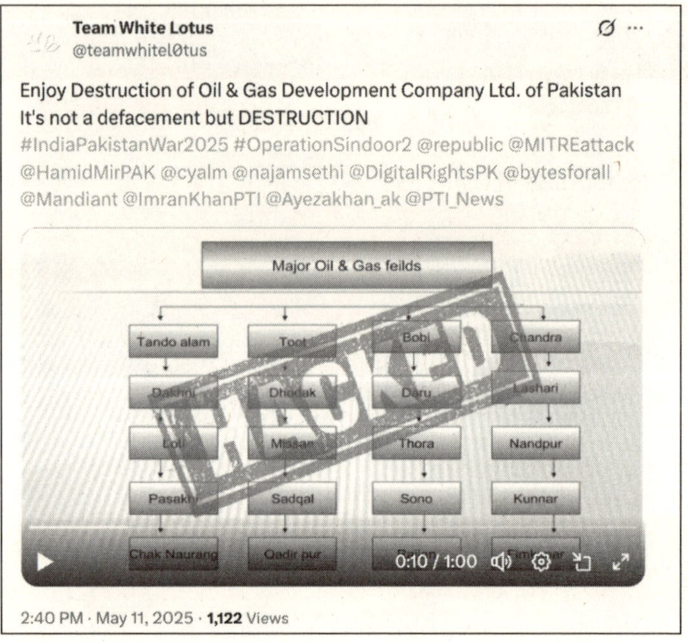

Source: Team White Lotus, 11 May 2025.[46]

Similarly, IT systems belonging to the Oil & Gas Development Company Limited (OGDCL), PAF Shaheen Foundation, Pakistan Army Welfare Trust, and the Defence Housing Authority (DHA) were impacted. Other sectors, including banking networks, paramilitary force systems, and capital development authorities, were also affected. The National University of Medical Sciences (NUMS) was among the institutions targeted, leading to a temporary disruption of its digital services. There were also instances of website defacements, including that of the Supreme Court of Pakistan, service outages on the Islamabad Police portal, and the reported compromise of official Twitter accounts belonging to various Pakistani ministries used for disinformation. In total, 230 cyber incidents were reported against Pakistan cyber space.[47]

Figure 3.17: Emergency response measures by India

THE DEFENCE

Hardening critical infrastructure

India ramped up cyber audits and real-time monitoring of power grids, defence networks, telecom etc. Sector-specific computer emergency response teams (CERTs) were activated

Offensive cyber-readiness

This involves pre-emptive and retaliatory cyber operations targeting known Pakistani hacker groups and command servers. Marks a shift from passive defence to active deterrence

Threat-Intelligence integration

CERT-In, NTRO and military intelligence created a joint cyber threat fusion cell to track and neutralise threats. Information-sharing with allies was scaled up

Cyber hygiene campaigns

Recognising Pakistan's focus on phishing, India launched targeted awareness drives across government offices, military and public sector units. Regular drills and simulated attacks are routine

Legal/ Diplomatic pushback

India is invoking international cyber norms to expose Pakistan's digital aggression in global forums. New legislation is in the works to empower agencies to prosecute foreign cyber attackers and freeze assets

Source: *India Today*, 28 July 2025.

It also included takedowns of social media troll farms, disruption of servers and digital forensics operations to trace and expose the origin of attacks. Pakistan's NCERT (National Cyber Emergency Response Team) was forced to issue a red alert for phishing targeting its organisations. Websites of Pakistan's Sindh Police and its airport systems were breached too.

India's robust response was put up rapidly, to include tripling the number of cyber defence teams, deploying real-time intelligence-sharing and activating a joint task force led by the Data Security Council of India (DSCI) to coordinate efforts by government agencies, private firms, and industry bodies. The cyber security measures included temporarily blocking vulnerable financial sites, issuing CERT-In alerts and monitoring suspicious command servers. I4C, under the MHA, spearheaded counter-hack operations, reportedly taking down over 150 hostile command-and-control servers. In this manner India was able to respond and react in this raging cyber war.

Operation Sindoor: A Legacy of Unity and Resolve

The closing message, frequently echoed in official statements, encapsulates the profound essence of Op Sindoor: "Peace is not absence of war, but presence of sacrifice." This powerful sentiment underscored the collective effort of every Indian, from the brave soldiers on the frontlines to vigilant citizens who acted as "cyber warriors" and "social media warriors", all playing an indispensable role in this "whole of nation" endeavour.

Pakistan's blatant ceasefire violation, immediately following its own proposal, unequivocally exposed its unreliability and its continued commitment to cross-border terrorism. In stark contrast, India's measured yet firm restraint, coupled with its decisive actions, solidified its global standing as a responsible and resolute nation. Op Sindoor, aptly subtitled "Taming the Rogue", effectively redefined India's security doctrine. It unequivocally demonstrated that India is no longer a passive victim of state-sponsored terrorism but a proactive and formidable force, capable of defending its interests and ensuring the security of its citizens with unwavering resolve. This operation marked a new chapter in India's approach to national security, characterised by strategic assertiveness and an uncompromising stand against the forces of terrorism.

Notes

1. Media Center, MEA, Govt of India, 23 April 2025, Statement by Foreign Secretary on the decision of the Cabinet Committee on Security (CCS). https://www.mea.gov.in/Speeches-Statements.htm?dtl/39442/statement+by+foreign+secretary+on+the+decision+of+the+cabinet+committee+on+security+ccs
2. Transcript of Special briefing by MEA on 23 April 2025, https://www.mea.gov.in/media-briefings.htm?dtl/39443/Transcript_of_Special_briefing_by_MEA_April_23_2025
3. Firstpost, 24 April 2025, Exercise Aakraman: Indian Air Force Conducts Drills Involving Rafales, Su-30s. Accessed on 3 August 25. https://www.firstpost.com/india/exercise-aakraman-indian-air-force-conducts-drills-involving-rafales-su-30s-13882822.html
4. Abhishek Chakraborty, NDTV, 24 May 2025, Pakistan Cites Right To Suspend "All Bilateral Pacts, Including Simla". https://www.ndtv.com/world-news/after-indias-big-steps-against-pak-islamabads-tit-for-tat-moves-8245017
5. *The Times of India*, 27 April 2025, Combat-ready Indian Navy Test Fires Anti-ship Missile in Arabian Sea. Accessed on 3 August 25. https://timesofindia.indiatimes.com/india/combat-ready-indian-navy-test-fires-anti-ship-missile-in-arabian-sea/articleshow/120662502.cms
6. Ministry of Foreign Affairs, Government of Pakistan, 27 May 2025, Statement by the Ministry of Foreign Affairs on the Recent Remarks by the Prime Minister of India. Accessed on 3 August 25. https://mofa.gov.pk/press-releases/statement-by-the-ministry-of-foreign-affairs-on-the-recent-remarks-by-the-prime-minister-of-india
7. Nistula Heebar, Dinakar Peri, and Vijaita Singh, *The Hindu*, 30 April 2025, PM Modi gives 'free hand' to armed forces to respond to Pahalgam terror attack. https://www.thehindu.com/news/national/pm-modi-key-security-meet-pahalgam-attack-rajnath-singh-ajit-doval-chiefs-of-armed-forces/article69505393.ece
8. DD News, 1 May 2025, Pahalgam Attack: India Shuts Airspace to Pakistani Aircraft and Military Flights. Accessed on 3 August 25.

https://ddnews.gov.in/en/pahalgam-attack-india-shuts-airspace-to-pakistani-aircraft-and-military-flights/

9. *The Statesman*, 30 April 2025, Pak Minister Holds Emergency Press Meet at 2 am, Says India's Military Action within 24 to 36 Hours. Accessed on 3 August 25. https://www.thestatesman.com/world/pak-minister-holds-emergency-press-meet-at-2-am-says-indias-military-action-within-24-to-36-hours-1503426623.html
10. Press Information Bureau, Government of India, 1 May 2025, PIB Press Release: PRID=2125837. https://www.pib.gov.in/PressReleasePage.aspx?PRID=2125837
11. Press Information Bureau, Government of India, 7 May 2025, PIB Press Release: PRID=2127370. Accessed on 3 August 25. https://www.pib.gov.in/PressReleasePage.aspx?PRID=2127370
12. *The Hindu*, 14 May 2025, Operation Sindoor and India's response to Pakistan's retaliatory strikes. https://www.thehindu.com/data/satellite-images-of-military-and-terror-targets-in-pakistan/article69567141.ece
13. *India Today*, 20 May 2025, Operation Sindoor: Indian Army Hits 7 Out of 9 Terror Targets in Pakistan. YouTube. https://www.youtube.com/watch?v=eKXDmAIfDI8
14. MIB Advisory No. DM/9/2025-DM, https://mib.gov.in/sites/default/files/2025-05/advisory_pakistan_origin_content_08052025nt_.pdf
15. Ministry of External Affairs, Government of India, 7 May 2025, Transcript of Special Briefing on OPERATION SINDOOR May 07. Accessed on 3 August 25. https://www.mea.gov.in/media-briefings.htm?dtl/39474/Transcript+of+Special+Briefing+on+OPERATION+SINDOOR+May+07+2025
16. https://www.aljazeera.com/opinions/2025/6/11/in-india-war-came-dressed-in-feminist-camouflage
17. https://ddnews.gov.in/en/wing-commander-vyomika-singh-and-col-sofiya-qureshi-steer-indias-operation-sindoor-briefing/
18. TASS, Russian News Agency, 7 May 2025, Pakistan blames India for future escalation in region. Accessed on 3 August 25. https://tass.com/world/1954299

19. Ministry of Foreign Affairs, Government of Pakistan, Press Release 7 May 2025, Pakistan Strongly Condemns India's Blatant Aggression. Accessed via VPN. https://mofa.gov.pk/press-releases/pakistan-strongly-condemns-indias-blatant-aggression
20. Press Information Bureau, Government of India, 8 May 2025, PIB Press Release: PRID=2127670. Accessed on 3 August 25. https://www.pib.gov.in/PressReleasePage.aspx?PRID=2127670
21. Press Information Bureau, Ministry of Defence, Government of India, 8 May 2025, Pakistan's Bid to Escalate Negated–Proportionate Response by India. https://www.pib.gov.in/PressReleasePage.aspx?PRID=2127670
22. ibid.
23. Ministry of External Affairs, Government of India, 8 May 2025, Foreign Secretary's Statement: Special briefing on OPERATION SINDOOR. Accessed on 3 August 25. https://www.mea.gov.in/Speeches-Statements.htm?dtl/39478
24. Press Information Bureau, Government of India, 18 May 2025, Operation SINDOOR: Forging One Force. https://www.pib.gov.in/PressReleasePage.aspx?PRID=2129453
25. DD News, 9 May 2025, BSF Foils Major Infiltration Bid Along International Border in Samba. https://ddnews.gov.in/en/bsf-foils-major-infiltration-bid-along-international-border-in-samba/
26. Sukalp Sharma, *The Indian Express*, 10 May 2025, Operation Sindoor: Pakistan Airspace Shut till Sunday Noon. Accessed on 3 August. https://indianexpress.com/article/business/aviation/operation-sindoor-pakistan-airspace-shut-till-sunday-noon-9994629/
27. X account, DG ISPR announces details of India's strikes, 10 May 2025. Accessed by VPN, https://x.com/OSPSF/status/1920967953580699891
28. Radio Pakistan, 10 May 2025, *Now you just wait for our response, DG ISPR warns India.* https://www.radio.gov.pk/10-05-2025/now-you-just-wait-for-our-response-dg-ispr-warns-india
29. https://x.com/OSPSF/status/1920967953580699891

30. *The Hindu*, 14 May 2025, Operation Sindoor and India's response to Pakistan's retaliatory strikes. https://www.thehindu.com/data/satellite-images-of-military-and-terror-targets-in-pakistan/article69567141.ece

31. *The Kathmandu Post*, 10 May 2025, Pakistan Summons Its Top Nuclear Body After Launching Offensive on India. https://kathmandupost.com/world/2025/05/10/pakistan-summons-its-top-nuclear-body-after-launching-offensive-on-india

32. Reuters, 10 May 2025, Pakistan PM Calls Meeting of Body That Oversees Nuclear Arsenal, Says Pakistan Military. https://www.reuters.com/world/asia-pacific/pakistan-pm-calls-meeting-body-that-oversees-nuclear-arsenal-says-pakistan-2025-05-10/

33. PIB Release, 14 May 2025, Operation SINDOOR: India's Strategic Clarity and Calculated Force. https://www.pib.gov.in/Pressreleaseshare.aspx?PRID=2128748

34. Dinakar Peri, *The Hindu*, 11 May 2025, Operation Sindoor objectives achieved; losses are part of combat but pilots are back home, says IAF. https://www.thehindu.com/news/national/operation-sindoor-objectives-achieved-losses-are-part-of-combat-but-pilots-are-back-home-says-iaf/article69564934.ece

35. *The Hindu*, 2 May 2025, Navy intensifies muscle-flexing against Pakistan even as small arms fire continues across LC. http://timesofindia.indiatimes.com/articleshow/120803512.cms?utm_source=contentofinterest&utm_medium=text&utm_campaign=cppst

36. PIB Delhi, 18 May 2025, Operation SINDOOR: Forging One Force, The Synergy of India's Armed Forces. https://www.pib.gov.in/PressReleasePage.aspx?PRID=2129453

37. Response to our requests for Inputs on Op Sindoor, from Naval HQ, email ID mprcnavy.321@gmail.com on 20 June 2025 to the lead author email bips_bak@hotmail.com

38. Shivani Sharma, *India Today*, 14 May 2025, INS Vikrant-led 36-ship armada was in position to hit Karachi. Accessed on 3 August 2025, available at https://www.indiatoday.in/india/story/ins-vikrant-

brahmos-equipped-warships-submarines-blockaded-paks-karachi-port-during-op-sindoor-sources-2724482-2025-05-14

39. Pradip Sagar, *India Today*, 28 July 2025, Cyber war | Outsmarting the hacker army. Available at https://www.indiatoday.in/india-today-insight/story/hacker-army-why-india-cannot-let-its-guard-down-2761646-2025-07-26?utm_source=story_twitter&utm_medium=twitter&utm_campaign=storyshareurl
40. https://x.com/DaKirito_o/status/1929054475060236527
41. https://x.com/qazizain698/status/1919876489140428944
42. https://x.com/qazizain698/status/1920768749042376863
43. *The Times of India*, 25 May 2025, How pro-India hackers defended country during cross border Cyberattacks amid Op Sindoor. Available at https://timesofindia.indiatimes.com/city/hyderabad/how-pro-india-hackers-defended-country-during-cross-border-cyberattacks-amid-op-sindoor/articleshow/121385229.cms
44. http://web.archive.org/web/20250509103515/https://mapp.dhamultan.org/mobileApp/
45. https://x.com/echo0fGulmarg/status/1920838565589618872
46. https://x.com/teamwhitel0tus/status/1921493042462097449
47. Grey Zone Escalation: The Strategic Role of Cyber Warfare in the 2025 India–Pakistan Conflict, https://www.linkedin.com/pulse/grey-zone-escalation-strategic-role-cyber-warfare-2025-indiapakistan-89x3f/

4

The Air Campaign

Space Surveillance and Nuclear Dimension

AIR MARSHAL RAJESH KUMAR

Planning of the Response to the Terrorist Attack

Detailed planning for a kinetic response to the dastardly attack on 22 April 2025 must have started in earnest even before the Cabinet Committee of Security (CCS) meeting on 23 April 2025. As the Foreign Secretary's statement on the decision of the CCS noted: "The CCS reviewed the overall security situation and directed all forces to maintain high vigil. It resolved that the perpetrators of the attack will be brought to justice and their sponsors held to account. As with the recent extradition of Tahawwur Rana, India will be unrelenting in the pursuit of those who have committed acts of terror, or conspired to make them possible."[1] Domestic outrage put intense pressure on New Delhi to retaliate, yet India's response had to balance punishment of the perpetrators with preventing uncontrolled escalation. India accused Pakistan of tolerating or sponsoring the terror infrastructure, signalling that "failure to deny space to terrorist groups on Pakistani soil is sufficient to legitimate military action"[2] across the border.

As military planners huddled to execute political direction of hitting significant terrorist targets and avoiding civilian casualties, they must have looked back at the lessons from the Balakot strike six years earlier, where questions were raised about the proof of the efficacy of the attack. Hence Battle Damage Assessment (BDA) became an imperative. The choice of targets would also depend upon the significance of the message, for example a terrorist headquarters should be occupied by terrorists as opposed to an empty building that should send a strategic signal not misunderstood by the adversary. The planners relied on a fusion of intelligence sources to validate targets. Human intelligence (HUMINT) and signal intercepts had identified increased militant activity at some sites after the Pahalgam attack. Imagery intelligence from satellites confirmed the locations and layout of the camps. Precision strikes were needed that would demonstrate India's ability to deliver pinpoint effects with minimal collateral damage. This was one of the most important considerations impacting the final selection of targets and the impact points within the target complexes. Utmost care was taken to avoid civilian population centres in close proximity like schools, hospitals, etc.

Target selection, therefore, was critical. Ultimately out of a shortlisted menu of about a score of targets, nine were selected for the maximum achievement of the above-stated objectives. Significantly, the planners did not restrict themselves to targets inside Pakistan Occupied Kashmir (POJK) but expanded the target area to the heartland region of Pakistan, i.e. Punjab. The choice of weapons was also carefully looked at. While the seven targets allocated to the Army were allocated to loitering munitions and unmanned aerial vehicles (UAVs) as the primary strike weapons, the two that were attacked by the Air Force were a mix of long and medium range weapons such as the SCALP cruise missile and Crystal Maze as well as SAAW glide bombs. Initially there was some consideration given to small-calibre weapons to cause smaller damage as escalation control was built into every step in the campaign while firmly retaining escalation dominance. Ultimately the trade-off for standoff range and precision capability won the argument on the day and the primacy of minimum collateral damage was upheld. It also suggested a plan "determined to signal its intent with clarity: India was not interested in initiating a conflict with the Pakistani state, but rather in degrading a specific ecosystem of terrorist violence that exists in the country".[3]

Planners were also acutely aware of the need for good timing to achieve operational surprise. It was well understood that this time round Pakistan would not be completely surprised like the Balakot strike six years ago and would be fully alert to the possibility of an Indian strike since it was fairly obvious by Indian statements that it was not a matter of if a kinetic response would come but when. In fact, Pakistan's Defence Minister Khawaja Asif in an interview to Yalda Hakim of *Al Jazeera* on 25 April stated that Pakistan is "already prepared" for strikes from India.[4] On 30 April 2025, Pakistan Federal Minister for Information and Broadcasting Attaullah Tarar held an emergency press meet at 2 am, saying that there were "intelligence reports of military action against their country within the next 24 to 36 hours".[5] Western commentators on news channels commented that "India holds all the cards" and its decision would determine the future status of the conflict. The only secrecy was the nature of attack and its timing. Thus, the early morning hour of 01:05 hours indicated a time when much of the civilian population would be firmly secured in their beds and would not be close to the places that were targeted. Deception was also an imperative in such a scenario to achieve operational surprise. Deception was part of the package and was achieved through decoys, UAVs, and Electronic Warfare. Battle Damage Assessment (BDA) was given redundancy to ensure that real time assessment of the strike could take place as well as adequate information about collateral damage and/or civilian casualties if any could be known in near real time to the planners and commanders. This was important as this information would help to manage escalation should things not go according to plan. Thus, escalation management was built into every stage of the plan right from the beginning despite the stated objective of striking terrorist camps. The planners needed to not only to demonstrate restraint but also India's willingness and capability to escalate horizontally and vertically should such a situation arise. The strike mission was to be surgical, precise and devastating, yet be something that could be justified as a proportional and befitting response to a most dastardly act. Not only the international community must be satisfied that it was a just response but at the same time the signal to Pakistan that terrorism on Indian soil will have costs should be unambiguous.

The First Strike

The Indian Air Force (IAF) took the lead in the kinetic response, bringing a formidable mix of combat aircraft, sensors, and command systems to bear. A package of IAF fighter jets—primarily Rafales and Su-30MKIs—was deployed to deliver precision strikes with stand-off munitions. These jets flew from forward air bases in western India under high alert; many had been pre-positioned during the preceding crisis days to shorten response time. Each strike mission was supported by aerial refuelling tankers (IL-78 MKIs) to extend endurance, and by airborne early warning and control (AWACS) aircraft like the IAF's Phalcon and Netra, which provided radar coverage and battle management. The IAF's Integrated Air Command and Control System (IACCS)—a secure network linking radars, AWACS, ground stations, and fighter aircraft—enabled real-time threat-tracking and coordination of these assets across multiple sectors. Indeed, a government statement highlighted that IACCS maintained "real-time threat identification, assessment, and interception across multiple domains" during

Operation Sindoor,[6] integrating Army and Navy elements as well. On 7 May 2025 at 01:05 hours, the Markaz Subhan Allah at Bahawalpur belonging to JeM, the Markaz Taiba at Muridke belonging to LeT, and other structures at Sarjal, Tehra Kalan; Mehmoona Joya, Sialkot; the Markaz Ahle Hadith at Barnala as well as two Markaz at Kotli and two camps at Muzaffarabad were attacked and successfully destroyed (see Figure 4.1). In addition to the IAF strikes on the two main targets at Bahawalpur and Muridke, the Indian Army also engaged the other seven targets with loitering munitions as well as direct artillery fire. Significantly, the Naval Palm series munition was also employed leading to a genuine tri-service effort. The precision of targeting was evident in the effects. All nine initial targets were hit with significant damage. Satellite imagery later revealed the Markaz Subhan JeM HQ in Bahawalpur had been reduced to rubble by a direct hit. The IAF's selection of weapons tailored to target type: hardened structures like concrete bunkers were struck by penetrator warheads, while softer targets (for example, militant camps in spread-out compounds) were hit by munitions with air-burst fragmentation for area effect. The main strike weapons used were the SCALP from the Rafale as well as the HAMMER air-to-surface weapon. BDA was near-instantaneous; within hours, satellites and drones captured images of burning buildings at the strike sites. The IAF also deployed a few weaponised drones to linger and perform post-strike reconnaissance, feeding live video back to command centres. At 01:44 hours Press Information Bureau (PIB) issued a statement confirming the attack. The statement also stated that "our actions have been focused, measured, and non-escalatory in nature. No Pakistani military facilities have been targeted. India has demonstrated considerable restraint in selection of targets and method of execution".[7] It is believed that the same message was conveyed on the Director General of Military Operations (DGMO) hotline to Pakistan. The message also conveyed that India's strike was complete and there would be no more kinetic action unless there was retaliation. Pakistan did not indicate that they would not retaliate. The Director General, Inter-Services Public Relations (DG, ISPR) of Pakistan, Lt. General Ahmed Sharif in a press briefing confirmed that Indian strikes on six different locations have so far claimed 26 innocent lives and left 46 others injured. It was also stated that Pakistan "shot down five Indian aircraft and one drone in its right to self-defence. The downed aircraft include three Rafale jets, one MiG-29, and one SU-series fighter".[8] India did not confirm or deny the losses. The claims and counterclaims have been hard to verify. In a press briefing on 11 May 2025, Air Marshal AK Bharti, Director General Air Operations (DGAO), IAF, stated that "losses are a part of combat".[9] He also categorically stated that all objectives of the strike were achieved and all the pilots were home safe. Therefore, losses if any were not from the strike force and perhaps from the deception force and may have included decoy UAVs.

Between 03:30 hours and 06:00 hours Pakistan Standard Time (PKT), on 7 May 2025, Pakistan's top military leadership, including Chief of Army Staff (COAS) General Asim Munir and Air Chief Zaheer Ahmad Babar, convened at General Headquarters (GHQ) Rawalpindi shortly after the strike. The meeting was convened within 2–3 hours of the Indian operation, likely around 04:00 hours PKT.[10] The DG of ISPR later confirmed that "the National Command and Operational Centre was active before sunrise". Official authorisation for retaliation was given at the National Security Committee (NSC) meeting chaired by Prime Minister Shehbaz Sharif; the government formally authorised the armed forces to retaliate under Article 51 of the UN Charter (right of self-defence).The meeting reportedly began around 09:00 hours PKT, and a public statement was issued by 11:00 hours. The NSC emphasised a "measured but resolute"response to India's "act of war".[11] The popular mood in Pakistan also favoured a response to the attacks that were seen in vivid detail by the population that lived close to these areas that were struck. According to Nishank

Motwani, an analyst with the U.S. branch of the Australian Strategic Policy Institute (ASPI), a government-funded think tank, "There's mounting public pressure in Pakistan to take some form of retaliatory action".[12]

Retaliation

When the action did finally come from Pakistan, it came in the form of a combined attack by drones, loitering munitions, and long-range weapons launched from aircraft especially the JF-17. In a bid to show credible retaliation in the eyes of the Pakistani populace, a sincere effort was made to strike some high-value targets in India. On the night of 7 May, Pakistan military tried to employ joint aircraft-missiles-drones strike tactics by attempting a Suppression of Enemy Air Defence (SEAD) trap for Indian EW and AD assets. Waves of UAVs and other munitions began a drone and missile attack on about 15 locations in western and northern India. These drone attacks continued into the next night (8–9May). Unfortunately for Pakistan, the strikes ran into the Indian Air Defence wall—a layered defence that had been prepared and synchronised well during the period after the Pahalgam attacks on 22 April. In the early stages of the strike itself two JF-17s were shot down using the S-400 system that was deployed tactically by the Indian Air Force. At the same time the drones and loitering munitions were engaged by Army Air Defence, short-range surface-to-air missile systems and counter drone systems deployed by the Indian Army. Of particular mention is the manner in which Akash of the IAF units proved their mettle by engaging low-flying drones that evaded detection until closer into the airspace. Legacy Soviet-era systems—the Pechora (SA-3) and OSA-AK (SA-8)—were also activated to cover gaps at lower altitudes. These older SAMs, though less advanced, still provided additional "rings"of defence and reportedly downed a couple of UAVs that slipped through the outer layers. Really small drones were mopped up by the L-70 and ZU-23 radar-guided guns of the Army Air Defence. There is large evidence comprising videos, and subsequent debris of AD firing both anti-aircraft guns and missiles as they responded to raids that sought to saturate Indian air defence through waves of attacks. Such was the failure in terms of effectiveness that Pakistan's official military spokesmen repeatedly denied conducting any such attacks.[13] In particular was an attempted attack on the Golden Temple in the city of Amritsar. Here locals reported explosions and bright flashes of light. On this Pakistan stated that India had attacked its own territory to stoke anti-Pakistan sentiment and create a "phantom defence".[14] This has been a recurring theme in the information domain by Pakistan where it has repeatedly accused India of attacking itself and blaming Pakistan. Unfortunately for Pakistan there are few takers for this theory.

As a result, it appears that the GIDS B-REK (Boosted Range Extension Kit) with a claimed range of 170 km, as well as missiles of Raad and CM400AKG variety, that were launched towards Indian territory were intercepted by SAMs along with their carrier aircraft and thus were either destroyed or they missed their targets. Subsequently, Pakistan appears to have resorted to launching several hundred drones to test the AD systems and gather intelligence. Other than the Turkish-origin Asisguard Songar, these attacks were largely composed of poor quality basic drones perhaps serving as flying chaff to clutter radars and probe air defence sites.[15] There is little evidence that Medium Altitude Long Endurance (MALE) UAVs like the Wing Loong or TB-2 were deployed in this phase of operations. Perhaps the vulnerability of such platforms as seen in the Ukrainian conflict as well as the Houthi experience by the Americans influenced the minds of the Pakistani planners. Even if some of these were attempted to be brought into the combat area, no wreckage of these platforms has been recovered in India, hence it is presumed that they were not in active use. Whatever be the logic of the composition of these attacks, it is clear that these attacks largely failed to hit any meaningful military targets and caused minimal damage on the Indian side. Satellite imagery supports that claim. What did cause some concern to the Indian side was the artillery shelling in the border areas and some drones that impacted in border areas on civilian population and caused casualties. Some places of worship were also targeted and damaged. As a consequence, civilian population in the areas of Jammu, Rajouri, and Poonch and their surrounding villages were relocated to safer areas.

Counterattack

In response to this wave of drone attacks, India undertook a counterattack in the morning hours of 8 May. The counterattack targeted air defence radars and systems at a number of locations in Pakistan. To signal non-escalatory intent, it was emphasized that India's response has been "in the same domain, with the same intensity as Pakistan".[16] There is overwhelming evidence (videos and subsequent debris) that an Air Defence Radar was neutralised at Lahore. This installation was attacked with a mix of Israeli-origin Harpy and Harop (a newer Harpy-variant) drones. Debris consistent with those platforms, as well as British-origin Banshee target drones (likely as decoys), was recovered in several spots across Pakistan.[17] Pakistan's military spokesperson acknowledged that the attacks injured four Pakistani soldiers and caused partial damage to equipment.

What this chaotic public denial of a drone attack on India on the night of 7–8 May by Pakistan and the subsequent 8 May morning Indian counterattack meant was that public in Pakistan perceived it as further Indian aggression. Pakistan's DG ISPR spokesperson complained that the attack was a sign that India had "lost the plot". Some among the Pakistani populace questioned their government on that day as to why did they not hit back the previous night. They reasoned that Pakistan should have struck back rather than have invited further Indian aggression. This non assuagement of the public mood ensured that Pakistan could not stop its operations and needed to continue fighting to follow the prevailing public sentiment. From India's vantage, it was merely responding to Pakistan's counterattack in a calibrated manner. Escalation control was built into Indian planning at all stages. The Indian forces focused mainly on Air Defence at this stage. Even the retaliatory strikes focused on taking out Pakistani Air Defence equipment rather than any meaningful military target that could cause large casualties and lead to further escalation. Amidst all this, misinformation had also gained centre stage: in fact, a leading South Asia analyst Michael Kugelman stated that the spread of "disinformation is escalating as rapidly as the hostilities". Amongst a bout of accusations and counter accusations Foreign Secretary Misri had to point out, "that we would attack our cities is the kind of deranged statement that only Pakistan could put out". The net result of such exchanges was that the Pakistani military spokesperson said at a news briefing that his country "will not de-escalate" with India. "With the damages India did on our side, they should take a hit. So far, we have been protecting ourselves, but they will get an answer in our own timing," he added.[18] Thus the die was cast for further escalation and Pakistan seems to have increased the firepower in this final night of attacks. Earlier the drone attacks were large, widespread, and probing with the intention of locating missile sites and neutralising some of the Air Defence systems especially the S-400. This was because the Indian AD systems had already inflicted a heavy cost on Pakistan Air Force (PAF) aircraft earlier and Pakistan did not want to risk exposure without creating some safe areas for the PAF to operate. By 9–10 May, there was more urgency to impose some cost on India. Pakistan now launched a much larger strike package using a combined missile, aircraft and drone attack in the early hours of the night of 9–10 May. As per reported intelligence, there was a plan for a follow-up larger attack a few hours later. In this launched attack Pakistan used larger kamikaze drones—in particular the Turkish-origin Yiha-III, which was not evident before the night of 9–10 May, and which was now in widespread use. It also appears that Pakistan used more short-range ballistic missiles on 9–10 May than it had on earlier nights, especially the Fatah-I and Hatf-I, both short-range ballistic missiles. Debris associated with these missiles was recovered on 10 and 11 May. An interesting missile was intercepted by Air Defence systems in the skies above Sirsa. This was established to be the Fatah II as the area of interception indicated that it was beyond the range of both the Fatah-I and Hatf-I. Ostensibly, in a desperate bid to create a sensational strike this missile had been launched towards Delhi. In addition, long-range munitions such as the CM400AKG cruise missile launched from Pakistani JF-17s were also used. Despite the change in tactics the result remained unfavourable for Pakistan and all major strike weapons were either intercepted or missed their targets. Small drones that got through did not cause any major damage and therefore till now Pakistan has not been able to substantiate any major hit on a target of substance claimed by them by satellite photos or even social media. Every piece of evidence that was put out was fact-checked and rebutted. One of the claims made by Pakistan was that the BrahMos storage facilities at Beas and Nagrota were destroyed. International media acknowledged that all such claims were false.[19] It was also during this period that many attempts were made to attack the S-400 and put it out of action. The S-400 has put the entire PAF on tenterhooks by its performance and deterrence capability. The PAF spokesperson called it the "centre of gravity". Despite many claims to have struck and disabled the S-400, all attacks on the system were unsuccessful and the S-400 continued to be in operation till the end of the conflict. All these claims indicate that there was not enough clarity in the minds of the Pakistani top brass as to the effectiveness of their strikes.

The Finale

This confusion and the sheer frustration at not being able to effectively furnish clinching evidence of a strike back at India forced Pakistan to give a go-ahead to a planned larger strike on Indian targets that would yield some impact. An indication that such a step could be considered by Pakistan was already in the minds of Indian top brass. A warning call from USA confirmed such fears. According to Christopher Clary quoting administration officials "around noon eastern on May 9 (9:00 pm in Pakistan, 9:30 pm in India), the Vice President (of the United States) called Indian Prime Minister Modi to express American concerns that "there was a high probability for dramatic escalation as the conflict went into the weekend".[20] This conversation has been confirmed by PM Modi's speech in the Indian Parliament on 29 August 2025,"When I returned the call, the US Vice President warned me of a big attack from Pakistan. I told him that if Pakistan attacks India, our attack would be much bigger as we will respond to bullets with cannons. This was my answer".[21] Having been forewarned, India took decisive action. India launched a pre-emptive strike of its own. Around 02:00 hours India struck the Nur Khan airbase. This airbase is a part of the Chaklala military cantonment near Islamabad. The blasts woke up residents in the nearby Rawalpindi and the Pakistani capital of Islamabad whose recorded videos are widely available on social media. Besides the Nur Khan attack, at least eleven other sites were struck on the night of 9–10 May. Other bases and sites that were struck included Rafiqui, Rahim Yar Khan, and Sukkur that were hit in the first wave of strikes, which was followed by strikes at Sargodha, Bholari, Rahim Yar Khan, and Jacobabad airbases. Also hit and destroyed were command-and-control or drone-related targets at Murid and radar sites at Chunian, Arifwala, and Pasrur. "Action taken reports show that the IAF fired 19 BrahMos supersonic cruise missiles at Pakistani airbases, along with nearly an equal number of French SCALP subsonic cruise missiles."[22] In addition, Crystal maze and HAMMER missiles were used. A summary of the attacks is detailed below:

Table 4.1 Attacks on Pakistani Targets by Indian Air Force

Target (Location)	Likely IAF Platform	Likely Weapon(s) Used	Reported Outcome
Nur Khan Airbase (Chaklala, near Islamabad)	Rafale / Su-30 MKI	BrahMos cruise missiles	Hangar, ATC, and command-and-control infrastructure damaged; C-130 aircraft destroyed
Sargodha Airbase	Rafale / Su-30 MKI	BrahMos / SCALP cruise missiles	Runway struck
Murid (Murid Camp / Air Facilities)	Rafale / Su30 MKI	BrahMos / SCALP / Rampage	Aircraft hangar; Drone command node and deployment infrastructure destroyed
Sukkur Airbase	Rafale / Su-30 MKI	BrahMos / SCALP cruise missiles	Radar destroyed; Hangar and support installations damaged

Target (Location)	Likely IAF Platform	Likely Weapon(s) Used	Reported Outcome
Chunian radar and command node	Decoy drones (Harop) + follow-up strikes	Loitering munition (Harop) + BrahMos	Air defence radar knocked out
Pasrur radar installations	Decoy + strike drones / jets	Harop drones, BrahMos	Radar destroyed
Jacobabad Airbase	Rafale / Su30 MKI	BrahMos / SCALP	Infrastructural damage to hangars and taxiways: Radar infrastructure
Bholari Airbase	Rafale / Su30 MKI	BrahMos / SCALP	High-value drone and surveillance assets destroyed; AWACS casualty
Rahim Yar Khan airbase	Rafale / Su30 MKI	BrahMos / SCALP	Runway damaged
Arifwala	Decoy + strike drones/ jets	Harop Drones, Rampage	Radar Destroyed
Nayachor	Decoy + strike drones/ jets	Harop Drones, Rampage	Radar Destroyed

Note: Also, see the photos of before-and-after pictures of struck targets on this chapter's page inserts.

Figure 4.1: Targets struck on 10 May 2025

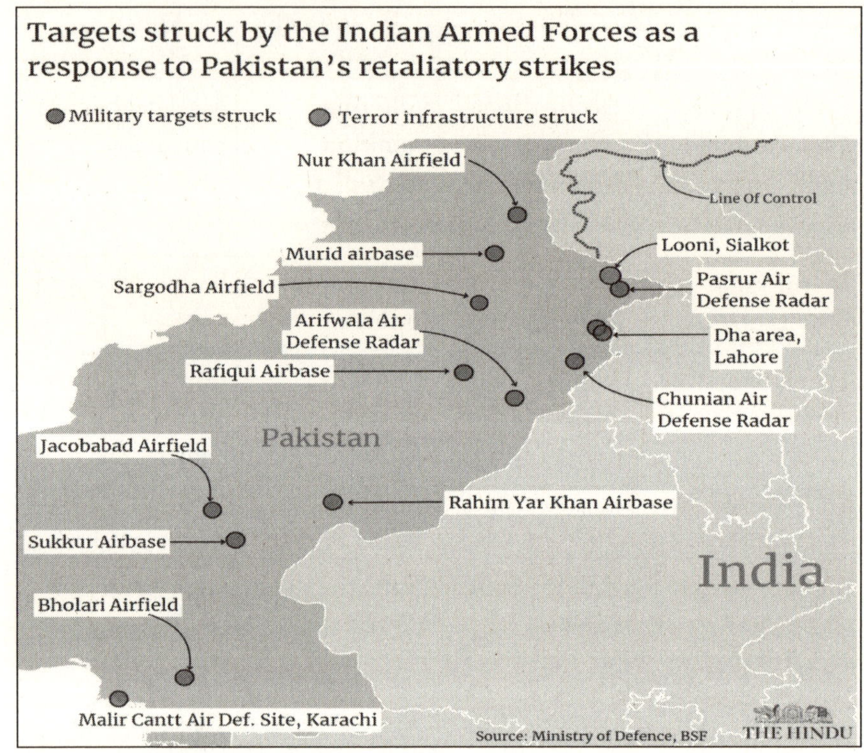

Source: *The Hindu*, 14 May 2025.[23]

The strikes were conducted in two waves and covered the entire span of the country from North to South and deep inside Pakistan, some as far away as 230 km inside Pakistani territory. Such a scale of attacks on Pakistan had not been carried out since 1971. In the photos it can be seen that the targets were struck with an accuracy not seen by Pakistan ever before. Six radar installations at Sukkur, Lahore, Arifwala, Chunian, Jacobabad, and Nayachor were taken out to create gaps for Indian strike aircraft to get through. The surface-to-air missile complexes at Lahore and Okara had already been struck earlier. At Sargodha and Rahim Yar Khan, the main targets were the runway. This was ostensibly to prevent further take-off of aircraft that were noticed to be taking off in earlier attempted strikes by Pakistan. At Murid, Bholari, Jacobabad, and Sukkur the runway along with aircraft hangars was targeted. This was based on specific intelligence on the aircraft and UAV assets being placed there. The collapsed hangars must have definitely been a demoralising sight for Pakistan. At Murid and Chaklala (Nur Khan) command-and-control centres were hit to prevent coordination of strike packages and UAV swarms. This was one of the most crippling blows on Pakistani operations.

The strikes had a serious impact on the planned Pakistani strike. Armed with intelligence obtained even before Vice President JD Vance's call, the IAF struck runways where a majority of the strike aircraft were due to take off. Combined with the downing of the command-and-control centre at Nur Khan, the planned Pakistani strike was called off. This was well before the documented call from DGMO. This sequence of events was confirmed by the Pakistani Prime Minister Shehbaz Sharif speaking in the presence of General (now Field Marshal) Asif Munir during a visit to Azerbaijan on 27-28 May, "Our armed forces were prepared to act at 4.30 in the morning (10 May) after the Fajr prayers to teach a lesson. But before that hour even arrived, India once again launched a missile attack using BrahMos, targeting various provinces of Pakistan, including the airport in Rawalpindi".[24]

In the words of India's DGAO Air Marshal Bharti that following sustained attempts to mount attacks on India "it was time to convey some message to our adversary" and that the attack was "swift, coordinated, calibrated". These strikes were strikingly successful and threw down the gauntlet to Pakistan. In its wisdom Pakistan decided to back down and sue for peace. India accepted the request having understood that its objectives as laid down before the conflict had been achieved. This was a widely criticised move that was questioned by many on social media as well as the main print and electronic media including members of the opposition.[25] The issue was discussed in Parliament as well in July 2025.[26] India also perhaps deliberated that the political advantages of further strikes were not worth the risk of a dangerous escalation to the crisis should it continue to persist.

What caused this sudden change in Pakistan's approach? Christopher Clary argues that backroom diplomacy may have played a part. He argues that during the night Pakistan was reasonably sure that their earlier drone strikes had been successful and they were, according to some sources (not Clary), confident of having hit the S-400, there were numerous calls from the US side including those from the US Secretary of State Marco Rubio to the Pakistani side. One such call occurred on the night of 9–10 May. "The readout of the Rubio-Munir phone call was released at approximately 11 pm on 9 May in Washington, which is 8 am on 10 May Pakistan time, suggesting the conversation must have occurred at least several minutes prior to the press release. It appears that Rubio secured Munir's agreement to pursue a ceasefire in that phone call or one shortly thereafter with Pakistan's Foreign Minister Dar, an agreement that he quickly set to work securing."[27] The Indian side was quite clear that any ceasefire would have to be requested for from the Pakistani side. This was well understood by the US who perhaps conveyed it to Pakistan. Pakistan's DGMO attempted to initiate a call around 09:15 hours which was not attended as India's DGMO was in a meeting. Subsequently this request was acceded to in a subsequent call. Immediately President Donald Trump tweeted the same. Around 17:00 hours on 10 May, the Foreign Secretary of India made a statement: "The Director General of Military Operations of Pakistan called the Director General of Military Operations of India at 15:35 hours IST earlier today. It was agreed between them that both sides would stop all firing and military action on land and in the air and sea with effect from 17:00 hours Indian Standard Time today. Instructions have been given on both sides to give effect to the understanding. The Director Generals of Military Operations will talk again on the 12th of May at 12:00 hours."[28] Besides the fact that diplomatic pressure was building on both sides, ultimately it was the early morning strike that broke the camel's back. The intensity and the ferocity of the serial attacks on Pakistan across the depth and breadth of the country left the Pakistani leadership rattled. Loss of the command-and-control centre meant that they could not strike back early enough even if they could get their runways up and running. There are also reports of aircraft lost in hangars that were hit which must have weighed on their mind. They decided to give up the ghost. This sequence of events was confirmed by the Deputy PM of Pakistan in an interview on TV on 20 June where he admitted that Pakistan was compelled to ask for a ceasefire after India struck the Nur Khan airbase. "Unfortunately, India once again launched missile strikes at 02.30 hours. They attacked the Nur Khan air base and Shorkot air base... Within 45 minutes, Saudi Prince Faisal called me. He said he had then just learnt about my conversation with (US Secretary of State) Marco Rubio. He asked if he was authorised to talk to (India's External Affairs Minister) S Jaishankar and convey that we are ready if they (India) stop. I said, 'yes, brother, you can'. He then called me back, saying he had conveyed the same to Jaishankar", Mr Dar said".[29] Thus, almost four days of kinetic action was brought to an end by a swift attack that provided shock and awe to the adversary.

Outcomes for the Indian Air Force

While the kinetic action ended, the IAF remained on alert and prepared to go back into action should the agreement not hold. Despite a few border violations, the agreement held. It is worthwhile to note that over the four-day operation, the IAF flew hundreds of sorties—from strike missions to combat air patrols (CAPs), escorts, reconnaissance, and electronic warfare. On the opening night of 7 May alone, multiple waves of strike aircraft hit targets in rapid succession. Each Rafale and Su-30 carried a heavy payload of precision-guided munitions. By avoiding deep penetration (strikes were launched from within Indian airspace or near the Line of Control using long-range weapons), the IAF minimised exposure to enemy air defences. Still, Pakistani fighters scrambled to challenge some of these strikes, leading to contested engagements. The IAF thus concurrently maintained CAPs with pairs of air superiority fighters (MiG-29UPG and Su-30) to deter PAF interceptors. Flight hours surged accordingly and some IAF squadrons operated almost round-the-clock. IAF pilots accumulated extensive flight time, with some crews flying multiple sorties per day thanks to mid-air refuelling and efficient turn-around on the ground. Behind the scenes, robust logistics chains sustained the tempo. Forward airbases were stocked with weapons and spares in advance (reflecting lessons from the 2019 Balakot strike, after which Pakistan's riposte highlighted the need for quick rearming). Munitions like the SCALP cruise missiles and Spice-2000 bombs were ferried from central depots under armed escort. Ground crews performed rapid rearming and refuelling (hot refuelling with engines running in some cases). The IAF's networked maintenance management allowed damaged aircraft to be rotated out and reserves brought in seamlessly. In sum, Op Sindoor's execution showcased a modernised IAF that could mobilise precision firepower on short notice and sustain high-tempo operations. It also emphasised the usefulness of air power. The Vice Chief of Air Staff Air Marshal N Tiwari stated at a recent seminar in July 2025 that "less than 50 weapons can bring the adversary to the talking table ...that is an example that needs to be studied and will be studied (by scholars)".[30]

The IAF enhanced its reputation for deep and precise strikes. Even after taking some losses on 7 May, it still struck with accuracy and achieved the desired hits. It came back stronger on 10 May with a set of devastating blows that shell-shocked the enemy and bludgeoned them into submission. The opening salvo of Op Sindoor made extensive use of long-range stand-off weapons to hit targets from within Indian airspace. The IAF's Rafales used SCALP air-launched cruise missiles while SU-30s and Mirage 2000s carried

Photo 1: Muridke Targets struck by IAF on 7 May 2025

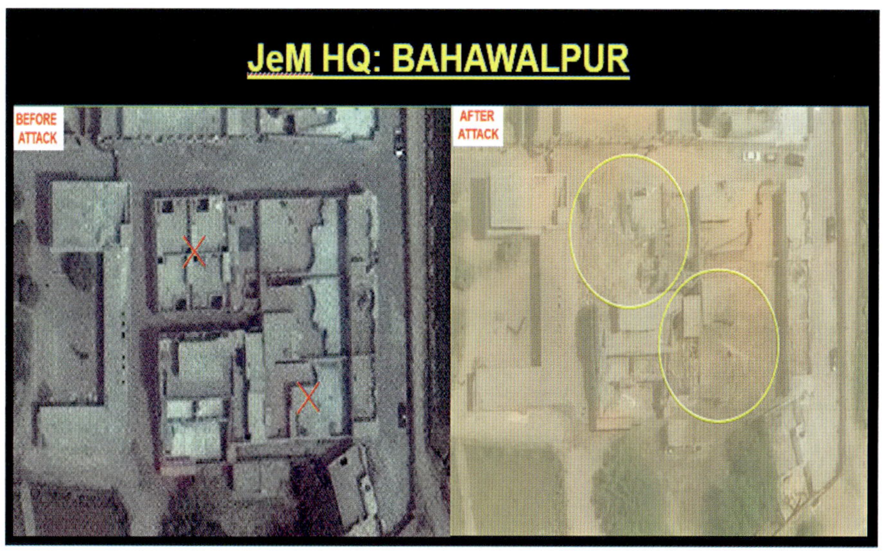

Photo 2: LeT Targets struck on 7 May 2025

Photo 3: Strikes by IAF on 7 May 2025 night

Source: IAF media briefing.

Photo 4: Radar at Pasrur struck by IAF on 10 May 2025

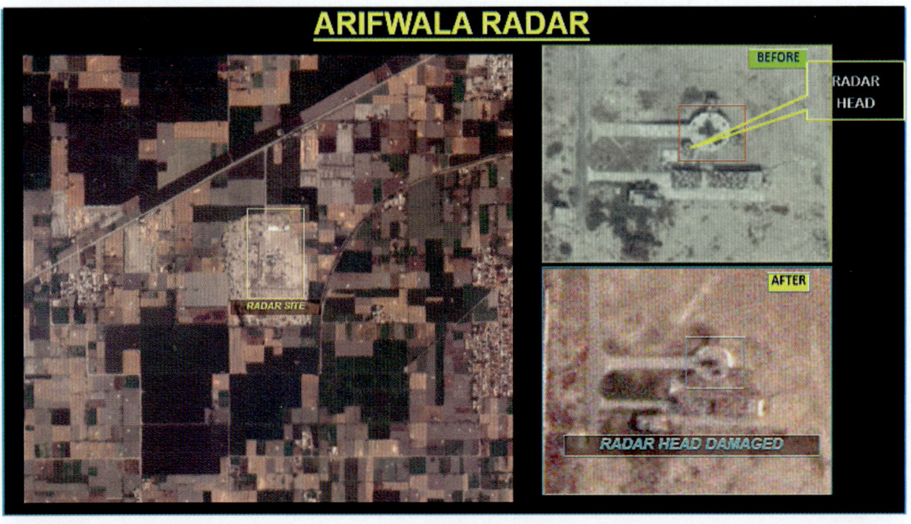

Photo 5: Strikes by IAF on 9/10 May 2025 night

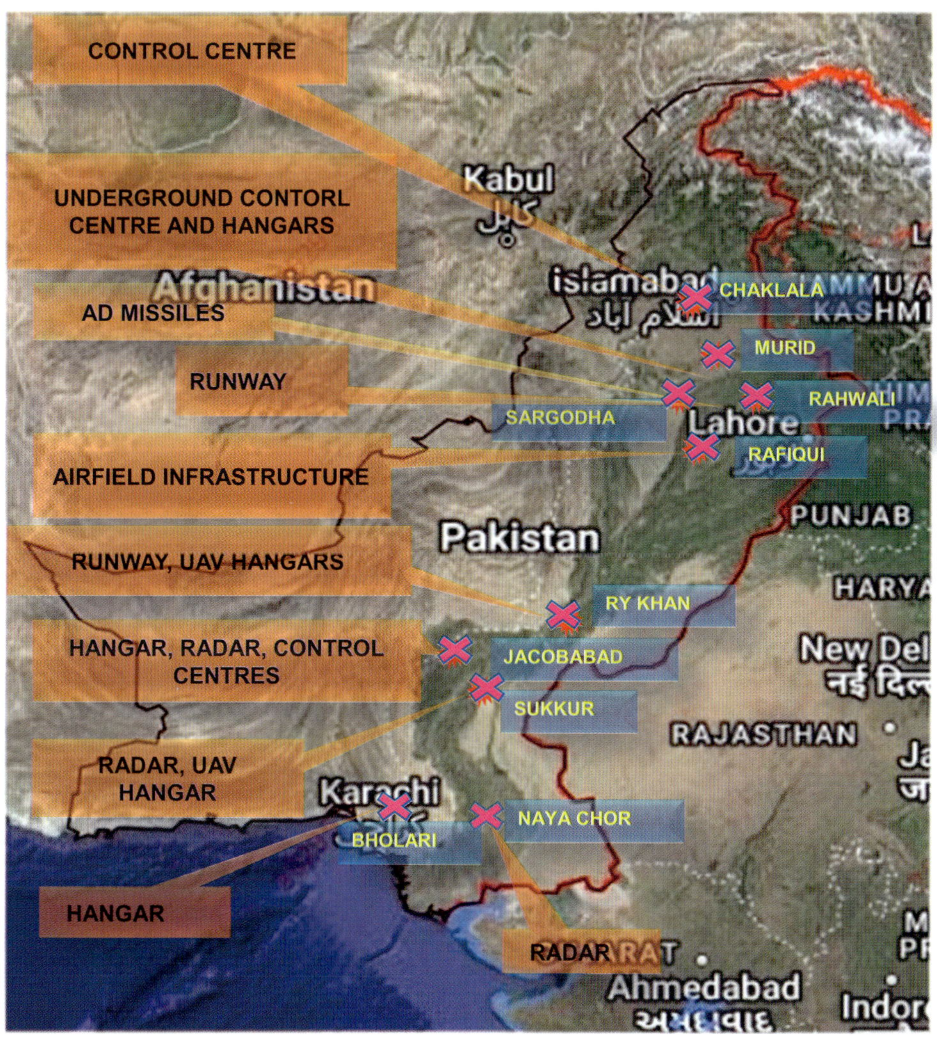

Source: IAF media briefing.

Photo 6: Radar at Naya Chor struck by IAF on 10 May 2025

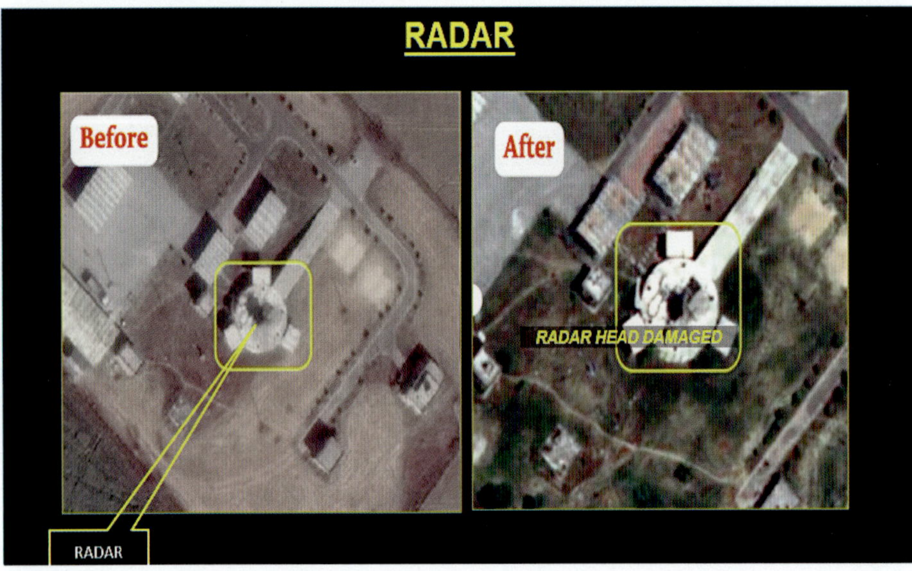

Photo 7: Radar at Chunian struck on 10 May

Photo 8: The mobile GMCC at Chaklala was destroyed

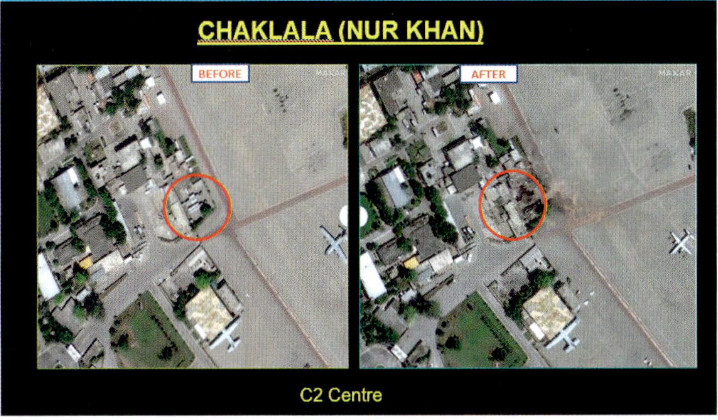

Source: IAF.

Photo 9: Sukkur radar and UAV hangar

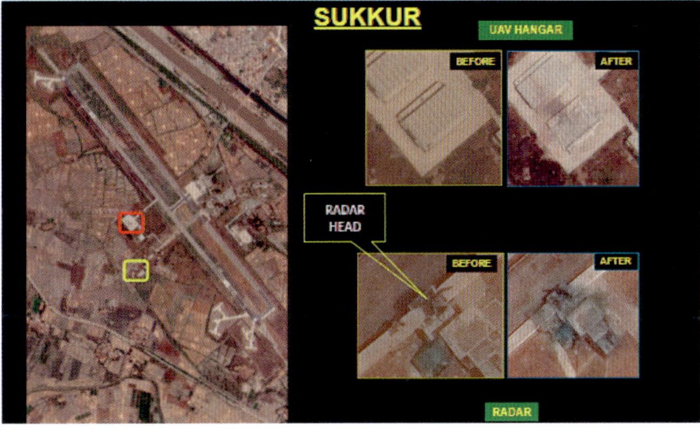

Photo 10: Sargodha runway and allied buildings

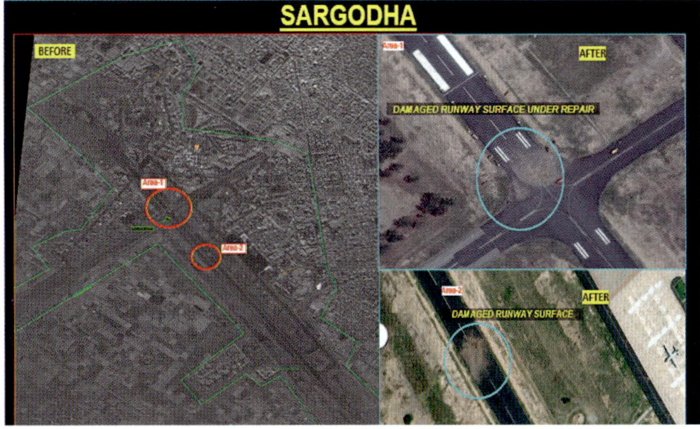

Source: IAF.

Photo 11: Bholari AWACS hangar

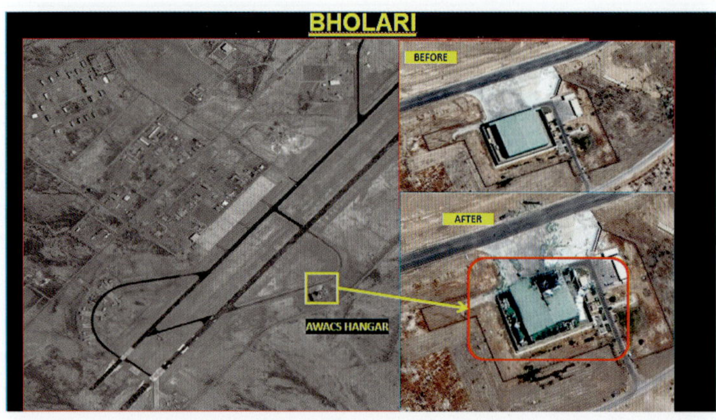

Photo 12: Jacobabad maintenance hangar

Photo 13: A ground view of the maintenance hangar before and after the strike

Source: IAF.

Photo 14: Murid drone command node

Photo 15: Rahimyar Khan UAV facility

Source: IAF.

Photo 16: Pakistan falsely claimed that the Fateh One missile engaged Indian targets; actually, no missile hit any target in India. Two missiles were intercepted over Sirsa, Punjab

Translate post

صبح 6 بجے کی ہیڈلائنز - 11 مئی 2025

دیکھنے مکمل ہیڈلائنز ہمارے یوٹیوب چینل پر؛ youtu.be/j6BajOMzwvk

Source: Accessed by VPN

Photo 17: Pakistan CAS grieves the loss of Sqn Ldr Usman

Source: Pakistani media report, accessed at https://x.com/DGPR_PAF/status/1924451878235947419

HAMMER and Rampage missiles. On 9–10 May the main strike weapon was the Air Launched BrahMos missile. All targets were successfully hit with precision and there were no misses. In fact, one weapon appears to have gone through the air conditioning vent to destroy an underground target. This speaks volumes of the professionalism with which these strikes were carried out.

In addition, air defence was a crucial component that got fine-tuned just months before the engagement. A suite of kinetic and non-kinetic anti-drone systems were integrated to existing air defence systems. Learning lessons from the Armenia-Azerbaijan and Russia-Ukraine wars, the Indian Air Force and the Indian Army designed a system and a set of operational procedures capable of minimising the damage from large, sophisticated attacks. It was a step that moved forward in its march from jointness to integration. Even the process of planning of the strikes on 7 May and allocation of targets that took into account the core competencies of each individual service served to enhance integration between the services. Joint planning is the bedrock on which joint operations and integrated actions can be based. The Sindoor experience will certainly accelerate the process of joint war fighting between the armed forces.

From a strategic impact perspective, the precision strike campaign achieved its aims. It degraded a specific ecosystem of terrorist violence by wiping out major terror hubs, thereby delivering a punitive lesson. Additionally, by escalating to hit Pakistan's military assets (after initial Indian losses), the IAF demonstrated that India could impose severe costs on the Pakistani military itself. This played directly into deterrence: Pakistan was left reeling under mounting losses and sought a ceasefire by Day 4. All this was accomplished with minimal collateral damage and without targeting civilian populations, reinforcing the operation's legitimacy. The high precision of IAF strikes—enabled by technology and careful planning—thus allowed India to send a dual message: resolve against terrorism and restraint against civilians. This approach reflects a maturation of India's precision strike doctrine since the Balakot episode in 2019. Then, questions arose over whether the bombs hit their mark; in 2025, Op Sindoor's strikes left little doubt of their effectiveness. The IAF's use of stand-off precision weapons, advanced ISR, and calibrated target selection in Op Sindoor showcases India's emergence into a capability for coercive precision operations—the ability to deliver punitive strikes with speed, accuracy, and controllable escalation. As Dr Walter Ludwig put it in his essay, "Operation Sindoor should be remembered not as a dogfight between airframes, nor as a stumble toward strategic instability. It was a calibrated use of force, intended to signal resolve, degrade terrorist infrastructure, and demonstrate capability—without crossing the line into broader war".[31] The fact that escalation control was carefully built into every stage of the operation indicated very clearly what the objectives of the operation were and why India accepted the ceasefire.

A significant discussion point among Pakistan and the western media in the aftermath of the strikes on 7 May was the reported downing of five military aircraft (including three Rafale aircraft) and one MALE UAV during the strike. Chinese media were agog with the effectiveness of a new method that outsmarted India. According to Micheal Dahm from Mitchell Institute of Aerospace Studies, Pakistan can "integrate ground radars with fighter jets and airborne early warning aircraft", and that "the Pakistani Air Force deployed ...'A' launched by 'B' and guided by 'C' and hit the target", as cited in a 12 May report from China Space News, a Chinese defense industry magazine. Dahm's theory is that maybe a surface-to-air missile system, or some other type of radar system illuminated the Indian target. Subsequently, a Pakistani J-10C fighter launched its missiles, probably at extreme range, and, finally, an airborne early warning and control aircraft used a midcourse datalink to update and guide the missile to the Indian fighter.[32] This created a great euphoria in the Pakistani media with reports indicating that they were winning the conflict. On 11 May, DGAO Air Marshal Bharti made two statements in this regard. Firstly, he said "losses are a part of combat" and secondly "all our pilots are home safe". In subsequent analysis it has become clear that India did not lose three Rafale aircraft. Speaking to CNBC–TV18 the Defence Secretary of India said, "You have used the term Rafales in the plural, I can assure you that is absolutely not correct".[33] Dassault Aviation CEO Eric Trappier, in an interview with *Challenges* magazine ahead of the Paris Air Show, said: "The Indians have not communicated, so we do not know exactly what happened. What we already know is that the words of the Pakistanis—three destroyed Rafales—are inaccurate."[34] Therefore it is fairly certain that the Indian losses are much lower than claimed by Pakistan. Further the so-called kill chain never made reappearance during the rest of the conflict especially on the night of 9–10 May.

What is lost in the conversation are the losses in aircraft terms by the PAF. Besides the humiliating strikes that forced a ceasefire, the PAF lost aircraft both in the air and on the ground. A post-conflict assessment of the military engagement during Op Sindoor has indicated heavy damage to Pakistani aerial and ground military assets. Quoting sources, NDTV has stated that five to six PAF fighter jets, two high-value surveillance aircraft, over ten armed drones, and a C-130 Hercules transport aircraft were destroyed in IAF's kinetic actions during Op Sindoor. Besides this there are multiple unspecified losses due to the attacks on hangars and allied aircraft infrastructure. The most significant was the loss of a SAAB AEW&C aircraft in the strike on a hangar at Bholari. Satellite pictures and statements by senior retired PAF officers virtually confirm the result. According to a video shared on the Internet, Retired Air Marshal Masood Akhtar stated, "they (Indian forces) fired four back-to-back BrahMos surface-to-surface missiles... surface-to-surface or air-to-surface, I am not sure. The (Pakistani) pilots rushed to secure their aircraft, but the missiles kept on coming and, unfortunately, the fourth one hit the hangar at Bholari (airbase), where one of our AWACS was standing. It was damaged and casualties were also reported".[35] Sqn Ldr Usman Yusuf along with an unspecified number of personnel were also killed in the attack.[36] PAF airborne losses were confirmed via radar tracking and thermal signatures captured by Indian ground-based missile systems and the consolidated air picture available in the IACCS.[37] Some of these losses occurred due to air-to-air engagements, others occurred due to engagement by SAMs principally the S-400 and MR-SAM supplied by Bharat Electronics Limited. In one instance, a long-range S-400 missile strike neutralised a high-value aerial target (suspected to be a Pakistani early-warning aircraft) at nearly 300 km distance.[38] These losses are not insignificant and it will take time, effort, and money to replace them.

The IAF's own Electronic Warfare capabilities were crucial in enabling its strikes. Right on Day 1, Indian Mirages, Mig-29s, and Su-30s flew with EW pods to confuse Pakistani ground radars and missile guidance. The Rafales flew with an internal EW suite that included airborne decoys. These EW tactics were partly why the initial wave of IAF attackers could survive Pakistan's HQ-9 SAMs and PL-15 AAMs envelopes, albeit not without losses. Once Indian strategy shifted on Day 2 to actively suppress enemy air defences, the anti-radiation missiles and Harop loitering drones took centre stage. By knocking out key components of Pakistan's integrated air defence—including destroying several SAM batteries and radars especially the ones situated at Lahore and Okara—the IAF achieved a degree of air superiority in some sectors. This claim is supported by the fact that IAF strike sorties faced progressively less resistance as the days went on. By 9–10 May, Indian fighters carried out strikes with impunity as Pakistan's radar coverage had been blinded in many sectors. Another factor that may have played out is the use of swarm drones to saturate PAF AD. According to the *Hindu*, "to overwhelm Pakistan's air defences, India also deployed swarm drone formations developed jointly by the Defence Research and Development Organisation (DRDO) and private contractors to create radar clutter, trigger premature defensive responses, and saturate surveillance networks".[39] Thus, the use of technology and electronic warfare played an important role in the success of Op Sindoor.

Intelligence, Surveillance, and Reconnaissance (ISR) also played a significant role for both India and Pakistan during Op Sindoor. ISR enabled pre-strike planning, battle damage assessment, and real-time situational awareness—critical in a short, high-tempo air campaign. The Indian side used integral assets like Heron and Heron-TP UAVs that were deployed along the western border to monitor troop and airfield activity. GSAT-7A (Rukmini), India's dedicated military communications satellite, allowed secure uplink/downlink to ground stations for real-time ISR coordination. AEW&C aircraft (Netra and Phalcon) monitored PAF combat air patrols, and directed Indian fighter ingress and egress paths. During the 9–10 May strikes, ISR enabled mid-course corrections and secondary target engagement. Heron drones and RISAT synthetic aperture radar imagery were used to assess damage to key targets like the Sargodha EW control centre and the Murid nuclear storage site perimeter. While Indian satellites such as the CARTOSAT and RISAT with good resolution were used, the long revisit times necessitated the use of commercial imagery obtained from open sources like Maxar, Planet M, as well as other US and European satellites. In addition, indigenous firms like Pixel and Soho were also used. Though this approach was useful, there was a time lag between the requirement and its receipt and analysis. By contrast, the Pakistani side had access to the Chinese satellites such as the China's Yaogan series comprising electro-optical (EO), synthetic aperture radar (SAR), and electronic intelligence (ELINT) sensors, which enabled persistent surveillance over northern India and the western Indo-Gangetic plain. Even though there was latency in information the PAF had, there was complete support from the Chinese side towards change of orbital dynamics to ensure information ability towards the operational needs of the PAF. Lieutenant General Rahul R. Singh, Deputy Chief of Army Staff (capability development and sustenance), speaking at the FICCI "New Age Military Technologies" event on 4 July 2025, stated that Pakistan had full visibility into Indian military deployments, which was made evident during the director general of military operations (DGMO)-level talks. "When the DGMO-level talks were going on, Pakistan actually was mentioning that 'we know that your such and such important vector is primed and ready for action. I would request you to perhaps pull it back'. So, he was getting live inputs ... from China", he disclosed.[40] In addition, according to *Jane's Defence Weekly* the Yaogan-30 series likely provided Pakistani command centres with real-time alerts on Indian radar activation and air defence posture.[41] These satellites (Yaogan-30 triplets) carry electronic intelligence payloads, capable of triangulating radar and communications emissions from Indian IACCS nodes.

Lessons

The foremost learning for the IAF is that indigenous weapons performed very well. The manner in which seamless integration of indigenous hi-tech systems into the national defence architecture was done was truly praiseworthy. Of particular note was the integration between the Army Air Defence network Akashteer and the IACCS of the IAF. Newly brought in anti-drone systems of indigenous origin were integrated too. Some legacy systems like the SPYDER of Israeli origin and the S-400 operated in standalone mode. They are in the process of being integrated and this should happen quickly. The networking of the airborne element has faced delays and needs to be completed quickly in order to make the entire system more robust and avoid losses. According to Air Marshal Anil Chopra, a leading expert on airpower, "Op Sindoor demonstrated the success of India's 'Atmanirbhar Bharat' (Self-

Reliant India) initiative, highlighting the country's increasing self-reliance in defence. India's indigenous counter-unmanned aerial systems, electronic warfare assets, and air defence weapons ensured multiple defensive layers from the international boundary to the hinterland. Indian multi-tier defence systems built over the last decade neutralised Pakistani attacks on our airfields and logistic installations".[42] He goes on to add that much more needs to be done in this area and the pace of fielding indigenous solutions needs to increase.

The next issue pertains to the manner in which Chinese support to Pakistan emerged during the conflict. Nearly 80% of Pakistani military hardware is of Chinese origin. Over the years, China has supplied aircraft, ships, submarines, tanks, missiles, drones etc; however, the greatest cooperation is in the field of aviation. It is reliably learnt that for all newly supplied systems, Chinese technicians and operational teams were in Pakistan, and reportedly guiding and supporting combat engagements.[43] With Pakistan being the leading recipient of Chinese armaments worth almost $20 billion, it was necessary for China to display the capabilities of these weapons. Hence, the "no holds barred" approach to the cooperation between the two sides. While the ISR cooperation leading to good battlefield transparency was a given, the reported supply of the non-export version of the PL-15E in the period between the Pahalgam attack and 7 May was a new level of collusion not seen before. India, therefore, needs to study all Chinese weapons and their capabilities carefully and develop counter mechanisms to deal with this double threat. In addition to catering for the difference in battlefield transparency that is likely to persist between India and its two principal adversaries for some time, there is a need to improve camouflage and concealment of critical assets that can deliver war-winning outcomes (like the S-400). Technologies to mask such assets already exist in the country and should be inducted expeditiously to retain the combat edge. Existing masking equipment is of vintage technology and needs to be upgraded at the earliest.

India's defence modernisation has chugged along steadily in the last few decades, albeit at a slow pace. This pace needs to accelerate. The number of fighter squadrons in the IAF has touched an all-time low. To enable effective targeting against a collusive threat the numbers have to increase. The defence spending in this geopolitical and neighbourhood environment needs to increase in order to be able to dominate the escalation ladder in such conflicts. The Ukraine war has shown that uncontrolled escalation can lead to long drawn-out conflict. In such a scenario domestic armament capacity becomes a dominant factor. Therefore, to both stimulate domestic capacities and to make up for shortfalls, an increased defence spending is a must. Larger funds have been recently authorised for emergency purchases, though there is a large backlog. The IAF's fighter fleet strength needs to be restored to the sanctioned 42 Squadrons at the very least, and acquisition of Flight Refuellers and AEW&C aircraft must be done on priority.

Drone warfare has had an effect on all conflicts in the recent past and Op Sindoor was no exception. In this operation drones were used for two main roles, viz., ISR and strike. ISR drones were pivotal in real-time battlefield awareness; both India and Pakistan employed ISR drones extensively. These platforms provided real-time battlefield mapping, target identification, and tracking, and post-strike BDA. High-quality ISR was critical for identifying targets, planning strikes, and conducting post-strike assessment. Hence, there is a need to improve fusion of airborne ISR (like Netra AEW&C, Heron TP drones) with space and HUMINT and harden and protect ISR assets against cyber/EW disruption. MALE UAVs due to their large size and slow speed are vulnerable in operations. However, till better solutions emerge they are invaluable in pre-conflict phases. India also needs to step up production of low-cost strike drones or loitering munitions to enable continued strike missions on vulnerable targets to keep up the pressure in a conflict situation. Counter-Drone Operations have also become critical – drones were successfully countered through kinetic and non-kinetic means and the IAF and AAD downed multiple Pakistani drones before they could engage targets. Therefore, drone defence is now a layered mission requiring integrated kinetic and electronic warfare assets. India must scale and harden its low-level air defence grid. Future developments in drone warfare point to use of drones for Electronic Warfare, Manned Unmanned teaming, use of AI/ML for drone swarming and drone interceptors. India must keep abreast of such developments and come up with indigenous solutions to develop these capabilities.

A factor in the multi domain operation that emerged was the narrative war that occurred during the conflict. Pakistan attempted to shape the global narrative, especially with videos, fake strike claims, and international lobbying. While the narrative war has been discussed elsewhere in the book, it is essential to understand that all future conflicts will be multi domain and there is a need to use open-source intelligence and independent verification to control narrative as well as deepen strategic communication planning across MEA, MOD, and PMO.

Finally technological self-reliance is now a strategic imperative. High-tech imported systems depend on spare parts, foreign data links, and political approvals. Therefore, fast-track development and integration of indigenous radar, missiles, avionics, and jammers is a pressing need. There is a need to incentivize private defence R&D, especially in drones, AI/ML for targeting, and hypersonic weapons; as well as, achieve supply-chain independence for long-duration conflict readiness.

Space Segment

The space segment contributed in three major ways during the conflict. ISR was the dominant role from space. However, navigation and communications were also important functions that needed space support during the operations. Therefore, during Op Sindoor, space-based surveillance played a vital role in ISR, BDA, and strategic situational awareness. India relied upon its growing military space infrastructure under the purview of the Defence Space Agency (DSA) and support from Indian Space Research Organisation (ISRO). In the years leading up to Sindoor, India had bolstered its constellation of military-capable satellites. This paid dividends during the operation. High-resolution electro-optical satellites of the Cartosat series and radar imaging satellites (RISAT) continuously monitored Pakistani territory for movement of troops, aircraft, and other indicators. Satellites such as the RISAT series were developed after the 2008 Mumbai attacks to keep tabs on militant threats; these were now being put to full use. During Op Sindoor, ISRO reportedly increased the imaging frequency, providing up-to-date snapshots of target areas. Obviously with the limited number of satellites and the long revisit time, there was a need to augment the same. Therefore, additional satellite images were sourced from commercial imagery providers like Maxar from USA and Sentinel from Europe and another commercial operator from the US.[44] Indian start-ups like Pixxel, GalaxEye, Suhora, Kawa, and Satsure also did phenomenal work during the conflict sourcing and processing images. Thousands of satellite images were processed in the span of the conflict, enabling real-time adjustments to targeting as needed (for example, detecting where Pakistan was moving assets like aircraft to alternate airfields, so those could be targeted). This space-based surveillance was the silent hero of the operation, turning the fog of war into a fairly clear picture for Indian commanders. Despite such success, the shortage of homegrown assets in space were keenly felt as sometimes entities like Maxar exercised tight control leading to delays. A need for additional satellite assets has already been projected by the armed forces. According to ISRO Chairman Mr V Narayanan, India would launch 100–150 satellites in the next five years. Among these would be 52 satellites as part of the Space-

Based Surveillance-3 (SBS-3) programme, and 31 of these will be developed by the private sector.[45] The focus will also shift from MEO to LEO to enable faster revisit times. While this is a welcome step, it may still fall short of the needs in a tactical scenario of fast-moving battlefield where minutes can make a difference.

By contrast, Pakistan had much better battlefield transparency thanks to the large constellation of satellites that China already has in orbit. According to Lt Gen AK Bhatt (Retd), Director General Indian Space Association, "open-source intelligence suggests Pakistan may have received real-time ISR feeds from China's Yaogan, Gaofan and Jilin satellite constellations. If true, that's not just passive support, that's direct enabler-level ISR, possibly even contributing live targeting data. That would have directly influenced Pakistan's tactical decisions during the conflict. Additionally, there's the ground side. China operates satellite control stations near Islamabad, specifically under the China-Pakistan Space Cooperation Centre. These stations manage telemetry and data relay and, by all accounts, they're tied into China's broader surveillance net that covers this entire region. With that, Pakistan isn't just using its own satellites; it's essentially borrowing reach from China, a space power with credible capabilities".[46] Looking at the close cooperation between the space-based assets of China and Pakistan, India will need to up its game of surveillance satellites in space and integration of these assets in the intelligence grid of the nation.

Communications were another critical contribution of space. India employed its dedicated military communication satellites (such as GSAT-7A for the Air Force and GSAT-7 for Naval links) to maintain secure data links between the theatre and New Delhi. The IAF's fighters and AWACS benefitted from satellite communications for beyond-line-of-sight connectivity, ensuring that even if Pakistan tried to jam traditional radio communications, the command chain remained intact. The use of satellite communication also allowed the tri-service coordination across vast geographies, for example, the Naval HQ and Air HQ could coordinate over secure SATCOM channels. This reflects India's recognition that space-based communications are vital for joint operations, especially given the need for real-time control in a fast-escalating crisis. Having said that, the terminals that are needed in the tactical battle area for satellite communication are still being rolled out. Also, the architecture of the network is still command-centric. A Starlink like architecture that brings tactical intelligence and communications to the last war fighter on the ground is the need of the hour.

As regards Position, Navigation, and Timing (PNT), the Indian forces relied on satellite navigation for their precision weapons. India's weapons (whether Spice bombs or the SCALP missile) typically use GPS/INS guidance. Anticipating possible GPS denial or spoofing the IAF was ready to fall back on India's own regional NAVSAT system NavIC (also known as IRNSS) for accurate positioning. Indeed, one benefit of India's investment in NavIC was seen in Op Sindoor—it provided an indigenous, jam-resistant navigation channel to guide Indian missiles if needed. In this conflict, outright GPS jamming by Pakistan was limited (perhaps to avoid affecting its own systems), but the IAF's preparation for a GPS-denied environment speaks to the increasing role of space in ensuring navigation sovereignty. The NavIC still has a limited number of satellites and with some of them being non-functional,it is necessary to launch additional satellites to make up for the shortfall.

For Pakistan the Beidou constellation with 30 satellites in the GEO and MEO orbit augmented with 120 ground stations provided a resilient Navigation System. Pakistan due to its arms purchases from China has inherited the Beidou architecture and it was easy for them to integrate their command-and-control as well as weapon systems for better effectiveness. India's domination in the conflict does not detract from the effective utilisation of space-based assets by Pakistan.

In essence, the need for utilisation of space-enabled support and the hardening against cyber onslaught in Op Sindoor show that India's war fighting doctrine needs to catch up with 21st-century realities, where dominance is required not just in air, land, and sea, but also in outer space and the electromagnetic spectrum.

The Nuclear Dimension

In any India–Pakistan conflict scenario, the reality of both powers having nuclear weapons is not lost on anyone, least of all on the two incumbents. Therefore, meticulous care has to be taken to avoid escalation to uncontrollable levels. Words have to be chosen slowly and utterances carefully calibrated to ensure that events do not spiral out of control. The international community watches very closely any development in tensions between the two nuclear armed states and does communicate with both sides on the prevailing situation. That India has a strict "no third party" rule does not deter from powers like the USA from having a conversation. Both India and Pakistan carefully calibrate their responses in the nuclear domain in accordance with their respective doctrines.

The nuclear doctrine of India rests on three major pillars—credible minimum deterrent, no first use (NFU), and massive retaliation in case of attack by nuclear weapons. Therefore, India does not specifically mention the nuclear word except when in response to utterances by Pakistani spokespersons or leaders especially in crisis situations. India has, however, questioned on many occasions the safety of nuclear weapons in the Pakistani state and the ability of Pakistani leaders to manage nuclear weapons. In a recent speech in May 2025 at Srinagar, India's Defence Minister Rajnath Singh said, "I raise this question before the world: Are nuclear weapons safe in the hands of such an irresponsible and rogue nation? Pakistan's nuclear weapons should be taken under the supervision of the IAEA".[47]

Pakistan, by contrast, has stated that its nuclear weapons are solely aimed at India and rejects and notions of "no first use". Pakistan does not have a formal doctrine but articulates its nuclear posture by released statements through DG ISPR and other senior leaders. Pakistan has a nuclear posture of full spectrum deterrence wherein it purports to use nuclear weapons early in a conflict in order to negate India's conventional superiority and thereby deter India. Pakistan claims that it crafted this strategy in response to India's cold start doctrine. Pakistan claims that it has developed its nuclear arsenal according to this posture that Full Spectrum Deterrence implies the following:

- "That Pakistan possesses the full spectrum of nuclear weapons in three categories: strategic, operational and tactical, with full range coverage of the large Indian land mass and its outlying territories; there is no place for India's strategic weapons to hide.
- That Pakistan possesses an entire range of weapons yield coverage in terms of kilotons (KT), and the numbers strongly secured, to deter the adversary's declared policy of massive retaliation; Pakistan's 'counter-massive retaliation' can therefore be as severe if not more.
- That Pakistan retains the liberty of choosing from a full spectrum of targets in a 'target-rich India', notwithstanding the indigenous Indian BMD or the Russian S-400, to include counter value, counter force and battlefield targets."[48]
- Therefore, according to Pakistan conventional war by India against Pakistan is impossible as the nuclear card comes into play as soon as Indian forces launch a ground offensive using conventional forces. Speaking at a seminar on 28 May 2025, DG, Institute of Strategic Studies Islamabad (ISSI),Ambassador Sohail Mahmood reaffirmed

> "that Pakistan's Full Spectrum Deterrence under Credible Minimum Deterrence ensures that no space exists for aggression below the nuclear threshold".[49] This self-belief that Indian conventional responses can be contained through nuclear brinkmanship became the basis of Pakistan's proxy warfare strategy of using cross-border terror against India.

However, nuclear taboos are not so easily crossed. The world has seen the horror of nuclear weapon use and despite humanity moving ever so closer to the doomsday clock nuclear weapons have remained firmly in the background. As with all India–Pakistan crises before and during the present one, the leadership on both sides has approached the nuclear issue rationally and with maturity. Despite the rhetoric, there is no evidence that any nuclear weapons were moved from peace time locations on either side. As stated, earlier escalation control was an essential element of planning at all stages. Therefore, despite "full freedom of action" being granted to the armed forces the decision not to attack military targets in the initial wave was taken to send a message of non-escalation to the adversary.

Nuclear signalling, however, is evident in any India Pakistan period of tension. During the Balakot Crisis of 2019, the nuclear signalling was very prominent. On 26 Feb 2019 at the ISPR briefing it was announced that Pakistan had summoned a special meeting of the National Command Authority (NCA), which controls the country's nuclear arsenal. For added emphasis, the ISPR spokesperson added "I hope you know what a meeting of the NCA means". The meeting was actually held at 13:00 hours on 27 Feb 2019 wherein Prime Minister Imran Khan "directed that elements of national power, including the armed forces and the people of Pakistan, remain prepared for all eventualities".[50] This was a clear signal to India to rein in its conventional response with underlying nuclear signals. By contrast, the nuclear signalling during Op Sindoor was more muted. There were no overt nuclear threats nor was there any indication of a meeting of the NCA. The DGMOs of both sides were in contact and no indication of nuclear escalation was passed on either side. After the Indian strike on the night of 9–10 May, it was reported by Reuters that Prime Minister Shehbaz Sharif had called for a meeting of the NCA.[51] However, Pakistan's defence minister Khawaja Asif later said that no such meeting was held. In an interview with ARY TV he later added, "This thing that you have spoken about (nuclear option) is present but let's not talk about it; we should treat it as a very distant possibility, we should not even discuss it in the immediate context".[52] Thus, Pakistan chose a different path on nuclear signalling this time. This was perhaps due to the phone calls that were going on between the USA and Pakistan. According to Christopher Clary, "indeed, while the timeline is not clear, it is not impossible that the key Munir-Rubio phone call was spurred by the National Command Authority announcement".[53] Another possibility is that learning from the various nuclear signals from the Ukraine–Russia war especially those emanating from the Russian side and their challenge by the West, Pakistan decided not to rattle the nuclear sabre. Nuclear signalling is both an art and a science—too subtle and the signals could be missed and if too aggressive it may provoke the adversary to challenge the enunciated red lines. A nuclear signal that Pakistan displayed was the launch of an Abdali Weapon System, a surface-to-surface missile with a range of 450 km on 3 May 2025. The launch was reportedly a part of "Ex Indus" and was witnessed by the commander of the Army Strategic Forces Command (AFSC). Hasan Askari Rizvi, a Pakistani military analyst, said, "it clearly indicates that we have the resources to counter India. This is not a message only for India but the rest of the world that we are well-prepared".[54]

Another issue that was hotly debated after the conflict ended was whether India struck any nuclear facilities of Pakistan. In this context two places were mentioned—Kirana Hills near Sargodha which is suspected to be a site of storage of nuclear weapons and Nur Khan airbase which is close to Islamabad where Strategic Plans Division is located. On the issue of Kirana Hills, the evidence is ambiguous in that it shows a missile strike on a hilly area that really cannot be confirmed as Kirana Hills. A military expert Tom Cooper, in an interview with Indian media speaking in context of Kirana Hills, claimed that "India hit two entrances to one of Pakistan's underground facilities, suspected or assumed to be a nuclear facility".[55] This, however, was denied by India. Air Marshal AK Bharti, DGAO, when questioned during a press briefing on 12 May 2025 about whether India targeted the nuclear facilities at Kirana Hills denied reports that the Indian Air Force struck there. He stated, "We have not hit Kirana Hills, whatever is there. I didn't mention it in my briefing yesterday or today".[56] There were also social media posts of a US radiation monitoring aircraft in the area of Sargodha and Kirana Hills. However, this radiation leak theory was debunked by IAEA. "Based on information available to the IAEA, there has been no radiation leak or release from any nuclear facility in Pakistan", an IAEA spokesperson told PTI on 15 May 2025.[57]All signs, therefore, point to non-targeting of nuclear facilities by India. This is also in consonance with India's policy to control escalation. Therefore, it can be safely assumed that the strikes carried out by India did not target any nuclear storage sites.

With regard to the strike on Nur Khan Airbase, The Strategic Plans Division is more than a kilometre away from the base and hence there was no targeting of the nuclear organisation of Pakistan. We do know, however, that a command-and-control centre was targeted. Whether this command-and-control centre was shared with Nuclear Command, Control and Communications (NC3) of Pakistan is not known in the public domain. Hence, it can be seen that if there are dual use facilities they can be targeted inadvertently. It must be remembered here that despite all tensions, Confidence Building Measures (CBMs) between India and Pakistan in the nuclear domain like the Agreement on the prohibition of

Attack against Nuclear Installation and Facilities have held since they were signed between the two states in 1988. A list of such facilities was exchanged between the two sides as recently as 1 Jan 2025.[58] These previously agreed CBMs have held despite many tensions in the India–Pakistan relationship over the last many decades. India can, therefore, hardly be expected to risk attacking nuclear storage sites that are likely to cause nuclear contamination especially in the early stages of the conflict. Hence, despite all the noise on social media there was no nuclear rhetoric or nuclear escalation on both sides during Op Sindoor. This is a feature of all India Pakistan crises wherein both sides have acted with maturity and restraint in nuclear matters.

What India has challenged in the nuclear domain is Pakistan's belief that there is no space for conventional kinetic action under the nuclear threshold. During Op Sindoor, India treated the Pahalgam terrorist attack originating from Pakistani soil as an act of war. Consequently, India did not allow Pakistan's nuclear capability to deter it from using kinetic action thereby creating space for military action below the nuclear threshold. Op Sindoor was characterised by clear definition of objectives, controlled escalation, and effective strategic messaging. In the conduct of Op Sindoor, India demonstrated the limitations of Pakistan's nuclear deterrent as a shield for the prosecution of terrorism.[59]

One of the many arrows that Pakistan has in its nuclear quiver is to project "irrationality" in its nuclear posture. While it may act rationally in crisis situations, the projection of irrationality is normally present in its public posture. During the current crisis this element was noticeably absent. It perhaps took a post-crisis analysis for the Pakistani leadership to realise that they had missed a trick. As Yossef Bodensky notes in his writings, "Islamabad is convinced that the mere threat of approaching the nuclear threshold will prevent India from seizing the strategic initiative and military dominance of events, permitting Pakistan to escalate the crisis at will without the fear of meaningful Indian retribution".[60]

Perhaps the Pakistani leadership had been so shell-shocked by the rapid strikes of the IAF that they did not have the mind space to use all available tools at their disposal. Hence in the post-crisis projection of their nuclear posture, a return to this tool of irrationality has been noted.

Two events indicate this posture. In the first instance, at a seminar hosted by the Arms Control and Disarmament Centre (ACDC) at the ISSI as a part of the commemoration of Youm-e-Takbeer on 28 May 2025, DG ISSI, Ambassador Sohail Mahmood, as stated earlier, had reaffirmed that "Pakistan's Full Spectrum Deterrence under Credible Minimum Deterrence ensures that no space exists for aggression below the nuclear threshold".[61] The seminar also noted that "Pakistan's credible nuclear deterrence will continue to constrain and limit India's political and operational choices."[62] This signals a return to the old playbook of irrationality.

The second and more recent development is Field Marshal Asim Munir's surprising nuclear threat against India during a speech to Pakistani diaspora in the United States. On 10 Aug 2025, at a dinner in Tampa hosted by businessman and honorary consul Adnan Asad, FM Munir reportedly stated, "We are a nuclear nation. If we think we are going down, we'll take half the world down with us".[63] Even though the subsequent official release, post the event, did not mention these threats, it was widely recounted to journalists by those present and was accordingly reported. The reaction of the Indian Ministry of External Affairs was immediate "Nuclear sabre-rattling is Pakistan's stock-in-trade. The international community can draw its own conclusions on the irresponsibility inherent in such remarks" the spokesperson stated at a media briefing on 12 May 2025.[64] Pakistan perhaps realised that by playing down the nuclear threat during the period of Op Sindoor had possibly given rise to the perception that there was space for conventional warfare under the nuclear umbrella. Forgoing such a potent tool in its deterrence strategy was not seen favourably in the strategic community in Pakistan. Hence there is a push-back towards the irrationality doctrine in the nuclear domain. The 27th Amendment to the Constitution of Pakistan, which, amongst other things, shifts the control of nuclear forces from the civilian leadership to the Chief of Defence Forces, also indicates a strategic signal to India that nuclear forces could be called upon at much earlier stages in future conflicts. This, coupled with the likelihood of Field Marshall Asim Munir becoming the Chief of Defence Forces, and his aggressive nuclear posture against India, sends a significant signal.

This shift in strategic signalling will continue to be a feature of future India Pakistan engagements and crises. As Syed Eesar Mehdi of International Centre for Peace Studies noted in a previous crisis "as the smoke cleared over Kashmir, the world was reminded that even in an era defined by nuclear deterrence and global diplomacy, conventional military power, strategic signalling, and crisis management remain indispensable to national security".[65]

Notes

1. Media Centre, Ministry of External Affairs, GOI, 23 April 2025, Statement by Foreign Secretary on the decision of the CCS. https://www.mea.gov.in/Speeches-Statements.htm?dtl/39442/Statement_by_Foreign_Secretary_on_the_decision_of_the_Cabinet_Committee_on_Security_CCS#
2. Dr Walter Ladwig, 21 May 2025, Calibrated Force: Operation Sindoor and the Future of Indian Deterrence, RUSI. https://www.rusi.org/explore-our-research/publications/commentary/calibrated-force-operation-sindoor-and-future-indian-deterrence
3. Ibid.
4. Yalda Hakim, 25 April 2025.https://x.com/SkyYaldaHakim/status/1915682394985709595
5. *The Statesman*, 30 April 2025, Pak minister holds emergency press meet at 2 am, says India's military action within 24 to 36 hours. https://www.thestatesman.com/world/pak-minister-holds-emergency-press-meet-at-2-am-says-indias-military-action-within-24-to-36-hours-1503426623.html
6. PIB Press release, 18 May 2025, Operation SINDOOR: Forging One Force The Synergy of India's Armed Forces. https://www.pib.gov.in/PressReleasePage.aspx?PRID=2129453
7. PIB Press release, 7 May 2025, Operation Sindoor: Indian Armed Forces Carried Out Precision Strike at Terrorist Camps. https://www.pib.gov.in/PressReleseDetailm.aspx?PRID=2127370
8. *The Nation*, 7 May 2025, 26 civilians martyred, 46 injured in Indian strikes on Pakistan: DG ISPR. https://www.nation.com.pk/07-May-2025/26-civilians-martyred-46-injured-in-indian-strikes-on-pakistan-dg-ispr
9. PIB, Govt of India, 11 May 2025, https://www.pib.gov.in/ViewVideo.aspx?V_ID=194344&MinID=33&VPRID=183232&Day=&Month=5&Year=2025
10. *Dawn*, 7 May 2025.
11. Pakistani Ministry of Information, 7 May Press release 69.

12. *The Washington Post*, 6 May 2025. https://www.washingtonpost.com/world/2025/05/08/india-pakistan-attack-response
13. *The Express Tribune*, 9 May 2025, DG ISPR challenges Delhi to produce evidence of Pakistan's missile, drone attacks in India. https://tribune.com.pk/story/2544936/pakistan-military-questions-indias-quick-accusations-following-border-tensions
14. *The Washington Post*, 8 May 2025. https://www.washingtonpost.com/world/2025/05/08/india-pakistan-attack-response
15. Amrita Nayak Dutta, 19 May 2025, *The Indian Express*, Pakistan deployed attack and surveillance drones hidden in swarms of basic drones.https://indianexpress.com/article/india/pakistan-deployed-attack-and-surveillance-drones-hidden-in-swarms-of-basic-drones-10014686/.
16. PIB, Ministry of Defence, Govt of India, Pakistan's Bid to Escalate Negated - Proportionate Response by India. https://www.pib.gov.in/PressReleasePage.aspx?PRID=2127670
17. The STRATCOM Bureau (@OSPSF), X, 9 May 2025. https://x.com/OSPSF/status/1920763519646994705;Farooq Bhai (@FarooqB90714421), X, May 8, 2025
18. *Al Jazeera*, 9 May 2025, India and Pakistan tension mounting amid attacks and accusations. https://www.aljazeera.com/news/2025/5/9/india-and-pakistan-tension-mounting-amid-attacks-and-accusations
19. RT.com, 21 May 2025, How Moscow's legendary S-400 missiles helped India outgun Pakistan. https://www.rt.com/india/617955-brahmos--s-400-india-pakistan
20. Christopher Clary, 28 May 2025, Stimson, Four Days in May: The India-Pakistan Crisis of 2025. https://www.stimson.org/2025/four-days-in-may-the-india-pakistan-crisis-of-2025
21. NDTV, 29 July 2025, Night Before Ceasefire, JD Vance Called PM Modi. Here's What They Discussed. https://www.ndtv.com/india-news/night-before-ceasefire-jd-vance-called-pm-modi-heres-what-they-discussed-8977128
22. Shishir Gupta, 8 June 2025, *Hindustan Times*, 19 Brahmos, Crystal Maze missiles: How India brought Pakistan to its knees during Op Sindoor. https://www.hindustantimes.com/india-news/19-brahmos-

crystal-maze-missiles-details-of-how-india-brought-pakistan-to-its-knees-during-operation-sindoor-101749345012318.html

23. https://www.thehindu.com/data/satellite-images-of-military-and-terror-targets-in-pakistan/article69567141.ece.
24. Dipanjan Roy Chaudhury, 30 May 2025, *The Economic Times*. https://economictimes.indiatimes.com/news/politics-and-nation/shehbaz-sharif-admits-pakistan-caught-unawares-by-brahmos/articleshow/121497528.cms?from=mdr
25. *The Hindu*, 27 May 2025, Congress poses questions about ceasefire conditions at Jai Hind rally in Barmer. https://www.thehindu.com/news/national/rajasthan/congress-poses-questions-about-ceasefire-conditions-at-jai-hind-rally-in-barmer/article69621978.ece#goog_rewarded
26. *The Hindu*, 30 July 2025, In Rajya Sabha, Opposition questions Centre on terms of ceasefire. https://www.thehindu.com/news/national/opposition-questions-centre-on-trumps-remarks-verbal-attack-on-colonel-qureshi/article69870728.ece
27. Christopher Clary, 28 May 2025, Stimson, Four Days in May: The India-Pakistan Crisis of 2025. https://www.stimson.org/2025/four-days-in-may-the-india-pakistan-crisis-of-2025
28. Media Center, MEA, Govt of India, 10 May 2025, Statement by Foreign Secretary (May 10, 2025). https://www.mea.gov.in/press-releases.htm?dtl/39488/Statement_by_Foreign_Secretary_May_10_2025
29. NDTV World, 20 June 2025, "Asked India for Ceasefire When...": Pak Deputy PM's Viral Admission on Op Sindoor. https://www.ndtv.com/world-news/asked-india-for-ceasefire-when-pakistan-deputy-prime-minister-ishaq-dar-viral-admission-on-operation-sindoor-8713973
30. *The Times of India*, 9 August 2025, Just 50 air-launched weapons pulverised Pak, says IAF Vice-Chief. https://timesofindia.indiatimes.com/india/just-50-air-launched-weapons-pulverised-pak-says-iaf-vice-chief/articleshow/122914122.cms
31. Dr Walter Ladwig, 21 May 2025, RUSI, Calibrated Force: Operation Sindoor and the Future of Indian Deterrence. https://www.rusi.org/

explore-our-research/publications/commentary/calibrated-force-operation-sindoor-and-future-indian-deterrence

32. John A. Tirpak, 19 May 2025, *Air and Space Forces Magazine*, The Biggest News from India-Pakistan Air Battle: the Kill Chain. https://www.airandspaceforces.com/india-pakistan-air-battle-kill-chain
33. *The Economic Times*, 7 July 2025, No Rafale Jets Lost: Defence Secretary Says ...https://economictimes.indiatimes.com/news/defence/no-rafale-jets-lost-defence-secretary-says-pakistan-paid-a-higher-price-over-100-terrorists-killed-in-operation-sindoor/articleshow/122300471.cms
34. Shivani Sharma, 15 June 2025, *Business Today*, Pakistan's claims are inaccurate': Dassault CEO on Rafale jets loss claims during Op Sindoor. https://www.businesstoday.in/india/story/pakistans-claims-are-inaccurate-dassault-ceo-rafale-jets-loss-claims-during-op-sindoor-480451-2025-06-15
35. *The Eurasian Times*, 16 May 2025, Pakistan's AWACS Aircraft Lost in BrahMos Strikes at Bholari Air Base, Pak Air Marshal Says in TV Interview. https://www.eurasiantimes.com/pakistans-awacs-aircraft-lost-in-brahmos-strikes-at-bholari-air-base-pak-air-marshal-says-in-interview
36. Ibid.
37. NDTV, 4 June 2025, 9 Pakistani Aircraft Were Destroyed In Operation Sindoor Strikes: Sources. https://www.ndtv.com/india-news/9-pakistani-aircraft-were-destroyed-in-operation-sindoor-strikes-sources-8583398
38. Purnima Mishra, 5 June 2025, *Bharat Express*, Op Sindoor: India Delivers Decisive Blow to Pakistan in Retaliation to Terror Attack. https://english.bharatexpress.com/india/op-sindoor-india-delivers-decisive-blow-to-pakistan-in-retaliation-to-terror-attack-205579
39. Rahul Bedi, 30 May 2025, *The Hindu*, Autonomous warfare in Operation Sindoor. https://www.thehindu.com/news/national/autonomous-warfare-in-operation-sindoor/article69633124.ece
40. *The Wire*, 5 July 2025, Five Key Revelations from Army's Deputy Chief on Operation Sindoor. https://thewire.in/security/five-key-revelations-lt-gen-rahul-singh-operation-sindoor

41. *Janes Defence Weekly*, Vol. 62, May 2025
42. Air Marshal Anil Chopra, 26 May 2025, *FirstPost*, Operation Sindoor: Indigenous systems gave India the edge, more needs to be done. https://www.firstpost.com/opinion/operation-sindoor-indigenous-systems-gave-india-the-edge-more-needs-to-be-done-13891706.html
43. Air Marshal Anil Chopra (r),31 May 2025, *Indian Aerospace and Defence Bulletin*, China's Military Aviation Support to Pakistan – Need to Watch India. https://www.iadb.in/2025/05/31/chinas-military-aviation-support-to-pakistan-need-to-watch-india
44. Chethan Kumar, 13 May 2025, *The Times of India*, Operation Sindoor: Domestic Strategic Space Assets https://timesofindia.indiatimes.com/india/operation-sindoor-domestic-strategic-space-assets-foreign-commercial-satellites-used/articleshow/121118997.cms
45. *The Economic Times*, 13 May 2025, Indian Armed Forces used domestic strategic space assets .... https://economictimes.indiatimes.com/news/defence/indian-armed-forces-used-domestic-strategic-space-assets-foreign-commercial-satellites-for-operation-sindoor-report/articleshow/121131502.cms?from=mdr
46. Interview with Defstrat magazine on 31 Jul 2025 transcript on https://www.linkedin.com/pulse/indias-space-power-operation-sindoor-challenge-zpoxe/
47. Rajat Pandit, 17 May 2025, *The Times of India*, Pak a rogue nation with nukes https://timesofindia.indiatimes.com/india/pak-a-rogue-nation-with-nukes-must-be-under-iaea-scanner-rajnath-singh/articleshow/121196819.cms
48. ISSI, 26 May 2023, Speech by Lt. Gen. (Retd) Khalid Kidwai, Advisor, National Command Authority and former DG SPD, on 25th Youme-e-Takbeer. https://issi.org.pk/speech-by-lt-gen-retd-khalid-kidwai-advisor-national-command-authority-and-former-dg-spd-on-25th-youme-e-takbeer/
49. ISSI, 28 May 2025, Press Release – Youm-e-Takbeer: Lt. Gen. Kidwai speaks at ISSI Seminar on "The Future of Deterrence and Emerging Challenges". https://issi.org.pk/press-release-youm-e-

takbeer-lt-gen-kidwai-speaks-at-issi-seminar-on-the-future-of-deterrence-and-emerging-challenges/

50. *India Today*, 27 February 2019, Imran Khan to chair Pakistan's nuke authority meeting after Indian Air Force bombs Jaish camps in Balakot. https://www.indiatoday.in/world/story/imran-khan-pakistan-nuke-authority-meeting-indian-air-force-airstrike-jaish-camps-balakot-1465988-2019-02-27

51. Reuters, 10 May 2025, Pakistan PM calls meeting of body that oversees nuclear arsenal, says Pakistan military. https://www.reuters.com/world/asia-pacific/pakistan-pm-calls-meeting-body-that-oversees-nuclear-arsenal-says-pakistan-2025-05-10

52. *The Times of India*, 10 May 2025, Pakistan PM Shehbaz Sharif calls National Command Authority meeting https://timesofindia.indiatimes.com/world/pakistan/pakistan-pm-shehbaz-sharif-calls-national-command-authority-meeting-body-that-oversees-nuclear-arsenal/articleshow/121047361.cms

53. Christopher Clary, 28 May 2025, Stimson, Four Days in May: The India-Pakistan Crisis of 2025. https://www.stimson.org/2025/four-days-in-may-the-india-pakistan-crisis-of-2025

54. *Dawn*, 3 May 2025, Pakistan successfully tests launch of short-range Abdali ballistic missile. https://www.dawn.com/news/1908176/pakistan-successfully-tests-launch-of-short-range-abdali-ballistic-missile

55. *The Economic Times*, 16 May 2025, Pakistan's ability to handle nuclear weapons is questionable https://economictimes.indiatimes.com/news/defence/pakistans-ability-to-handle-nuclear-weapons-is-questionable-military-analyst-tom-cooper/articleshow/121203217.cms

56. *Business Today*, 12 May 2025, 'Didn't know what is there, didn't hit': Air Marshal denies rumours of action at Pakistan's Kirana Hills. https://www.businesstoday.in/india/story/didnt-know-what-is-there-didnt-hit-air-marshal-denies-rumours-of-action-at-pakistans-kirana-hills-475919-2025-05-12

57. *The Hindu*, 15 May 2025, No radiation leak from any nuclear facility in Pakistan: IAEA. https://www.thehindu.com/news/

international/no-radiation-leak-from-any-nuclear-facility-in-pakistan-iaea/article69578556.ece

58. MEA Press release, 01 Jan 2025, India and Pakistan exchange list of Nuclear Installations. https://www.mea.gov.in/press-releases.htm?dtl/38877/India+and+Pakistan+exchange+list+of+Nuclear+Installations
59. Arun Sahgal, 21 May 2025, BASIC, Operation Sindoor establishes India's New Response Doctrine towards Pakistan. https://basicint.org/operation-sindoor-establishes-indias-new-response-doctrine-towards-pakistan/
60. Yossef Bodansky, Pakistan's Nuclear Blackmail. https://www.oocities.org/collegepark/library/9803/pak_strategic/bodansky3.html
61. ISSI, 28 May 2025, Press release – Youm-e-Takbeer: Lt. Gen. Kidwai speaks at ISSI Seminar on "The Future of Deterrence and Emerging Challenges". https://issi.org.pk/press-release-youm-e-takbeer-lt-gen-kidwai-speaks-at-issi-seminar-on-the-future-of-deterrence-and-emerging-challenges/
62. Ibid.
63. *India Today*, 11 August 2025, Will take half the world down with us: Asim Munir threatens nuke wipeout from US. https://www.indiatoday.in/world/story/well-take-half-the-world-down-pak-army-chiefs-nuclear-threat-to-india-from-us-glbs-2769228-2025-08-10
64. Shubhajit Roy, 12 August 2025, *The Indian Express*, After Pakistan army chief Asim Munir's anti-India rhetoric in US, Delhi calls it 'nuclear sabre-rattling'. https://indianexpress.com/article/india/india-pakistan-asim-munir-united-states-nuclear-sabre-rattling-10182699/
65. Syed Eesar Mehdi, 11 June 2025, Retaliation and Restraint: Op Sindoor, India's War Within Limits, International Centre for Peace Studies. https://www.icpsnet.org/comment/Retaliation-and-Restraint-Op-Sindoor

5

Pounding the Earth and Guarding the Sky

The Indian Army

BRIGADIER AKHELESH BHARGAVA

"A Nation has security when it does not have to sacrifice its legitimate interests to avoid war and is able, if challenged, to maintain them by war."

—Walter Lippmann

In the previous chapter, the air battle, as well as the nuclear aspects, during Operation Sindoor has been covered in detail. This chapter examines the following aspects:

- The attack on terror camps by the Indian Army on the night of 6–7 May 2025
- The destruction of Pakistan assets along the Line of Control (LC) by infantry and artillery
- Action by the defenders of the Indian sky, "The Army Air Defence (AD)"

Synergised Targeting of Terrorist Camps

Between 23 April and 6 May 2025, Pakistan was kept in suspense, in that the Indian reprisal will come from land, sea, or air. On 6 May 2025, it was announced that there will be rehearsals for "black-out" drill across many cities. Under the CDS, a list of 21 camps,[1] belonging to Jaish-e-Mohammed (JeM), Lashkar-e-Taiba (LeT), and Hizbul Mujahideen (HM), located in POJK and Pakistan had been prepared. This included indoctrination camps, training camps, terrorist holding areas (post-training waiting area), and headquarters (HQ). Op Sindoor was launched on the night of 6–7 May 2025.

Figure 5.1: List of terrorist camps identified by the Indian Armed Forces

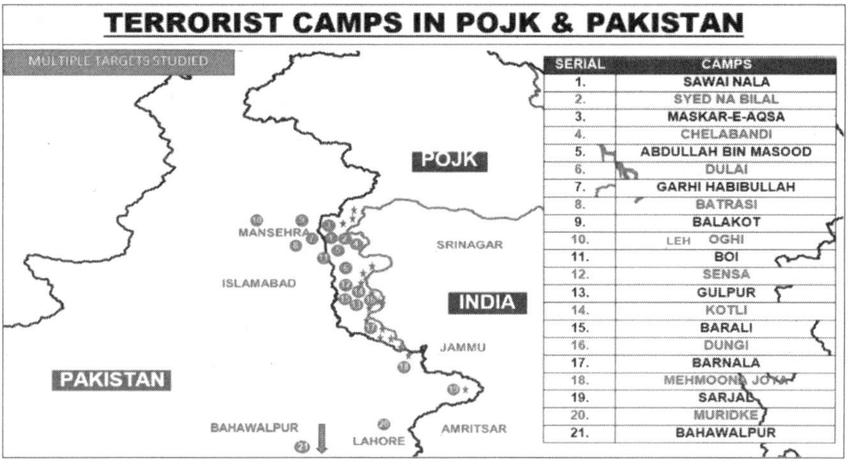

TERRORIST CAMPS IN POJK & PAKISTAN

MULTIPLE TARGETS STUDIED

POJK
MANSEHRA
ISLAMABAD
SRINAGAR
INDIA
JAMMU
PAKISTAN
BAHAWALPUR
LAHORE
AMRITSAR
LEH

SERIAL	CAMPS
1.	SAWAI NALA
2.	SYED NA BILAL
3.	MASKAR-E-AQSA
4.	CHELABANDI
5.	ABDULLAH BIN MASOOD
6.	DULAI
7.	GARHI HABIBULLAH
8.	BATRASI
9.	BALAKOT
10.	OGHI
11.	BOI
12.	SENSA
13.	GULPUR
14.	KOTLI
15.	BARALI
16.	DUNGI
17.	BARNALA
18.	MEHMOONA JOYA
19.	SARJAL
20.	MURIDKE
21.	BAHAWALPUR

Source: Media briefings during Operation Sindoor.

India had the advantage of the first move, while for Pakistan the suspense continued—suspense about which targets would be hit, which weapons would be used, and from where? The daily routine at each camp was studied thoroughly and continuously, mapping the move pattern of cadres coming in and out of camps, their prayer timings, and other activities. Refer to the terrorist camp Photos 1–8 on the page inserts of this chapter. The whole idea was to destroy the camps and send a message to Pakistan that the location of camps is known to the Indian intelligence agencies. Collateral damage to civilians, residential areas, schools, mosques close to the respective camps, was to be avoided. The Pakistan Air Force (PAF) air activity was also monitored around the clock. Based on these inputs, the time between 01:30 and 02:00 hours was selected, when there would be minimum activity. The 21 camps that were identified and kept under surveillance are as under:

- **In POJK**, 12 locations were identified: Maskar-e-Aqsa, Sawai Nala, Syed-na-Bilal, Chelabandi, Abdullah Bin Masood, Dulai, Sensa, Kotli, Dungi, Barali, Gulpur, and Barnala.
- **In Pakistan** there were nine locations: Balakot, Oghi, Garhi Habibullah, Batrasi, Boi, Mehmoona Joya, Sarjal, Muridke, and Bahawalpur.

From among these camps, nine camps were shortlisted based on value. Seven were to be addressed by the Army and two by IAF.[2] The terrorist camps destroyed by the Indian Army are as under:[3],[4]

- Sawai Nala, Muzaffarabad, POJK (30 km from LC): This is a key LeT training facility in Tang Dhar sector. It was responsible for the ideological indoctrination and combat training of operatives destined for cross-border infiltration and attacks. The attack on civilians and security forces in Sonmarg on 20 October 2024, in Gulmarg on 24 October 2024, and in Pahalgam on 22 April 2025 were carried out by the terror module from here.
- Syedna Bilal, Muzaffarabad, POJK: This is a significant staging area of JeM facility, also used to train terrorists in weapons, explosives, and jungle-cum-survival techniques.

This camp was directly linked through intelligence intercepts to the planning and execution of the 2019 Pulwama attack.

- Abbas Camp, Kotli, POJK (13 km from LC): This was identified as a nerve centre for training LeT suicide bombers (fidayeen) and providing their logistical support. It had a terrorist training infrastructure for about 50 terrorists.
- Gulpur Camp, Kotli, POJK (30 km from LC): This was a known base for LeT terrorists operating in the Rajouri-Poonch sector. Intelligence confirmed its direct involvement in attacks in Poonch on 20 April 2023, and on bus pilgrims on 9 June 2024. Zaki-ur-Rehman Lakhvi, the 26/11 mastermind, frequently visited this camp for indoctrination and motivational speeches.
- Barnala Camp, Bhimber, POJK (9 km from LC): This was a training centre for LeT, focused on the fabrication and handling of Improvised Explosive Devices (IEDs), advanced weapons training, and jungle survival techniques for infiltrators. It was opposite the Rajouri-Poonch sector.
- Mehmoona Joya Camp, Sialkot, Pakistan (12 km from the international border [IB]): This was a key training facility and control centre of HM for operation in Kathua-Jammu region. Intelligence linked this facility directly to the planning and logistical support for the 2016 Pathankot airbase attack.
- Sarjal Camp, Tehra Kalan, Chak Amru, Sialkot, Pakistan (6 km from IB): This was a JeM training facility for operation in Samba-Kathua region. It was deceptively disguised as a health centre to evade detection but was a clandestine terror camp. The terrorists who killed four personnel of Jammu and Kashmir Police in March 2025 were trained here and launched the operation from this camp.

It was after 15 days of the terror strike at Pahalgam on 22 April that India struck these nine terror bases commencing around 01:30 hours IST.[5] It was well coordinated as all camps were struck within a span of 23 minutes. Of these nine camps, five belonged to JeM, three to LeT, and one to HM. The strategy adopted by India was to cause camp destruction from stand-off distance, without using ground troops.

Figure 5.2: Nine terror camps destroyed on 7 May 2025

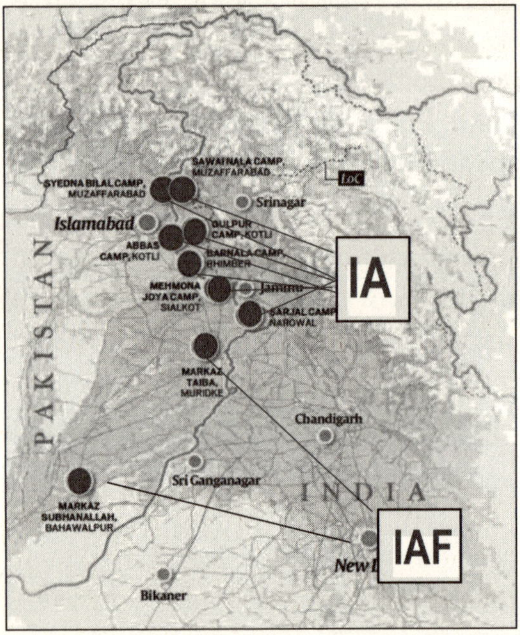

Source: MEA briefing.

Seven of the nine terror camps were close to LC, and the Indian Army was made responsible for their destruction. Long range artillery and loiter ammunition were used to destroy these camps. The tri-service synergy was at its best in the destruction of the nine terror camps.

The M982 Excalibur precision-guided artillery shells can be fired from 155 mm/52 calibre M-777 howitzers and the K-9 Vajra self-propelled howitzer. Depending on the configuration, its range varies from 40 to 57 km and it has a circular error of probability (CEP) of just around 3 m. Its warhead is high-explosive blast-fragmentation that is used to target structures like bunkers. Using its precision and penetrating heavy structures capability, using shaped charge warhead, terrorist launch pads located in PoJK could be destroyed during Op Sindoor.[6]

Sky Striker is a fully autonomous loitering munition that can locate, acquire, and strike operator-designated targets with a 5 or 10 kg adapted warhead installed inside the fuselage, enabling high-precision performance. With the capability to dive towards targets at speeds exceeding 500 km/h, the Sky Striker is difficult to detect and intercept. It has an electro-optical (EO) system that gives it multiple roles of either gathering intelligence, delivering powerful strikes, or providing post-strike damage assessment (PSDA). Its electric engine (having low acoustic signature) and the ability to operate in ground positioning system (GPS)-denied environment enables stealth operations at low altitude. It has abort mission facility too. As a silent, invisible, and surprise attacker, Sky Striker delivered the warhead with utmost precision and reliability during Op Sindoor.[7]

The Palm 120 is a bunker-bursting loitering munition and has tandem warhead technology that neutralises the roof before delivering the main charge with pinpoint accuracy. It has a range of 40 km, endurance of 60 min and a 4.5 kg warhead.[8] The Palm 400 is an advanced version of Palm 120. It has a longer range and is artificial intelligence (AI) enabled for target recognition and an autonomous decision-making capability. It continues to function in jamming environment and even if there is breakdown in GPS and communications. It has a range of 150 km, endurance of 120 min and an 8 kg bunker buster warhead.[9] Both Palm 120 and Palm 400 have a man in loop command and control systems allowing the operator to maintain visual contact with targets, perform precision strikes, and abort mission if necessary. The Navy used these weapons complementing the Army at two locations.

India claimed "over 100 terrorists killed with no collateral damage to civilians or military infrastructure".[10] It seems that a large number of terrorists returned to the two HQs after initial dispersion, as so many close relatives of Masood Azhar were killed. However, Pakistan had ample warning of an impending Indian attack and the authorities may have worked to reduce the number of people in all camps.

Another highlight of the terror camp strikes was the real-time coverage of each attack using satellites imagery and intelligence, surveillance, and reconnaissance (ISR) drones. Such was the planning and coordination that these satellites and drones were prepositioned over the target locations. Where not feasible, commercial satellites like MAXAR were used. The pictures and videos of the weapons being "dropped," and destruction caused were relayed in real-time for the world to acknowledge. Post this action, no one had any question to ask on the veracity of the claims made.

As stated by an Indian spokesperson, the 7 May strikes only hit "terrorist infrastructure" and were "focused, measured, and non-escalatory in nature".[11] India gave Pakistan a chance to call it quits. But Pakistan continued to show its façade of false bravado backed by China, Türkiye, and probably USA. Op Sindoor improved India's global standing and signalled to the world that it is self-sufficient in dealing with a rogue state like Pakistan. Op Sindoor also revealed the half-hidden nexus between USA and Pakistan.

Action on the Border (LC and IB Sectors)

The ceasefire on LC was last re-negotiated on 25 February 2021. The moment the terror camps were attacked in the early hours of 7 May 2025, Pakistan activated the entire LC from Kupwara to Bhuj, firing artillery barrages and sending multiple armed drone strikes. The ceasefire had no meaning and Indian troops retaliated using artillery fire assault in the Kupwara, Baramulla, Poonch, Rajauri, and Jammu sectors.[12] The aim was to have moral ascendency over the other by causing destruction of military equipment, infrastructure, and inflict casualties on soldiers. On the night of 7 May Pakistan attempted attacks on 15 cities including Uri, Baramulla, Men Dhar and Rajouri, Amritsar, Pathankot, Kapurthala, Ludhiana, Adampur, Jallandhar, Chandigarh, Nal (Bikaner), Phalodi, Uttar Lai, and Bhuj.[13]

Around Srinagar, Pakistan attempted drone incursions against military installations, but Indian defence systems intercepted these threats. In Jammu, no direct casualties were reported from missile or drone attacks. Cross-border shelling resulted in civilian injuries and caused power outages in parts of the city. Emergency blackout protocols were activated, and civilians were advised to stay indoors.[14] At Avantipur, drone threats were effectively countered by Indian forces.[15]

Amritsar faced missile threats, all of which were intercepted without causing harm. No casualties were reported at Pathankot, but attempted drone strikes were intercepted. A blackout was implemented, air raid sirens were tested, and emergency services were placed on high alert. Kapurthala, Ludhiana, and Adampur cities were on high alert due to attempted drone attacks, which were successfully thwarted. Similarly, in Jalandhar, Pakistani drones attempted to fly over the Jalandhar cantonment area but were shot down before entering the inner perimeter.[16]

At Chandigarh, air sirens sounded, and a citywide blackout was enforced following the Pakistani missile strikes in Jammu, prompting emergency safety measures. Power was restored after midnight once the threat level subsided. Sirens were sounded again on Friday morning, warning of a potential aerial attack. The Air Force Stations at Nal, Phalodi, and Uttar Lai were targeted but remained unharmed. At Bhuj, no casualties were reported, and drone threats were intercepted.

Pakistan increased the intensity of its unprovoked firing across the Line of Control using mortars and heavy calibre artillery in areas around Kupwara, Baramulla, Uri, Poonch, Men Dhar, and Rajouri sectors. Uri and Baramulla experienced shelling and reports of drone sightings. Gurudwara, Madrassa, concrete houses, and hutments came under indiscriminate firing. Intermittent power disruptions were reported, and schools and public places were temporarily closed. Heavy shelling occurred in both Men Dhar and Rajouri. The Indian Army responded by targeting and destroying multiple enemy posts involved in the attacks.[17] Indian troops fired Bofors gun, mortars, Army AD guns in direct ground role, ATGMs in bunker/post destruction role, and other weapons. The fire was very effective and the destruction caused was kept under surveillance by Long Range Reconnaissance and Observation System (LORROS). The system uses Forward Looking Infrared (FLIR) and Charge-coupled device (CCD) image sensors.

All the firing by Pakistan was initiated despite being told that the Indian Army actions are non-escalatory in nature. It was clarified to Pakistan that if they continue to fire, then retaliation will be in the same measure and with the same intensity. Here too, India was compelled to respond and bring mortar and artillery fire from Pakistan to a halt. On the morning of 7 May, the Indian Army briefing was done at 10:00 hours, followed by top government officials and Cabinet Committee on Security (CCS) meeting. The families of the victims of Pahalgam attack thanked the Indian Armed Forces for taking revenge. Israel was the first to support India's action. USA, Russia, and UK too supported India's fight against terrorism.[18]

On the night of 7–8 May, Pakistan increased the intensity of its unprovoked firing across the LC using drones, mortar, and heavy-calibre artillery. Locations on the Indian side which came under artillery fire were Srinagar, Baramulla, Avantipur, Rajouri, Jammu, and Nag Rota. Locations which came under drone and missile attacks were Pathankot, Gurdaspur, Amritsar, Hoshiarpur,

Ferozepur, Fazilka, Lalgarh Jattan, Pokhran, Jaisalmer, Barmer, Kuar Bet, Lakhi Nala, and Bhuj.

In Jammu and Kashmir, the places attacked were Kupwara, Baramulla, Uri, Poonch, Men Dhar, and Rajouri sectors in Jammu and Kashmir. Pakistan resorted to indiscriminate firing. Sixteen innocent lives were lost, including three women and five children, due to the Pakistani firing.[19] In retaliation, India too resorted to heavy firing.

On the intervening night of 8–9 May, "Pakistan military carried out multiple violations of Indian airspace along the entire western border with an intent to target military infrastructure. Pakistan also carried out artillery shelling across the Line of Control using heavy-calibre artillery guns and armed drones at Tang Dhar, Uri, Poonch, Men Dhar, Rajouri, Akh Noor, and Udhampur in J&K area, which resulted in some losses and injuries to Indian Army personnel. Pakistan Army also suffered major losses in Indian retaliatory fire in the sectors mentioned above."[20]

The International Border (IB) sector, where there had been no fire exchanges previously, also had an exchange of cross-border firing with the Border Security Force (BSF). BSF foiled a major infiltration attempt along the IB in Samba district, Jammu and Kashmir, at around 23:00 hours on 8 May 2025. Acting on detected suspicious movement, BSF personnel swiftly engaged armed infiltrators and successfully prevented a significant breach. They also intercepted drones of various kinds across the Jammu and Punjab border areas and remained alert to thwart many infiltrations attempt during Op Sindoor. The relentless vigil and successful operations underscored the BSF's vigilance, operational preparedness, and its crucial role in maintaining border security during heightened tensions.[21]

On the night of 9–10 May, Wg Cdr Vyomika Singh stated, "Heavy exchange of artillery mortars and small-arm fire in Kupwara, Baramulla, Poonch, Rajouri, and Akh Noor sectors continued. Indian Army has responded effectively and proportionately, causing extensive damage to Pakistan Army. Pak military has been observed to be moving their troops into forward areas, indicating offensive intent to further escalate the situation. Indian Armed Forces remain in a high state of operational readiness. All hostile actions have been effectively countered and responded appropriately. Indian Armed Forces reiterate their commitment to non-escalation, provided it is reciprocated by the Pakistan Military".[22] The impact of Indian retaliation can be seen in Photos 9–13 of the page inserts of this chapter. A medicare centre in Srinagar and schools in Avantipur and Udhampur were targeted. An airman was killed in Udhampur airbase.

In retaliation to Pakistan firing on each day, the Indian troops along the border retaliated with small arms fire, mortars, and field guns, anti-tank guided missile and Army AD guns deployed along the LC, medium guns, and drones. At no point in time were the Pakistani forces allowed to have morale ascendency. The destruction caused on Pakistan side on their military post and infrastructure were at the same level of escalation. However, unlike Pakistan, Indian troops did not direct fire at civilian areas. The Pakistani posts across the LC were subjected to very heavy degradation by all available weapons of the Indian Army. An unprecedented amount of destruction was caused to Pakistani positions in areas like the Lipa Valley and Kotli areas opposite Rajouri and Baramulla sectors. Videos of this action were provided to media and were seen on various TV channels. Some photographs taken as stills from these videos are in the photo pages of this chapter. Through these four days, Pakistan Army suffered more than 100 casualties due to intense retaliatory firing by the Indian Army.

AD Operation: Akashe Shatrun Jahi

Op Sindoor was a non-contact operation where aerial threat manifested in various forms. The drone warfare, so far heard in distant wars, was brought to our doorstep by Pakistan and in good numbers and variety. The use of loitering munition, air-to-air missiles (AAM), surface-to-surface missiles (SSM), etc, were used in large numbers by Pakistan. The ground-based AD systems (GBADS), available with both Army and Air Force, enabled an effective use of the Network-Centric Warfare (NCW). The integrated AD was successful in foiling Pakistan's attempts to cause damage to our key assets.

While India has been progressing gradually in indigenous production of AD systems, albeit at slow pace, Pakistan remains dependent on weapons provided by China. It seemed as if Pakistan AD was ready to fight a proxy war for China. On one hand, India has been upgrading technology in newly manufactured AD weapon systems though not yet battle-proven. On the other hand, China had been supplying Pakistan with advance technology in the field of AD weapons, communications (optical fibre and 4G), electronic warfare (EW), satellite-based navigation system and satellite-based real-time processed intelligence inputs.

Post the Azerbaijan–Armenia and Ukraine–Russian wars, the drones got added to the list of multi-spectral air threat. Even as Pakistan proliferated the battle zone with drones in hundreds, alternate methods were designed and manufactured by India to engage these low-cost drones. These methods ensured a relatively cost-effective method of dealing with radar-resistant small-sized drones. Currently some more anti-drone systems are being manufactured and being tested for future use.

Both the opponents had limited AD weapons and the inventory was mostly of foreign origin. India, with the delivery of Russia's S-400 SAM system, was able to deploy a reasonably good "area AD" or outer layer. Similarly, Pakistan, who was supplied with Chinese Hong Qi (HQ)-9 (a replica of S-300 SAM system), too had a good area AD cover. What was expected to be an evenly balanced war and continue for long ended in just four days.

Knowing the range and the effectiveness of S-400 SAM, Pakistan decided to conserve its aircrafts by moving them away from front-line bases located near LC / IB and make do with only a part of its air force. In hindsight, Pakistan's poor planning, related to the use of its AD systems, had a telling effect on failure to safeguard its air-space resulting in major losses at various air bases.

The message was clear to Pakistan that a decisive response is both necessary and justified when reason and diplomacy are met with continued aggression. Op Sindoor has lessons that India needs to learn too. With the mass use of drones, the importance of Army AD has become significant. Low-cost countermeasures, satellite-based communications, data links, AI-based data handling and ingenious ways of ramping up the ammunition production line are essential steps that India needs to take.

The "Atmanirbharta" in the field of AD has to be further expedited as the drone threat now extends to non-military and hinterland targets (as in case of Pakistan's drone attack on Guru Harmandir Sahib and many other civil areas).[23]

The Army AD responsibility compliments the AD provided by IAF. The IAF has the overall responsibility of India's AD. The Army and the Navy are responsible to provide AD to their respective assets within defined "rules of engagement". As per the laid down rules, the Army AD's responsibility is to provide AD up to a low-level altitude or up to 1500 m in the entire battle zone including the airfields. Basically, the guns systems cater to this air threat. Further, they may provide AD up to a medium-level altitude or 5000 m in tactical battle area (TBA), especially where offensive elements are deployed / move. A mix of guns and surface-to-air missiles (SAMs) cater to this air threat.

AD Battle is Unique

In any operation, before a country goes in for an offensive, it has to ensure its defence to ward off any riposte. The air component being the most flexible normally leads this offensive operation. Consequently, the AD assumes much greater importance as it has to protect its own assets against the opponent's counter strike. To ensure this, the ground-based AD systems (GBADS) get deployed first to take on the opponent's pre-emptive air strikes if any. Thus, AD acts as a shield and the stronger it is, the better would be the subsequent performance of the armed forces. However, no AD can ever be 100% foolproof as was seen in the case of Israel, whose air-space volume is a fraction as compared to India's and yet the acknowledged "Iron Dome" AD system could not safeguard it from the "rain" of Iran's ballistic missiles. This gives an idea about how challenging is the task of AD in Indian context.

Even as India announced its intention, Pakistan geared up fully with all the arsenal in its kitty. Just a few days before the operations, transport aircrafts, notably C-130 from Türkiye and China, had landed in Pakistan for further beefing up the war-waging resources. Fearing the overwhelming advantage of the IAF, Türkiye and China provided Pakistan with hundreds of armed and unarmed drones and real-time satellite-based intelligence inputs.

The GBADS' role is to defend a country's key assets and areas (both military and civilian) from enemy air threat. The multi-spectral air threat includes fighter aircrafts, bombers, helicopters, long-range air-to-surface missiles (ASMs), long-range surface-to-surface missiles (SSMs) (both ballistics and cruise), glide bombs, loiter munition, and a variety of drones including the kamikaze.

AD battle involves an integration of multiple functions which are essential to keep the assets safe from damage or destruction. A typical aircraft or missile flies at sub-sonic, sonic or super-sonic speed which means that the AD battle is fast-paced and is executed in seconds. At one Mach (330 m/s or 19.8 km/min or 1188 km/hr), a gun system having a range of 2.5 to 4 km will have a reaction time of just five to eight seconds before an aircraft reaches its weapon release line (WRL) (typically aircraft guns and rockets are fired at approximately 800 m distance from the defended location).

The stand-off weapons may be fired from long distance, in which case they will be intercepted by SAMs.

The nerve centre of an AD battle is the AD control and reporting system (ADCRS). In a defined air space there are multiple users, like aircraft, helicopters, drones, missiles, artillery shells of both—your own and that of the enemy. The basic aim of ADCRS is the prevention of fratricide. It also ensures that all air and land components operate in an efficient, integrated, and flexible manner with minimum mutual interference.

AD involves a series of complex steps and for each of them only a short reaction time (two to four secs) is available. The complexity of these procedures increases as the number of simultaneously attacking aerial target increases from 1's and 2's to 10's and 100's over a defined area. These steps include, firstly, surveillance[24] and detection by a grid of radars, deployed all across the country. The selected IAF, Indian Navy (IN), and the civilian radars are deployed 24×7 and they operate as per a pre-planned schedule even during peace time. During active operations, some IAF and Army radars are additionally deployed to either superimpose or to fill in the gaps. These radars carry out surveillance, and on detection of an aerial object report to the nearest control centre of the Integrated Air Command and Control Centre (IACCS)[25] of the IAF or the Akashteer[26] system of the Army AD. At IACCS or Akashteer, all tracks are integrated to create a single real-time air situation picture (RASP).

Secondly, identification of a friend or foe (IFF) is carried out by matching the flight plan data of the detected aerial object with all friendly aerial movement which is continuously fed and available in IACCS. A link of the same is available at Akashteer too. When any aerial object is detected, in a defined air space, its parameters (location, speed, altitude, and direction) are matched with the available data. In case it matches, then it is considered friendly, and if not then the interrogation protocol will be set in motion using electronic or visual means.

The third step is the designation post confirmation of the unidentified object as hostile; the target is assigned to the nearest and most appropriate AD weapon system (AD gun or SAM). The entire process of threat evaluation and weapon designation is AI-enabled. Algorithms for this process are pre-fed and constantly upgraded. Simultaneously, the system is given the order "weapons free".

The fourth step is tracking once the weapon receives the target parameters either from IACCS or Akashteer (ADC&RS). The process for radar-controlled or manual engagement is initiated. For radar-controlled engagement, the weapon system's fire control (FC) radar starts tracking the target while for manual systems, the operator visually tracks the target in sight. The last step is engagement on the orders of the weapon in-charge. The AD gun/s or SAM/s will engage the target and destroy it.

Weapon Systems with the GBADS are a mix of gun and missile family. Guns normally are either single or multi-barrel with a very high rate of fire. The SAMs may be very short (less than 10 km), short (10 to 30 km), medium (30 to 100 km) or long-range (beyond 100 km). The SAMs have different height coverage too.

Since AD is about dealing with radars (radio frequencies [RF]), electronic warfare (EW) is an important component to be considered. The AD battle is all about "who sees first gets to shoot first". To ensure this, a credible EW strategy is required. It is about enabling one's own troops to effectively use the electro-magnetic (EM) spectrum while denying the enemy from using it. Intelligence on enemy's electronic order of battle (e-orbat) is collated using electronic support measures (ESM), and then put it to effective use in an offensive role through electronic counter measures (ECM) and a defensive role through electronic counter-counter measures (ECCM).

Akashteer: Army AD Control and Reporting (C&R) system

Prior to the induction of Akashteer C&R system, the whole process of control and reporting was being done in a semi-automatic mode using Tactical AD Integrated Display System (TADIDS).[27]

This, however, was subject to interruptions, as manual feeds were required which in turn were dependent on communication using VHF and HF radio sets. The old system could rarely provide adequate reaction time at the weapon end for successful engagement.

Akashteer[28] is an AI-driven autonomous ADCRS, developed jointly by Indian Satellite and Research Organisation (ISRO), Defence Research and Development Organisation (DRDO), and Bharat Electronics Limited (BEL) under the "Atmanirbhar Bharat" initiative. It is an Army AD-network-centric warfare (NCW) system which was approved for induction on 30 March 2023. As of November 2024, 107 modules had been delivered to Army AD. Army AD units, which were allotted modules, conducted validation trials of Akashteer, simulating scenarios as expected in future wars. The entire order of 455 modules is expected to be delivered by April 2027. As of January 2025, integration between Akashteer and IACCS for one site was complete while that for others was underway. Priority for allocation of Akashteer modules was given to units deployed in the Northern and Western theatres. Without the support of Akashteer, the story would have unfolded differently.

Akashteer integrates all inputs from the Army AD surveillance radars (including Reporter radar, 3D Tactical Control Radars, Low-Level Light Weight Radars [LLLWR], Akash Weapon System's Rajendra Radar and others), acquisition radars, and ISRO's Earth Observation Satellites. Its flexibility to integrate with IAF, IACCS, and the Indian Navy's TRIGUN enables it to get a complete picture of the entire Indian Airspace (the IACCS integrates all IAF and civilian radar inputs while TRIGUN integrates all Navy radars inputs). This enhances coordination and situational awareness across the three forces. Based on target parameters, AI eliminates all duplicate inputs and the system creates a RASP. The RASP provides a comprehensive view of the airspace to the intermediate and lowest operational sub-units of the Army AD. Since the flight track plans of all friendly flying objects are known, the IFF process easily enables the detection of the approaching hostile object. The use of Navigation by Indian Constellation (NavIC)[29] for giving exact location of the target, ensures accurate targeting and makes Akashteer much more efficient.

The heart of Akashteer is its threat evaluation and weapon assignment (TEWA) software. Based on target parameters (direction, height, range, and speed), the TEWA software automatically assigns it to the most appropriate weapon system's command post (CP) either directly or via intermediary regimental command post (RCP). The commander at CP will start his/her battle drills to include the cueing in of the weapon on to the target for tracking to begin. The procedure depends on the weapon system used, which could be radar-controlled, EO sight-controlled or visually controlled. On receipt of target parameters, the fire control (FC) radar or the EO sight will start tracking the target. For visual engagement, the gunner will acquire the target in his optical sight. As the aerial target approaches within range, "order to fire" is given and engagement is initiated.

During Op Sindoor, Akashteer proved to be a game changer; it has many advantages. Effectiveness of the Army AD weapons can be attributed to it. Being AI-enabled and fully automated, Akashteer could make at least two engagements possible, resulting in higher efficiency and reduced reaction time. Since all friendly tracks are known, the safety of friendly aircraft in contested airspace is ensured. Conversely, for low-level targets appearing suddenly or for recovery of our own damaged aircrafts, the facility of upward interrogation can be easily used by the operator. Since the inputs to Akashteer, as also to IACCS, are from a large number of sensors working in different frequency bands, frequency diversity is achieved. Being spatially spaced out, electronic jamming has no effect on target detection. The TEWA AI algorithms have been indigenously prepared, its source code is known and therefore foreign power cannot meddle with it. The entire navigational data is based on NavIC which now has satellite clocks with an accuracy of 10 nanoseconds resulting in better accuracy of sub-meter. Lastly, it ensures cost-effectiveness and economy of effort as the system chooses the most appropriate weapon system for a specific air threat.

Pakistan Drones/UAVs

Pakistan's employment of drones/UAVs[30] during Op Sindoor involved all the three types of drones, viz., the ISTAR, the UCAVs, and the Kamikaze. With an emphasis on increasing its inventory, Pakistan had acquired drones from many countries, besides having their indigenous production. During Op Sindoor, around 15 types of drones were used by Pakistan with many being from China and Türkiye. Pakistan procured low-cost drones from Türkiye, to be used in swarm mode and in multiple waves. The modus operandi of Pakistan was firstly to launch drones in swarm mode, expecting maximum AD radars to open up, resulting in disclosing their locations and frequency bands. This would reveal the e-orbat and initiate ECM activity. Secondly, to make the sensors less effective by saturating them and diverting them from detecting missiles or larger drones. Thirdly, to deploy UCAV and target the AD sensors as part of the Suppression of Enemy AD (SEAD) operations. This was aimed at creating a favourable environment for Counter Air Operations (CAO) and cause maximum destruction to selected ground assets.

Pakistan has a long history of manufacturing drones at various public and private companies. These companies include Air Weapon Complex (AWC), Pakistan Aeronautical Complex (PAC), Integrated Dynamics, Surveillance and Target Unmanned Aircrafts (SATUMA), Associated Consulting Engineers (ACES), and Global Industrial & Defence Solutions (GIDS). Some known drones are Bravo (and Bravo+) UAS, "Jasoos" series of ISTAR UAS, "Mukhbar", Vision Mk I and II surveillance drones,

"Uqaab" tactical drone with a range of 300 to 350 km, "Shahpar" reconnaissance (recce) and strike drones, "Sarfarosh", canister launched kamikaze drone with a range of 1000 km and endurance of 2 hours and "Turah" stealth loitering munition.

Pakistan also imports drones from many other countries. The ones that were used during Op Sindoor included the Chinese Wing Loong II which has a range of 4000 km and endurance of 20 hours. It can loiter over the target for a sufficiently long time before releasing its payload. The payload capacity is 480 kg and can be guided bombs, guided rockets precision munitions, anti-radiation missiles (ARMs), air-to-surface missiles (ASM), and laser-guided cluster bombs (LGB). The "CH 4A and 4B" drones have a range of 1000 km and an endurance of 6 hours. Türkiye made a fresh supply before the commencement of Op Sindoor by C-130 aircraft. They were used in swarms during the operation. The variety of drones that were supplied included Bayraktar TB2 that has a range of 300 km and endurance of 27 hours. Its payload includes laser-guided rockets, 81mm mortar, anti-tank missiles and laser-guided smart bombs. However, the Indian AD could get the better of it; Baykar's Akinci is a high-altitude long endurance (HALE) UCAV. It can achieve an altitude of 12000 m, and has a maximum take-off weight of 5500 kg including a payload of 1350 kg. It can carry a variety of payloads that include EO / IR / laser designation (LD) pod, AESA radar, SIGINT system, EW systems, Gokgogan and Bozdogan AAMs, several types of locally made ammunition, stand-off missiles, and ASM. However, due to slow speed and large surface area, it became a vulnerable target to AD system; Asisguard Songar drones with a range of 10 km and endurance of 35 min were delivered in large numbers to Pakistan and used during the operations; YIHA-III is a kamikaze variety drone and they were used in large numbers during the operation. These are also being locally produced in Pakistan by GIDS.

Multi-layered and Multi-tiered AD

The Indian AD is based on the "concept of layered and tiered defence", which has basically four layers and combines both static and mobile elements. With every layer the altitude coverage also increases. The multi-tier is about being organised in depth starting from border towards the hinterland. Supporting these layers are a wide range of ground and airborne-based sensors. These feed data about target tracks to Akashteer and enable threat neutralisation. In recent years, India has strengthened its AD shield and it is evolving continuously by incorporating emerging technologies like AI and data analytics. These improve threat assessment and response time.

The first layer of the Army AD has anti-drone and very short-range systems. The second layer is of SRSAM category, and the third layer is of MRSAM category. The fourth and final layer is of LRSAM category.

In India, military and civil assets have been assessed for their vulnerability to air threat. Accordingly, these are nominated as vulnerable areas (VA)s / vulnerable points (VPs). These assets merit either dedicated AD or area AD cover and sometimes both. However, due to paucity of AD resources, only a small percentage of VAs / VPs, based on priority criteria, are allotted point AD cover. Conversely, AD protection to a significant number of assets is not available and many gaps exist. During Op Sindoor, Pakistan used small drones which were immune to detection by radar, thereby increasing the vulnerability of these VAs/VPs.

Drone Warfare Systems

The Integrated Drone Detection and Interdiction System (IDD & IS) also referred to as Drone, Detect, Deter, and Destroy (D4) Anti-Drones System is an anti-combat unmanned aerial vehicle (C-UAV), developed by DRDO. After integration of the sub-systems, it was handed over to BEL for manufacture. Limited numbers were ready before Op Sindoor commenced and they were deployed along the LC / IB from Kupwara to Amritsar. They were used in both mobile and static mode. It targeted micro- and mini-sized drones during Op Sindoor. The system proved its mettle during this operation by successfully neutralising and destroying several drones over a short range.

Zen Anti-Drone System (ZADS) are manufactured by a private company Zen Technologies Limited. These successfully neutralised Chinese Wing Loong-II and CH-4 besides the Türkiye Yiha-III drones. The system works on drone detection, classification, and tracking on passive surveillance, camera sensors, and neutralisation of the threat through jamming the drone communication.

Sensors

Many Sensors were integrated with Army AD Akashteer and IAF IACCS. The success of BEL in incorporating both active and passive steered phased array beam technology in a wide range of radars is a big success story. Some of the important acquisition / surveillance Army Radars include:

- Rohini (Revathi for IAF) Acquisition Radar, which is a 3D-S Band medium-range (180 km) radar, capable of detecting low-altitude supersonic aircrafts and has high resolution;
- Central Acquisition Radar (3D-CAR), which is used for long-range surveillance and target acquisition for Akash SAM;
- Rajendra FC radar, which is part of Akash AD system, with multi-function PESA used for tracking and guidance to Akash missiles;
- Reporter Tactical Control Radar (TCR) manufactured by BEL, which has a 40 km range and has multi-target handling and engagement capability;

- Swathi Weapon Locating Radar (WLR) with phased array technology meant for artillery which has limited capability for detecting aerial targets;
- Low Level Light Weight Radar (LLLWR), which being light weight can be deployed in any terrain and is very effective for low-level coverage.

The Impenetrable AD Spider Web

The Army AD along with IAF AD acted as first responders and swiftly mobilised with effect from 25 April 2025 in Op Sindoor to counter any possible air threat in both the manned and unmanned domain. It was the AD operations that guaranteed India's operational integrity. Indian air space was infiltrated not by the Pakistani jets crossing the borders, but by a sustained barrage of drones, UCAVs, long-range guided rockets, cruise missiles and loitering munitions.

The Army AD emerged as the silent but resolute shield on the modern battlefield. To manage an acceptable level of AD cover, unconventional deployment patterns were employed. The homogeneity of standard fire units comprising 6/4 guns was given a pass. Instead, guns were deployed in single as well as in pairs to create a grid and cover the assessed likely air avenues. IDD & IS were interspersed and this crucial tactical decision proved to be a great success as AD engaged swarms of drones very effectively. The bulk of these swarms came in the Jammu–Pathankot–Amritsar region where the AD density was reasonably good.

In the aftermath of the strikes on nine terror camps on 7 May by the IAF and IA (supported by IN), Pakistan decided to carry out counter strikes. Despite being informed to not escalate, Pakistan pressed on with the attacks in various forms. At this stage, had Pakistan accepted India's proposal to stop further escalation, the operation would have ended. Possibly, Pakistan armed with Chinese aircraft and AD systems wanted to prove a point.

Drone Warfare and AD Effectiveness

On 7 May, during the day time all was quiet but later, on the night of 7–8 May Pakistan commenced sending unarmed drones—DJI Mavic mini quadcopter, Yiha III loitering munitions and missile attacks in waves. The aim of using unarmed drones was perhaps to saturate the Indian AD systems as well as reveal their locations. Drones would also create a diversionary for Pakistan missiles. The Yiha-III drones carried little explosives and were employed to cause minor damage. These were neutralised by the integrated C-UAS grid (using both kinetic and non-kinetic means) and other AD systems. The debris of these elements were recovered from a number of locations that proved the origin of these attacks.[31]

In response to Pakistan's drone strikes on the night of 7–8 May, India resorted to a drone counter attack in the morning hours of 8 May. The official Indian brief stated, "Today morning, Indian Armed Forces targeted AD Radars and systems at a number of locations in Pakistan. Indian response has been in the same domain and with same intensity as Pakistan. The AD radar at Lahore was damaged / destroyed".[32] Debris of the drone attack by India (found in Pakistan) indicated employment of Israel origin Harpy and Harop loitering munition.[33] The attack likely injured four Pakistani soldiers.

As part of the propaganda war, Pakistan denied having carried out any drone attack on India on night of 7–8 May and highlighted the Indian counter attack of the morning of 8 May as an act of aggression. The intended Indian targets were military installations, air bases, command-and-control centres, logistics nodes, and population centres. Playing the victim card, Pakistan accused India of escalating the operation. However, enough evidence was presented to call the Pakistani bluff. Indian AD systems had been successful in engaging Pakistan drones and missiles.

A number of guns were deployed in civil areas especially in Jammu. The locals got an experience of watching live firing of

Army AD guns. The tracer-laced ammunition enabled accurate firing from these guns resulting in destruction of the intended aerial targets. The visual effects also provided succour and confidence to border populations that they were being kept safe.

The videos made by civilians became a testimony of Pakistan drones being engaged and destroyed by L/70 and ZU-23-2B and ZSU-23-4B guns (many videos of live firing are in circulation).[34] Eyewitness accounts and drone debris were also evidence to prove and counter Pakistan claims. It was amply clear that the "wave" attacks by drones and missiles were to "saturate" the AD systems, as stated by Director General Air Operations (DGAO), Air Marshal Bharti.[35] Photos 16–25 on the page inserts of this chapter contain photographs of Army AD weapons and debris of the drones shot down.

The unarmed drone attacks mixed with missiles continued again on the night of 8–9 May. The numbers were greater than the previous night, and the aim probably was to tire out the Indian AD gunners. There were very few C-UAV and more of DJI Mavic mini quadcopter (used for surveillance) drones. The Indian integrated Army AD grid, alert as they were, again neutralised the drones, neutralising Pakistan's game plan. Minor damage happened at some civil locations. The daily briefing stated, "In response to the Pakistani drone attack, India retaliated the next day with armed drones at four AD radar sites in Pakistan. One of the drones was able to destroy an AD radar".[36] Over two days, Indian drone attacks, being more focussed, were able to damage or destroy two AD radars of Pakistan. This implied that a gap was created in the Pakistan's air surveillance grid.[37] In a way this was part of the IAF SEAD / DEAD operation before bigger things were to come.

On the night of 9–10 May, Pakistan further increased the intensity of drone and missile attacks. Increasing number of Yiha-III loitering munition were used.[38] During media briefing, Wg Cdr Vyomika Singh stated, "Along the IB and LC, drone intrusions were attempted from Leh to Sir Creek at 36 locations with approximately 300 to 400 drones. Indian Armed Forces brought down a large number of these drones using kinetic and non-kinetic means. The possible purpose of these large-scale aerial intrusions was to test the AD systems capability and gather intelligence.[39] Forensic examination of the drone debris was undertaken. Preliminary reports indicated these to be Asisguard Songar drone of Türkiye. Later in the night, an armed UAV of Pakistan attempted to target Bathinda military station, which was detected and neutralised.[40] As such, these attacks failed to cause any damage".

The missiles being fired along with drones were being intercepted by AD systems. Missile debris was found in agricultural fields in Sirsa, Barmer, and Jalandhar. These developments coincide with reports that shortly after midnight of 9–10 May, Pakistan fired its Fateh-II short range ballistic missile (SRBM) at a strategic Indian location, which was intercepted successfully by AD units in Sirsa (approximately 130 km from IB). The Fateh-II missile has a range of up to 400 km and can carry both conventional and potentially nuclear warheads. The Fateh-II ballistic missiles were employed for the first time.[41] Seeing the escalatory ladder which Pakistan was climbing gradually, called for a quick decision—to hit where it hurts the most. The action was undertaken by IAF with effect from 01:40 hours on 10 May as described in the previous chapter.

The IAF held S-400 SAM missile shot down multiple Pakistani ALCM and UCAV, and proved its real worth during the operations. It was revealed that S-400 made a historic kill by engaging AEW&C SAAB 2000 Erieye at a range of 314 km.[42] This reduced the Pakistan's NCW capability to detect Indian aircrafts and loitering munitions.

Pakistan accused India of carrying out attacks inside its territory for the fourth consecutive night, launching ballistic missile strikes on at least three air bases. Islamabad said that in response it launched a major military campaign, "Operation Bunyan-al-Marsoos" (Arabic for "a structure made of lead") on 10 May

2025 targeting at least six Indian military bases. Pakistan claimed that they hit Artillery gun position, Drangyari; field supply depot, Uri; BrahMos battery and missile storage at Nag Rota and Beas respectively; and air bases at Udhampur, Pathankot, Adampur, and Bhuj. The attacks caused hardly any significant damage.[43]

Wg Cdr Vyomika Singh during the 10 May briefing stated, "Pakistan employed UCAV, drones, long-range weapons (SRBM), loitering munitions and fighter aircrafts to target civilian areas and military infrastructure. Along the IB and the LC, air intrusions and harassment attacks were attempted from Srinagar till Naliya at more than 26 locations. There were also several high-speed missile attacks noticed subsequently, on 10 May after 01:40 hours, at several air bases in Punjab. In a swift and calibrated response, Indian Armed Forces carried out precision attacks on identified military targets. Radar sites at Pasrur and Sialkot aviation base were also targeted using PGM".[44] The details of the precision attacks on identified military targets by the Indian Armed Forces have been covered in the previous chapter.

Indian drone attacks and operational changes to reduce emissions and vulnerability to anti-radiation munitions (ARM) may have weakened Pakistani AD grid. IAF surprise attack on 10 May appears to have bypassed Pakistan AD.

Pakistan claimed "major damages" at 15 Indian airbases it targeted. However, Indian officials acknowledged "limited damage" from drone attacks at four locations, viz., Udhampur, Pathankot, Adampur, and Bhuj.[45] Yiha III was the largest drone employed by Pakistan and its warhead is much smaller than that of BrahMos/SCALP. Obviously, the degree of damage achieved is corresponding. As stated, the larger Pakistan missile Fateh II was intercepted and destroyed.

The integrated NCW for AD obtained by linking two independent service NCW—Akashteer for Army AD and IACCS for IAF—proved to be a "strong spider-web". Every Pakistani aerial intrusion was detected and engaged using kinetic and non-kinetic means. As compared to cost per drone engagement, during wars between Azerbaijan-Armenia, Russia-Ukraine or Israel-Iran (including its proxies Hamas, Houthis, and Hezbollah), India achieved an abysmally low cost.

The integrated AD deployment can be credited for the success of Op Sindoor at the national level and Army AD had a major role to play. As appreciated, Pakistan's drone-centric aggression, involved approximately 1000 drones (all types) that were sighted. Majority of the engagements were carried out by gun systems of Army AD and their performance left everyone spellbound. These included the radar-controlled L/70 guns, 23mm Zu Guns equipped with night sights, and upgraded Shilka Gun system.[46] The Army AD majorly engaged Yiha III, Asisguard Songar, and DJI Mavic drones while IAF AD systems engaged Bayraktar TB2 and Akinci. The Army AD units destroyed approximately 100–150 drones from 7 May 2025 till ceasefire was announced on 10 May 2025 late evening.

Failure of Pakistan AD

Pakistan AD

AD, as a separate arm in Pakistan, was created on 10 October 1989, while that of India on 10 January 1994. The Pakistan Air Force (PAF) and Army control the Pakistan's AD systems. Similar to India, even their AD regiments are equipped with different AD platforms depending on their tasks. To overcome the problem of ageing equipment and the emerging modern air threat, Pakistan decided to have an LTPP called "Comprehensive Layered and Integrated AD (CLIAD) (2007–2025)".

CLIAD is the outcome of a decade-long initiative by Pakistan Army to build its own multi-layered GBADS and enable the Army to efficiently distribute its SAM deployment and management across its hierarchy, from Corps level to Brigade level. The CLIAD[47] involves five layers which include Close in Weapon Systems (CIWS), Short-Range AD System (SHORAD), Extended-Short-Range AD System (E-SHORAD), Low to Medium AD System (LOMADS), and High to Medium AD System (HIMADS).

Post the Balakot air strike by IAF in 2019, Pakistan initiated the upgradation of its GBADS. However, challenges remained in terms of integrating new systems and addressing systemic issues. At present, while India has slowly started to migrate to indigenous manufactured AD systems, Pakistan continues to rely on foreign-origin equipment, especially Chinese-made systems, like HQ-9P, LY-80 and FM-90. After the failure of Chinese sourced systems during Op Sindoor, Pakistan needs to hunt for a better and more suitable AD system and has initiated talks with USA and Germany.[48]

Till the mid-1990s, Pakistan C&R relied on semi-auto Siemens Integrated Low Level Air Control System (SILLACS) and at that point it was far superior to the Indian manual C&R. Pakistan had an integrated radar network, based on Mono-Pulse Doppler Radar (MPDR) (three types) with ranges of 45 km, 60 km, and 90 km, and other surveillance radars in smaller numbers which included ANTPS 43, ANTPS 77, Giraffe, Sky-Guard, YLC-2, YLC-6, and YLC-8E. These radars were sub-networked under Sector Operations Centre (SOC). The SOC set-up has now been digitised with data connectivity on optical fibre (laid with the help of China) and Chinese satellite communication network. However, during Op Sindoor, it performed miserably as it failed to intercept any of the Indian missile launched against various targets in Pakistan.

Pakistan AD NCW[49]

Around 2010, Pakistan embarked upon the futuristic AD warfare and decided to switch over from SILLACS to AD NCW involving "CLIAD". AD NCW aims to achieve information superiority over the enemy in a combat environment, enabling rapid decision-making and mission accomplishment. An auto-synchronisation of the sensor grid, communication, data grid and finally the shooter grid is needed. All inputs are integrated using AI tools to enable real-time decisive response to enemy actions. In all this, China was a great enabler. The AD NCW consists of three grids. The first is the Sensor grid composed of diverse sensors to include radars, other RF emitters, IR sensors and low light, and other optical devices of PAF. The radar sensors of Army, Navy, and civil aviation are also networked. The inputs from SAAB AEWACS and ZDK-3 AWACS were also integrated into AD network. This enabled the PAF and Pakistan AD to display and control operations from anywhere in Pakistan.

The second is the Information grid which integrates inputs from computer systems, data transmission lines, microwave relays, optical fibre, and communication satellites to ensure 24×7 connectivity. Commanders could plan, monitor, and execute operations more effectively, efficiently, and responsibly in real time. The third is the Engagement grid which uses inputs from other two grids to designate appropriate weapon system to engage and damage or destroy the target. The unified information is disseminated in real time through AD operation centres (ADOC) or sector mission control centres (SMCC) or general mission control centres (GMCC). Once inputs are received at the combat operation centre (COC), they are segregated in two, one for defensive AD operations and the other for offensive PAF operations, for further action.

Pakistan AD Nemesis

India decided to conduct a non-contact operation. On 6–7 May 2025, the IAF and IA carried out attacks from a stand-off distance. As per known dispositions, the radar and satellite coverage duly backed up by inputs from China was deep into Indian territory all along the border. It is surprising that despite the elaborate arrangements for NCW and involvement of China (in the field of

4G, optical fibre network, and satellite communication support), Pakistan AD remained non-effective during the first stage of operations.

The Indian retaliatory drone attacks on the morning of 8 and 9 May were successful in that two surveillance radars were damaged or destroyed. Pakistan AD deployed for their protection failed to intercept the loitering munition.

On 9–10 May 2025, the IAF carried out attacks, again from stand-off distance, on eleven airbases, command centres, radar stations, SAM systems, and hangars. Pinpoint accuracy was achieved and every point of impact resulted in substantial damage to each asset. In hindsight, the destruction of two SAAB 2000 Erieye AEW&C, two command centres at Murid and Chaklala, two AD systems at Lahore and Okara and six radars at Sukkur, Lahore, Arifwala, Chunian, Jacobabad, and Nayachor by the IAF weakened the AD sensor grid of Pakistan substantially.

The irony was that both Pakistan AD and PAF could not prevent the damage that India could inflict on the night of 6–7 May or on 10 May. What possibly went wrong during Op Sindoor that rendered PAF and Pakistan AD ineffective? The reason could be many. Some that can be stated are—one is that Pakistan failed to utilise the NCW arrangement efficiently. Besides, in trying to maintain electronic silence, Pakistan AF and AD radars failed to switch on in time. Another reason is that the key radar systems were damaged or destroyed or jammed by India before major attacks, and another important point is that the surprise factor while executing the operations was very skilfully managed by IAF and ground forces.

Recommendations

Training is an important facet for an AD gunner and radar operator. The quality of training has to be made more simulator-based where all permutations and combinations can be worked out in terms of aerial attack profile of weapons and EW activities for the radars. Ever since I commanded my unit, way back in 2003–2005, equipped with L/70 guns, there was a paucity of practice targets (KD2R5). During annual practice firing, the unit procured aeroplane models and innovatively modified it as a target. It was remotely controlled with limited range. Since then, the rudimentary target has been modified many times over and the parameters tweaked to match the actual targets. The Army AD gunners were used to firing on slow moving (subsonic speed) aeroplane models of varying size, speed, and flying profiles. When the same gunners were provided with upgraded L/70 guns and PFFC ammunition, the Pakistan swarm drones were no match and were brought down very easily. Similar was the case with Zu-23-2B guns too.

With the availability of simulators, they can be trained to engage a variety of drones (shape and size) and fly them at different speeds and approach angles. These simulators should be procured in every AD unit. The drone lab at Army AD College is an important and well-equipped training venue. The radar operator has to learn to work through ECM environment, identify the type of jamming or deception and be able to use the various ECCM facilities available on the radar system. The EW lab at Army AD College is very well kitted to provide this training. However, simulation packages should also be made available to every AD unit.

After years of perseverance, Akashteer was finally delivered by BEL. Like any newly inducted system, Akashteer too has some teething problems. Though BEL has done a good job, it must ensure that the practical problems faced by the user are addressed. Since the IACCS is also being integrated with it, both should be compared sub-system by sub-system. The better one should be retained and a common system created. During Op Sindoor and other ongoing wars, it has been proven time and again that whoever has a better AD NCW capability will have an upper edge.

With new AI tools available, the response time of TEWA software should be improved further.

The ISR capability based on visual, infra-red (IR), and electronic sensors have made battlefields transparent and immune to any camouflage or concealment. The proliferation of sensors such as recce drones and remote-sensing satellites along with communication satellites and optical fibre data links have ensured foolproof coordination between sensors and shooters. All this generates voluminous data but AI and quantum computing has the capability to compress, filter, and make it available in a "ready to use format" within split seconds. Anything that moves will be picked up by a sensor and can be hit. To be effective as a whole, command and control elements have to synthesise the picture, using AI, of the entire operational area, update it in real time, and engage the enemy simultaneously rather than sequentially.[50]

India is surrounded by hostile neighbours on its land frontiers. China openly supports Pakistan, and also indulges in anti-India activities in collusion with our other neighbours. The Indian coastline is also exposed with Chinese spy ship frequenting Hambantota, Male, Karachi, and Gwadar ports. The multi-layered AD coverage needs to be enhanced to meet the current air threat. For varied reasons, Army AD procurement has been delayed and neglected. The procurement process has to be both simplified and accelerated. Various Army AD systems which urgently require procurement include:

- MANPADS: These are a low-cost option to engage larger drones. India is dependent on Russia and there is an urgent requirement to enhance our war wastage reserve (WWR). For long term, India should develop indigenous capabilities or do transfer of technology (TOT) to manufacture MANPADS as they will be required in thousands in a full-scale war.

- Upgraded L/70: Op Sindoor has proved the effectiveness of the upgraded L/70 gun. Only, limited numbers of these guns were upgraded. Therefore, there is a need to upgrade the balance L/70 guns in the interim, to fill the gap, till some new system is procured or indigenously manufactured. These radar-controlled guns are best suited to protect civilian areas, besides the military VAs/VPs. The FC radar technology needs to be fully indigenised and integrated with 30 mm / 40 mm AD guns.
- Anti-drone system: Systems like hybrid D4 anti-drone system should be available with all front-line forces including the CAPFs along the IB, LC, and line of actual control (LAC) as well as for hinterland. The system has proved its operational capability during Op Sindoor. These need to be produced in batches. Every batch should be an improved version over the previous one in terms of range for soft and hard kill. The jammer power and the laser gun intensity need to be increased till a range of 5 km is achieved.
- PFFC ammunition: PFFC ammunition for 40 mm AD gun proved phenomenal during Op Sindoor. The pre-formed fragments are contained in a casing / shell which on activation ensure certain damage or destruction of the aerial target. Their "proximity fuse" enhance detonation sensitivity at the target end, resulting in a high degree of damage or even destruction. Steps should be taken to indigenously manufacture the PFFC post TOT.
- Pan India sensor grid: A pan India multi-tiered sensor grid should be established with an overlap to ensure a gap-free radar coverage as the effectiveness of an AD grid is dependent on its efficiency. The most suited for all types of terrain and jam proof are the AESA and PESA radars. During Op Sindoor, Rajendra radar and LLLWR have proved that

radars designed and manufactured by BEL, LRDE, and ISRO combine are among the best. India should ramp up the radar production. The EO and TI detection system have excellent drone detection capability and India should have them in sufficient numbers. All sensors should be networked using satellites or optical fibre with AI-enabled Akashteer to create a RASP.

- Drone warfare: UCAV are being modified to simply ram into enemy drones to destroy or damage them (kinetic kill). In India, dogfight drones are now being designed. Even commercially available low-cost, low-altitude drones can be used for this purpose. Sophisticated drones use technology to precisely fire nets that trap enemy drones. Some may be modified to act as virtual flying Improvised Explosive Devices (IEDs) that have the advantage of springing the enemy drones. Due to their relative low cost, they are expendable but incorporation of "return to home" capability can increase their efficiency. All the drones mentioned above should be procured insufficient numbers as low-cost anti-drone systems.

The drone technology has made the job of Army AD ever so difficult as it adopts the role of an "Autonomous / Semi-autonomous Weapon System (AWS)". Systems like Harpy and Nagastra-1, fitted with a NavIC suite and supported by ECCM measures, should be procured to destroy the enemy AD systems, drone launch pads, and sensors. Anti-drone jamming guns can jam the drone control link to deceive, manipulate, disable control, or "capture" control. The jamming effect depends upon the power output of the jammer and its frequency. India needs to develop these guns in big numbers.

ISRO operated at least 10 satellites like CARTOSAT, EMISAT, and RISAT during Op Sindoor. They were used for target detection, PSDA, and data links. The data links were used in both IACCS and Akashteer and increased the efficiency of AD NCW. As a result, detection of approaching Pakistan missiles could be quickly processed and were effectively intercepted. The Defence Space Agency (DSA), which functions under the Integrated Defence Staff (IDS), is leading the Space-Based Surveillance (SBS) programme. Some of these satellites should have faster revisit time. The project needs to be fast-tracked.[51]

Just like Ukraine used "Star Link" web for data and communication link resulting in multi-fold improvement in targeting, so should our armed forces get access to Bharti's OneWeb, India.[52] Gradually, India should strive to have its own independent system. AD NCW effectiveness and efficiency will improve manifold if a foolproof secure connectivity is available.

Tri-service AD integration: Preparing for the future[53]

In view of the NCW requirement for IAF, Army AD, and Naval AD (including on ships) and the multi-dimensional air threat cutting across the three services, it is proposed that Tri-service AD integrated structure be created for better homogeneity, coordination, and effectiveness. Optimisation of AD weapons is the need of the hour. Simultaneously, there is an urgent need to take other stakeholders like DGCA and CAPF in view of the likely threat to assets in the hinterland. This integrated-structure should have direct control over the strategic AD weapons (LRSAM and ASAT) while delegating control of tactical AD weapons to respective services as hitherto fore.

It will bring about much-needed cohesiveness between AD elements of the three services and ensure optimal functioning. IAF being the main stakeholder should become the lead coordinator for a viable AD in the country. Each service has a few core competencies and they should be made responsible for that vertical either singly or jointly but within the laid-down guidelines legislated by this integrated-structure. Important considerations for the proposal are as under:

The three NCW—IACCS, Akashteer, and Trigun—were created in isolation. It's time to integrate all three on one single platform or structure. All operators should maintain cyber hygiene. An audit of surveillance radars available with the three services and ATC in the country should be carried out. A gap-free multi-tiered deployment should be re-worked and implemented. The complete NCW should be AI-enabled to create a RASP and carry out TEWA efficiently.

The integrated-structure should create Tri-Service units for Barak-8, S-400, Prithvi AD, and Advanced AD (BMD) and ASAT weapon systems. Their peacetime and operational locations need to be decided and infrastructure created.

The users of air space, especially at the low level (below 300 m), are many. To ensure their maximum freedom of action, a single control agency is needed. Air Space Control (ASC) should be formalised with dedicated staff.

Air threat to all assets of the three services and Joint Parliamentary Committee (JPC) tasks should be reassessed and prioritised. Similarly, stock of all AD weapons under various categories and those in the pipeline should be taken. Thereafter, reallocation of AD weapons should be carried out based on relative priority. Alongside, the indigenous manufacture and procurement ex-import needs to be expedited. A regular interaction with DRDO, Defence Public Sector Undertaking (DPSU), and private industries dealing with the manufacture of AD weapons is the need of the hour and should be held. Shortcomings, modifications, and upgrades wherever required, should be timely conveyed and feedback taken to avoid delays.

The training at IAF AD School /Army AD College/Naval AD School should be integrated based on respective core competency. Training for strategic AD weapons should commence at the earliest. Training of paramilitary forces' personnel on AD aspects (to include drones) needs to be considered in view of the growing drone threat.

PAKISTANI TERRORIST CAMPS TARGETTED BY INDIAN ARMY

Photo 1: Sawai Nala Camp, Muzaffarabad (LeT)

Source: Indian Army.

Photo 2: Syedna Bilal Camp, Bagh, Muzaffarabad (JeM)

Source: Indian Army.

Photo 3: Markaz Raheel Shahik Camp, Kotli (JeM)

Source: Indian Army.

Photo 4: Markaz Abbas Camp, Gulpur, Kotli (JeM)

Source: Indian Army.

Photo 5: Markaz Ahle Hadith Camp, Barnala, Bimber (LeT)

Source: Indian Army.

Photo 6: Mehmoona Joya Camp, Sialkot (HM)

Source: Indian Army.

Photo 7: Sarjal Tehra Kalan Camp, Chak Amru (JeM)

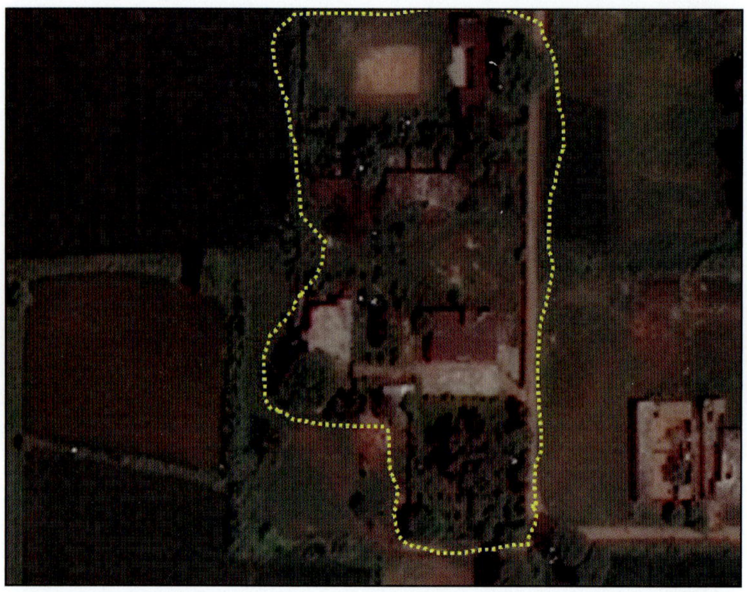

Source: Indian Army.

Photo 8: Syedna Bilal Camp destroyed by Indian Army

Source: Indian Army.

Photo 9: Battalion Tactical Headquarters before and after strike

Source: Indian Army.

Photo 10: Terrorist launch pad before and after strike

Source: Indian Army.

Photo 11: Pakistani post before and after strike

Source: Indian Army.

DESTRUCTION OF PAKISTANI POSTS OPPOSITE BARAMULLA AND RAJAURI SECTOR

Photo 12 A

Photo 12 B

Photo 12 C

Source: Indian Army.

Photo 13 A

Photo 13 B

Photo 13 C

Source: Indian Army.

Photo 14: Indian multi-layered AD system graphically explained

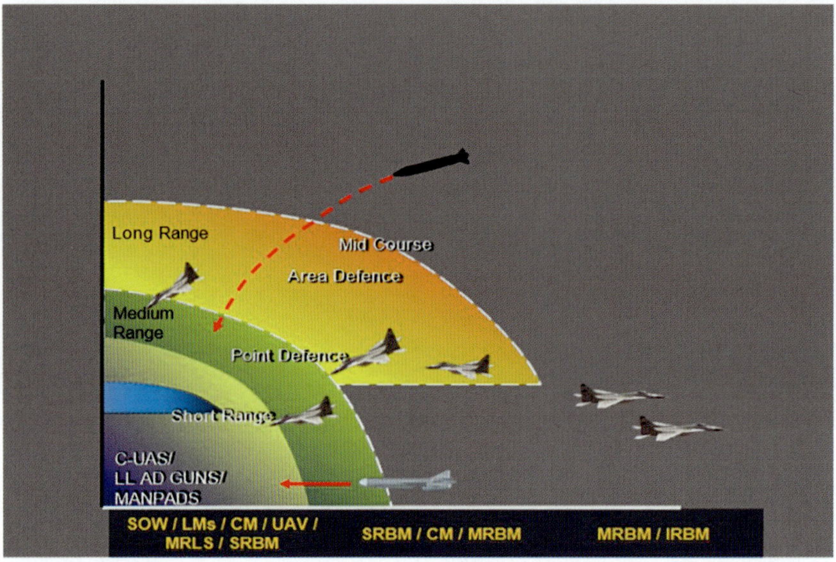

Source: Indian Army.

Photo 15: Indian multi-tiered AD system explained schematically

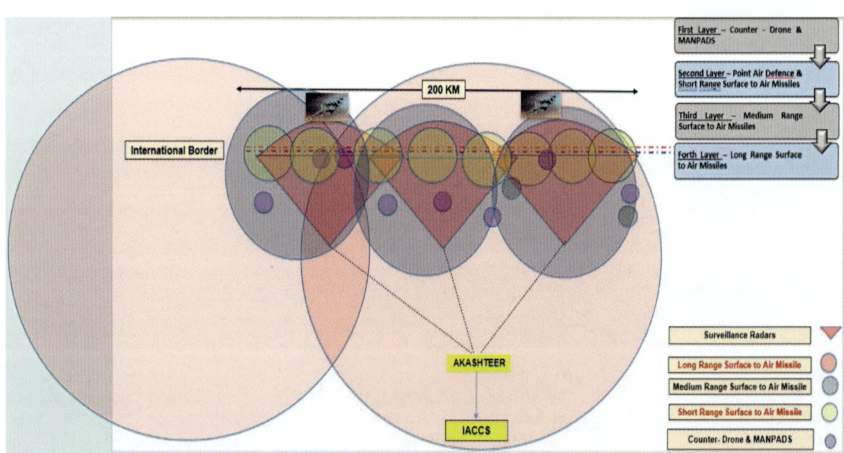

Source: Indian Army.

ARMY AD GUN SYSTEMS: DRONE KILLERS

Photos 16 A and 16 B: Upgraded Shilka 23mm-4B weapon system

Source: Indian Army.

Photos 17 A and 17 B: Upgraded L/70 40mm Gun

Source: Indian Army.

Photos 18 A and 18 B: ZU 23mm-2B Gun

Source: Indian Army.

Photos 19 A and 19 B: Akash SAM

Source: Indian Army.

Photos 20 A and 20 B: Igla MANPADS

Source: Indian Army.

Photos 21 A and 21 B: Soft and hard kill low-cost system

Source: Indian Army.

PAKISTANI DRONES DESTROYED BY INDIAN ARMY AIR DEFENCE

Photos 22 A and 22 B: Yiha III and Asissongar Guard drones of Pakistan meet their end

Source: Indian Army.

Photos 23 A and 23 B: Parts of Pakistan's destroyed drones recovered

Source: Indian Army.

Photos 24 A and 24 B: Pakistan sent drones in swarms but their fate was same

Source: Indian Army.

PAKISTANI DRONES DESTROYED BY INDIAN ARMY AIR DEFENCE

Photo 25 A

Photo 25 B

Photo 25 C

Photo 25 D

Source: Indian Army.

Due to the low population of certain AD equipment, it is suggested to pool in resources of the three services for base repairs and maintenance. Specialists need to be identified and data on their profile be shared.

Conclusion

The effectiveness of the AD NCW has made the adversaries take note. Some known reactions include Pentagon analysts being surprised by the Akashteer's detection and destruction capability of Pakistan and Chinese systems. It has prompted the USA to order an internal review of its underestimation of Indian defence technology.[54] Among others, China Aerospace Science and Technology Corporation (CASC) and Beidou teams are urgently working to counter Akashteer algorithms, while Beijing officials seems to be shocked.[55] Türkiye Bayraktar drones were outsmarted which has prompted their urgent upgrades.[56] Pakistan experienced critical failure of its radars and control centres, as they failed to detect Indian aircrafts. AWACS and USA surveillance radars also malfunctioned, triggering panic and a loss of confidence in their AD system.

The success of indigenous systems covering the AD spectrum in terms of range and capabilities has been noted by all global powers. The success of indigenous PESA and AESA radar systems alongside indigenous production of a variety of missiles under the "Make in India" programme allows India to enjoy increased autonomy in the AD domain. The accuracy of Akashteer is dependent on indigenous NavIC which has proved its mettle.

In conclusion, we can say that "Op Sindoor is not just a story of tactical success. It is a validation of India's defence indigenisation policies. From AD systems to drones, from counter-UAS capabilities to platforms, indigenous technology has delivered when and where it mattered the most". That India has successfully "asserted its role as a hi-tech military power in the 21st century"[57] is a very apt statement.

However, the AD warfare is continuously evolving and there is no time to rest on past laurels. It is time to act on the gaps and shortcomings noticed, addressing the observations of the user and looking at areas where we still lack.

The most intense AD operation happened in the area of responsibility of the "Rising Star" Corps. The commander stated, "Pakistan attempted hitting civil and military targets. With our proactive, dynamic deployment nature, we made sure that Army AD was able to defend successfully including two air bases (where Army AD was deployed). None of the drone or missile strike could reach any target. The soft and hard kill mechanisms were very effective".[58]

This was the first non-contact operation where fighting was mostly aerial in nature and Army AD stood by its motto "Akashe Shatrun Jahi".

The effectiveness with which the destruction of terror camps was conducted is an example of synergy between the three services ably led by the CDS himself. As per the political directive, "Targeting was precise, measured, non-escalatory in nature. It was to send a message to Pakistan loud and clear". That Pakistan chose to further escalate and extend the operation, ultimately, was at the cost of its own nemesis. The world watched the capability of India in dealing with the terror organisation. Indeed, a proud moment for India and Indian AD.

Notes

1. Media briefing by Foreign Secretary on 7 May 2025.
2. Ibid.
3. Mayank Singh, 8 May 2025, Operation Sindoor: Nine targets neutralised with clinical efficiency, *The Indian Express*, available at https://www.newindianexpress.com/nation/2025/May/08/operation-sindoor-nine-targets-neutralised-with-clinical-efficiency, accessed on 10 August, 2025
4. Kalyan Ray, 7 May 2025, Operation Sindoor, the nine terror camps that India destroyed, *Deccan Herald*, available at https://www.deccanherald.com/india/operation-sindoor-the-nine-terror-camps-that-india-destroyed-3528958, accessed on 10 August, 2025
5. AIR, 7 May 2025, New Delhi asserts it is well prepared to retaliate if Islamabad escalates situation after 'Operation Sindoor', available at https://www.newsonair.gov.in/indian-armed-forces-launches-operation-sindoor/, accessed on 29 July 2025
6. Debjit Sarkar op. cit.
7. Elbit Systems op. cit.
8. Dinakar Peri op. cit.
9. CDS op. cit.
10. Press Information Bureau, 14 May, 2025, Global Solidarity with India: A United Front Against Cross-Border Terrorism, Ministry of Information and Broadcasting, Government of India, available at https://www.pib.gov.in/PressReleasePage.aspx?PRID=2128747, accessed on 10 August, 2025
11. Press Information Bureau, 7 May 2025, Operation Sindoor: Indian Armed Forces carried out precision strike at terrorist camps, Ministry of Defence, Government of India.
12. Press Trust of India, 13 February 2025, Pak Army Suffered 'Heavy Casualties' After Ceasefire Violations along LoC, published in NDTV, available at https://www.ndtv.com/india-news/pak-army-suffered-heavy-casualties-after-ceasefire-violations-along-loc-7697155#google_vignette, accessed on 29 July 2025

13. Money Control, 8 May 2025, Pakistan attempted attacks on these 15 cities, available at https://www.moneycontrol.com/news/india/pakistan-attempted-attacks-on-these-15-indian-cities-on-may-7-check-full-list-13019454.html, accessed on 29 July, 2025
14. NewsX, 7 May 2025, Heavy firing along LoC as India launches Operation Sindoor targeting PoK camps, available at https://www.youtube.com/watch?v=yGyge0tlPfM&ab_channel=NewsXLive, accessed on 6 August 2025
15. PIB dated 14 May 25 op. cit.
16. PIB dated 14 May 25 op. cit.
17. PIB, 8 May 2025, Pakistan's bid to escalate negated - proportionate response by India, Govt of India, available at https://www.pib.gov.in/PressReleseDetailm.aspx?PRID=2127670, accessed on 7 August, 2025
18. Ibid.
19. Ibid.
20. MEA media briefing by Wg Cdr Vyomika Singh on 9 May 2025, available at https://www.mea.gov.in/media-briefings.htm?dtl/39482/Transcript_of_Special_briefing_on_OPERATION_Sindoor_May_09_2025, accessed on 7 August 2025
21. *Economic Times*, 9 May 2025, BSF foils 'major' infiltration bid along international border in Samba amid Pakistan air raids, available at https://economictimes.indiatimes.com/news/defence/bsf-foils-major-infiltration-bid-along-international-border-in-samba-amid-pakistan-air-raids/articleshow/121009237.cms?from=mdr, accessed on 12 August 2025
22. Ibid.
23. *The Hindu*, 19 May 2025, Pakistan drones and missiles attack targeting the Golden Temple were thwarted, available at https://www.thehindu.com/news/national/pakistans-drone-and-missile-attacks-targeting-the-golden-temple-in-amritsar-were-thwarted-indian-army/article69594333.ece, accessed on 29 July 2025
24. Surveillance involves keeping a defined air space under continuous observation using visual, electronic or satellite means.

25. IACCS was made operational in its current form in 2012. Earlier, it was a semi-automated system and resulted in wasted opportunities to engage in an aerial threat.
26. Akashteer was approved after intensive trials in March 2023. The first 100 modules were delivered by September 2024 and by March 2025 only 25 percent was expected to be ready. It was still in process of being deployed during the operations. DGAAD interview to ANI dated 19 May 2025, available at https://www.youtube.com/watch?v=uVS81eljVjY&ab_channel=ANINews, accessed on 20 July 2025
27. Tactical Air Defence Integrated Display System was designed in-house by IAF officer Sqn Ldr Praveen Patil in 1998 during Kargil operations. Bharat Shakti. available at https://www.bharat-rakshak.com/indianairforce/database/16981, accessed on 20 July 2025
28. *Financial Express*, How India's New Air-Defence Web Defeated Pak Drone Threats | Akashteer vs Pakistani Missiles. available at https://www.youtube.com/watch?v=2i2-lVGMKlY&t=49s&ab_channel=TheFinancial Express, accessed on 1 August 2025
29. ISRO, 24 January 2025, Advancing India's Regional Navigation Capabilities, available at https://www.isro.gov.in/NVS-02_Advancing_Navigation_Capabilities.html, accessed on 20 July 2025
30. Pakistan Drone Force, available at https://www.warpowerpakistan.com/droneforce.php, accessed on 1 August, 2025
31. MEA, GoI, 8 May 2025, Transcript of Special Briefing on Operation Sindoor, available at https://www.mea.gov.in/media-briefings.htm?dtl/39479/Transcript_of_Special_briefing on Operation Sindoor_May_08_2025, accessed on 29 July 2025
32. PIB, 8 May 2025, Pakistan's bid to escalate negated - proportionate response by India, available at https://www.pib.gov.in/PressReleasePage.aspx?PRID=2127670, accessed on 30 July 2025
33. ANI, *The Economic Times*, 8 May 2025, Harpy Drones Used by Indian Military to Target Enemy Air Defence Systems, available at https://economictimes.indiatimes.com/news/defence/harpy-drones-used-by-indian-military-to-target-enemy-air-defence-systems/articleshow/120996897.cms, accessed on 30 July 2025

34. One India News, YouTube, India Foils Pakistan's Drone Attack: 500 Drones Shot Down in 210 Minutes Across 4 States, available at https://www.youtube.com/watch?v=jxVq17eZqYw&ab_channel=OneindiaNews, accessed on 1 August 2025
35. Director General Air Operations on *Times Now*, 11 May 2025, available at https://www.stimson.org/2025/four-days-in-may-the-india-pakistan-crisis-of-2025/, accessed on 30 July 2025
36. Transcript of Special briefing on Operation Sindoor, 9 May 2025, available at https://www.mea.gov.in/media-briefings.htm?dtl/39482/Transcript_of_Special _briefing on _OPERATION_Sindoor_May_09_2025, accessed on 30 July 2025
37. Sansad TV, 11 May 2025, Press Briefing by DGMO of All Three Services on #OperationSindoor, available at https://www.youtube.com/watch?v=pGYME4HFgRs&ab_ channel=SansadTV, accessed on 30 July 2025
38. *The Express Tribune*, 21 May 2025, Only Targeting Indian Posts on LoC: DG ISPR, available at https://tribune.com.pk/story/2544927/only-targeting-indian-posts-on-loc-dg-ispr, accessed on 29 July 2025
39. Ministry of External Affairs, Government of India, 9 May 2025, Transcript of Special Briefing on Operation Sindoor, available at https://www.mea.gov.in/media-briefings.htm?dtl/39482/Transcript_of _Special_briefing_on_OPERATION_Sindoor_May_09_2025, accessed on 30 July 2025
40. Ibid.
41. Abhishek De, 10 May 2025, Missile debris found in Haryana, Rajasthan, Punjab as Pak ramps up strikes, *India Today*, available at https://www.indiatoday.in/india/story/india-pakistan-conflict-debris-missiles-sirsa-barmer-jalandhar-fateh-2722597-2025-05-10, accessed on 30 July 2025
42. *The EurAsian Times*, 24 May 2025, Historic Kill: S-400 Shot Down Pakistan's AEW&C Aircraft 314 KM Away, available at https://www.eurasiantimes.com/exclusive-s-400-secures-furthest-kill-during/, accessed on 1 August 2025
43. *Al Jazeera*, 10 May 2025, Pakistan launches Operation Bunyan Al Marsoos: What we know so far, available at https://www.aljazeera.

com/news/2025/5/10/pakistan-launches-operation-bunyan-marsoos-what-we-know-so-far#:~:text=What%20does%20Operation %20 Bunyan%20Marsoos, accessed on 12 August 2025

44. MEA, GoI, 10 May 2025, Transcript of Special Briefing on OPERATION Sindoor, available at https://www.mea.gov.in/media-briefings.htm?dtl/39486/Transcript+of+Special+briefing +on+OPER ATION+Sindoor+May+10+2025, accessed on 30 July 2025
45. Ibid.
46. Appreciation by Army AD Directorate vide their note received by email on 12 August 2025
47. Bilal Khan, Quwa, 1 November 2024, When Pakistan intensified its Air Defence Investment, available at https://quwa.org/pakistan/pakistan-air-defence-system/, accessed on 3 August 2025
48. YouTube, Pakistan has Started Asking US for Missile Defence System, available at https://www.youtube.com/shorts/bmBwfOXkEs8, accessed on 4 August 2025
49. MG Sudhakar Jcc, India Sentinels, 21 July 2025, Network-Centric Warfare: Pakistan's edge and India's wake-up call, available at https://www.indiasentinels.com/opinion/network-centric-warfare-pakistans-edge-and-indias-wake-up-call-6933#, accessed on 2 August 2025
50. Brig Akhelesh Bhargava, 2024, *Ukraine War*, Chapter 7, Significance of Army AD in the Ukraine conflict, IDSA.
51. *Economic Times*, 30 June 2025, Operation Sindoor triggers India's space shield push with 52 defence satellites by 2029, available at https://economictimes.indiatimes.com/news/defence/operation-sindoor-triggers-indias-space-shield-push-with-52-defence-satellites-by-2029/articleshow/122151610. accessed on 31 July 2025
52. Bharti, Eutelsat and One web merges to create World's first Geo-Leo Satellite Space connectivity company, available at https://www.bharti.com/press-release-2023-2024-eutelsat-and-oneweb-merges-to-create-worlds-first-geo-leo-satellite-space-connectivity-company.html, accessed on 31 July 2025
53. Brig Akhelesh Bhargava, 2 July 2020, Air Defence Command: A Step in Right Direction, CLAWS, Issue Brief.

54. Indian Defence Research Wing, 14 May 2025, India's Akashteer Drones redefine warfare, stunning global powers in India-Pakistan conflict, available at https://idrw.org/indias-akashteer-drones-redefine-warfare-stunning-global-powers-in-india-pakistan-conflict. accessed on 31 July 2025
55. Ibid.
56. Ibid.
57. PIB, 14 May 2025, Operation Sindoor: The Rise of Aatmanirbhar Innovation in National Security, available at https://www.pib.gov.in/PressReleasePage.aspx?PRID=2128746#, accessed on 30 July 2025
58. Gaurav Sawant, *India Today*, YouTube, Operation Sindoor: Indian Army Hits 7 Out Of 9 Terror Targets In Pakistan, available at https://www.youtube.com/watch?v=eKXDmAIfDI8&ab_ channel=India Today, accessed on 31 July 2025

6

Diplomacy Redefined

Geopolitical, Indus Water Management, and Information Dimensions

AMBASSADOR ANIL TRIGUNAYAT

Introduction

India has suffered from cross-border terrorism from Pakistan for at least last four decades. After decisively losing various conventional wars, from around the mid-1980s, Pakistani deep state ensconced in Rawalpindi, decided to indulge in "proxy by terrorism" wars against India to bleed her through the proverbial "Thousand cuts", as mentioned in Chapter 1 of this book, titled State-Sponsored Terror, a Prelude. Using terrorism, as an instrument of Pakistan's foreign policy, especially against India, became the prominent vector with plausible deniability in their security doctrines. The ulterior cause has been the unrest in Jammu and Kashmir (J&K) where every effort has been made by Pakistan-based terrorists and their Inter-Services Intelligence (ISI) and military to recruit and radicalise the youth in Kashmir to carry out terror attacks in the state and elsewhere. The normalisation in J&K is not acceptable to them as it would take away their logic of India threat and will cause more unrest in POJK and elsewhere, as in Balochistan, which are far less developed and suffer from inequities and discrimination as well as exploitation inflicted by the Pakistani elites and deep state. Hence, the barbaric Pahalgam terror attacks of 22 April 2025. It is often heard that in Pakistan "terrorism is sustained by 3 As—Allah, America, and Army".

The list is quite long but even then some of these stand out; these include Pathankot, Parliament attacks, 26/11 Mumbai attack, Uri and Pulwama and most recently the heinous and dastardly killing of 26 innocent tourists in Pahalgam based on their religion by the Pakistan-based terrorist group, The Resistance Front (TRF), an offshoot of the dreaded Lashkar-e-Taiba (LeT), which has already been internationally proscribed. However, India's response against terror, terror outfits and their sponsors has undergone a qualitative change in recent years. India has stopped giving the benefit of doubt to Pakistan which shelters, nurtures, and uses these terror groups against India as an instrument of its foreign policy. Now New Delhi takes it head-on and hits them wherever they are. This has been a paradigm shift in India's "Zero Tolerance for Terror" policy. From Uri surgical strikes to Balakot crossing the Line of Control (LoC) and the international border after Pulwama, and now precision aerial strikes on nine terror hideouts of Jaish-e-Mohammed (JeM) and LeT, killing over a hundred terrorists deep inside Pakistan, without crossing the LoC (Line of Control) dictate India's resolve and dynamic strategy to counter terrorism. This is a paradigm shift involving multi-domain and integrated deterrence with increasing reliance on indigenous technologies and defence equipment.

It is also an imperative, in view of the standardised responses of the international community especially our very close partners to "Op-Sindoor", which needs a careful analysis. We also need to understand the real dynamic of the so-called "Strategic Partnerships" and calibrate our expectations of them. From the lukewarm responses at least at overt diplomatic levels, it is clear that India will have to follow the "Ekla Chalo Re" (walk alone) policy as far as the fight against terrorism and terror infrastructure and sponsors of cross-border terrorism is concerned, as was done recently in the response to Uri, Pulwama, and Pahalgam terror attacks. Of course, we will have to continue to persuade our partners to see reason and not apply double standards. It does not obviate the need to continue to pursue on the adoption of the Comprehensive Convention on International Terrorism (CCIT) gathering dust in sanctum-sanctorum of the United Nations Security Council (UNSC). In the end, we must be sure ourselves that while we are informing our international partners and interlocutors exposing Pakistani sponsorship of cross-border terrorism, we are neither seeking their approval nor their validation.

An effort has been made in the following paragraphs to analyse the foreign policy and military diplomatic strategy, and Indian response leading to a "New Normal" declared by the Prime Minister Narendra Modi–led government. The reactions from our friends and foes and those sitting on fences have been analysed. A leading commentator, Dr Brahma Chellany, while decrying India's alleged "half pregnant approaches", said on 10 May 2025, "India won that three-day war but ceded the narrative, largely because it was slow to rebut Pakistan's empty boasts and outright lies, which the international media eagerly amplified". To what extent the current Indian foreign policy has been able to address the gaps in this, including the lack of a robust communication strategy, has been deliberated in this chapter. The diplomatic outreach by multi-party and multi-faith parliamentary delegations to nearly three dozen countries in the aftermath of "Op-Sindoor" and its success—limited or otherwise—needs to be assessed. Finally, some suggestions have been offered. The most important one is the institutional adoption of military diplomacy as the tool to deal with modern-day challenges and complexities.

India's Decisive Response to Pahalgam

The dastardly terror attacks and heinous killing of 26 innocent persons, on the basis of their religion, by the Pakistan-based terrorists of TRF, and the inhumane manner that these were carried out in broad daylight, shocked the conscience of the nation and the world. It needed a comprehensive and conclusive response. The perpetrators and their sponsors had to be punished and taught a lesson or at least create "Pause and Think" deterrence for the Pakistani deep state, although like the proverbial dog's tail it is unlikely to be straightened. Hence, India's policy responses have been well calibrated through a concentric-circles approach to expose, punish, and isolate the terror-sponsoring devious state of Pakistan. That there will be costs to this cheap proxy option, which Rawalpindi has adopted for the last four decades against India, was the clear message.

Diplomatic Strikes

India's diplomatic stroke was masterful with far-reaching consequences as it legitimately placed the lifeline for Pakistan, especially its Punjab and Sind provinces—the "Indus Water Treaty (IWT)" of 1960s—in abeyance. This clearly stipulated that "Blood and Water" cannot flow together. India has always been more than benevolent to Pakistan for decades as far as water supplies are concerned under the Treaty even though there has been significant discontent in India on its being partisan to Pakistan, a lower riparian state, which has taken it for granted and continued to object on all Indian dam projects especially in J&K. In view of the changed material circumstances, as permitted under the Treaty, India has been requesting Pakistan for discussion and review which until recently have been ignored or denied by Islamabad. Hence, New Delhi decided to hold the treaty into abeyance causing a societal stir in Pakistan. It is important for the people of Pakistan to understand that in their blind pursuit of anti-India stance their deep state has led them into avoidable difficulties and danger. This is not likely to go away until Pakistan and its deep state change course and take credible action against proscribed and wanted terror groups and designated terrorists in their country, like a normal international actor. They cannot continue to hide behind the shield of hypocrisy of major powers often taking umbrage by qualifying "Good Terrorist and Bad Terrorist" theory which provides sustenance to terrorists and their sponsors.

Immediately after terror attacks, the angry Indian Prime Minister Narendra Modi declared that India will "identify, track, and punish" every terrorist and their "backers" involved in the Pahalgam carnage and pursue the killers to the "ends of the earth". The Cabinet Committee on Security Affairs, led by PM Modi, took punitive and decisive diplomatic measures which can be summarised as follows:

- On 23 April, India announced a raft of measures against Pakistan, including the suspension of the Indus Waters Treaty. The Indus Waters Treaty, brokered by the World Bank, has governed the distribution and use of the Indus River and its tributaries between India and Pakistan since 1960. The Indus River system comprises the main river, the Indus, and its tributaries. The Ravi, Beas, Sutlej, Jhelum, and Chenab are its left-bank tributaries, while the Kabul river, a right-bank tributary, does not flow through Indian territory. The Ravi, Beas, and Sutlej are collectively referred to as the eastern rivers, while the Indus, Jhelum, and Chenab are known as the western rivers. The waters of this river system are crucial to both India and Pakistan. The Indian government said it will remain suspended unless Pakistan credibly and irrevocably stops support for cross-border terrorism.

- As part of the punitive measures, India also announced that it would expel Pakistan's three military Attaches and directed Islamabad to downsize the staff strength at its High Commission in New Delhi from 55 to 30. The Foreign Secretary, announcing the retaliatory measures, said "the defence, military, naval and air advisors in the Pakistani High Commission in New Delhi are declared persona non grata" and they have a week to leave India. India will be withdrawing its own defence, navy, and air advisors from the Indian High Commission in Islamabad.
- Foreign Secretary Vikram Misri said Pakistani nationals will not be permitted to travel to India under the SAARC visa exemption scheme (SVES) and any Pakistani national currently in India under the SVES visa has 48 hours to leave India.
- The CCS meeting that lasted for two-and-half hours decided to close the Integrated Check Post at Attari with immediate effect. It was the only operational land border crossing between the two countries. On closing of the Integrated Check Post at Attari, Misri said those who have crossed over with valid endorsements may return through that route before 1 May.
- In quick succession, on 24 April, India announced suspending visa services to Pakistani nationals with immediate effect. The ministry of external affairs (MEA) said all existing valid visas issued by India to Pakistani nationals stand revoked with effect from 27 April. It said medical visas issued to Pakistani nationals will be valid only till April 29. The MEA said all Pakistani nationals currently in India must leave the country before the expiry of visas.[1]

- The Border Security Force confirmed that it had "scaled down" the retreat ceremony held at Attari, Hussaini Wala, and Sadki along the India-Pakistan border in Punjab. Hundreds of visitors, foreign tourists, and locals visit the Attari-Wagah border on either side daily to watch the flag-lowering and retreat ceremony that is being held since 1959.[2]

Several of these measures had not been invoked earlier despite the two countries going to at least four overt wars and scores of covert operations and terror attacks on India. Of these, the most significant happens to be the one related to keeping the Indus Waters Treaty in abeyance as New Delhi aggressively started exploring options and expeditiously develop infrastructure to utilise the waters, which were as such due to India under the Treaty, and Pakistan was benefiting by default and took it for granted.

Terror and Talks Can't Continue

Pakistan has a unifocal foreign policy objective which is totally "India-centric" and is aimed at undermining the security and stability of India through terrorism and proxies. This has been done since 1947–48 when Mujahedeen extremists with Pakistani Army support marched onto Kashmir and illegally occupied a large part of the state of Jammu and Kashmir, which had already acceded to India as per the norm and choices given to the princely states. Raja Hari Singh chose India and signed the instrument of accession. Then Prime Minister Jawahar Lal Nehru decided to take it to the UNSC which ensured the ceasefire and the Line of Control (LoC) became the line of perennial problem. India and Pakistan have fought several wars over Kashmir as Islamabad and deep state in Rawalpindi have continued to use all means to destabilise India. Terrorism became the convenient tool in their arsenal. However, both sides had signed up to the Simla Declaration in 1972 and Lahore Declaration in 1999 which clearly underscored the need to resolve all issues bilaterally. But Islamabad would keep on making efforts to internalise the issues by raking up the demised UNSC Resolutions at nearly every United Nations General Assembly (UNGA) meeting. The chorus becomes much louder, even though irrelevant, at the Organisation of Islamic Cooperation (OIC), the second largest body after the UN. India, although originally invited, is not a member of the OIC even though today with nearly 230 million Muslims, India is the second largest Muslim nation in the world after Indonesia. India has often condemned the extraneous intervention and references by the OIC on India's internal affairs at the behest of Pakistan.

Pakistan even declared a suspension of the Simla Agreement on 23 April 2025, which was later denied. As far as trade is concerned, Pakistan never accorded the Most Favoured Nation (MFN) treatment to India as mandated by the WTO. Pakistan also closed the air space to Indian carriers as a reciprocal measure. But it kept Kartarpur Saheb corridor open on its side.

Pakistan Prime Minister Shehbaz Sharif has often expressed a willingness to engage in a "meaningful dialogue" with India to resolve all outstanding issues, as reported by PTI. The statement was made during a phone call with Saudi Crown Prince Mohammed bin Salman on marking a diplomatic overture, a little over two months after the 22 April Pahalgam terror attack that killed 26 people and sharply escalated tensions between the two countries. "Pakistan is ready to engage in a meaningful dialogue with India on all outstanding issues, including Jammu and Kashmir, water, trade, and terrorism", Sharif said, as quoted by Radio Pakistan. During the conversation, Sharif also thanked the Saudi Crown Prince for the Kingdom's continued support amid the recent India-Pakistan standoff, according to Pakistan's state-run broadcaster. India has now said that it will talk only on terrorism and POJK.

This sham is not the first time that Sharif has signalled openness to dialogue. He had earlier made similar remarks during his visits to Iran, Azerbaijan, and in a telephone call to US Secretary of State, Marco Rubio, stating Pakistan's readiness to discuss a range of issues with India, including Kashmir, terrorism, water, and trade.[3] India, however, has maintained a firm stance. The Ministry of External Affairs has reiterated that talks with Pakistan can only focus on the return of Pakistan-occupied Kashmir and ending terrorism. Ministry spokesperson Randhir Jaiswal said the Indus Waters Treaty will remain in abeyance until Pakistan permanently halts support for cross-border terrorism. "Just like Prime Minister Narendra Modi said: 'terror and talks cannot go together, terror and trade cannot go together, and water and blood cannot flow together'," Jaiswal added.

Pakistan has been facing increasing diplomatic isolation even at the Shanghai Cooperation Organisation (SCO) summit, with even traditional allies like China and Russia refraining from offering support amid growing concerns over Islamabad's role in regional instability. Thcy both condcmned the Pahalgam attacks.

The change in demeanour was evident when National Security Adviser (NSA) Ajit Doval explicitly named Pakistan-based terror groups LeT and JeM as major threats to regional security. The statement went unchallenged by any SCO member—including China—which has historically blocked attempts to single out Pakistan at multilateral forums.[4]

India's National Security Adviser Ajit Doval and Raksha Mantri Rajnath Singh attended the respective Shanghai Cooperation Organisation (SCO) meetings in China during June 2025, in the run up to the Summit in China. While both India and Pakistan attended the Shanghai Cooperation Organisation (SCO), New Delhi did not hold any bilateral meeting as part of the tactical disengagement from Pakistan in the wake of the 22 April Pahalgam attack. Ironically, and as in the past, the SCO Defence Ministers' meeting was driven by Sino-Pak combine to not include the reference to Pahalgam attack, while they wanted to include the references and attacks in Pak-occupied Baluchistan on Pakistan forces by the Baloch Liberation Army (BLA) fighting for their independence. Raksha Mantri Rajnath Singh vehemently criticised the double standards and refused to sign the communique. It is ironical that the SCO was essentially established as a security organisation whose primary objective was to fight against terrorism, but they have a RATS collaborative mechanism, which allows a terror-sponsoring member to get away with its nefarious activities. It is becoming increasingly evident that like the vertically divided UNSC, we may have a similar dynamic playing out in China-centric SCO.

Pakistan in its typical style has tried to project itself as an innocent regional actor which has also suffered from terrorism, and has often claimed to have the mischievous intent and readiness to enter into a dialogue with India. The Global South, including most of our neighbours, was guarded and pretty muted as they do not want to get caught in a war between India and Pakistan.

Global Response to Terror Attacks and India's Retaliation

Major powers

Here is an analysis of the response of some of the dominant powers to India's retaliation of the Pahalgam terror attacks.

USA

USA is India's Global Comprehensive Strategic partner with an exceptional convergence on issues of mutual importance and global concern between the two largest and greatest democracies. India figures prominently in the foreign policy priorities of USA despite Trumpian affair with Pakistani military leadership. Counter-terrorism, security, cyber and intelligence cooperation are the key fulcrum of the bilateral relationship. These have acquired a greater salience and bi-partisan support across the US political spectrum as they value friendship with India in no uncertain terms. But still gaps have been often magnified, as also during Pahalgam attacks and Operation Sindoor.

PM Narendra Modi, who shares a good friendly relationship with President Donald Trump, was one of the first leaders to visit White House (13 February) when both sides underscored the importance of the relationship between the two democracies encapsulating the essence in the White House statement, "As the leaders of sovereign and vibrant democracies that value freedom, the rule of law, human rights, and pluralism, President Trump and Prime Minister Modi reaffirmed the strength of the India-U.S. Comprehensive Global Strategic Partnership, anchored in mutual trust, shared interests, goodwill and robust engagement of their citizens". On counter-terror cooperation, it was categorical in pointing at Pakistan and its terrorist allies "The leaders reaffirmed that the global scourge of terrorism must be fought, and terrorist safe havens eliminated from every corner of the world. They committed to strengthen cooperation against terrorist threats from groups, including Al-Qaida, ISIS, JeM, and LeT in order to prevent heinous acts like the attacks in Mumbai on 26/11 and the Abbey Gate bombing in Afghanistan on 26 August 2021. Recognising a shared desire to bring to justice those who would harm our citizens, USA announced that the extradition to India of Tahawwur Rana has been approved, which happened soon thereafter. The leaders further called on Pakistan to expeditiously bring to justice the perpetrators of the 26/11 Mumbai, and Pathankot attacks, and ensure that its territory is not used to carry out cross-border terrorist attacks".[5] But soon there was a change in tracks and tact as the ownership of arranging ceasefire controversy began and there is no sign of it dying down. India continues to maintain that the temporary ceasefire was agreed at the behest and request of Pakistan, and through the direct talks between the DGMOs of the two countries for de-escalation, while Trump continues to claim it.

There is no doubt that USA and its senior officials including Secretary of State Marco Rubio and Vice President JD Vance were engaged in talking to both sides as well as their counterparts in India and Pakistan. On the US State Department's website there are several references to their role in de-escalation, let alone the Truth Social of Trump. The prominent one that pops up first is entitled "Announcing a U.S.-Brokered Ceasefire between India and Pakistan" at 5.25 pm on 10 May 2025 even before India and Pakistan made their announcements. It elaborates further that "Over the past 48 hours, Vice President Vance and I have engaged with senior Indian and Pakistani officials, including Prime Ministers Narendra Modi and Shehbaz Sharif, External Affairs Minister Subrahmanyam Jaishankar, Chief of Army Staff Asim Munir, and National Security Advisors Ajit Doval and Asim Malik. I am pleased to announce the Governments of India and Pakistan have agreed to an immediate ceasefire and to start talks on a broad set of issues at a neutral site. We commend Prime Ministers Modi and Sharif on their wisdom, prudence, and statesmanship in choosing the path of peace".

On 8 May Rubio spoke to Pakistan PM Sharif. According to Spokesperson Tammy Bruce, Secretary Rubio spoke with Pakistani Prime Minister Muhammad Shehbaz Sharif and emphasised the need for immediate de-escalation. He expressed US support for direct dialogue between India and Pakistan, and encouraged continued efforts to improve communications. The Secretary expressed sorrow for the reported loss of civilian lives in the current conflict. He reiterated his calls for Pakistan to take concrete steps to end any support for terrorist groups.[6] Likewise, Bruce referred to calls between Rubio and External Affairs Minister (EAM) Jaishankar stating that the Secretary emphasised the need for immediate de-escalation. He expressed US support for direct dialogue between India and Pakistan and encouraged continued efforts to improve communications. The Secretary reiterated his condolences for the horrific terrorist attack in Pahalgam and reaffirmed the United States' commitment to work with India in the fight against terrorism.[7]

As per US Administration, it was US President Donald Trump's Truth social post that told the world that India and Pakistan have agreed to a "full and immediate" ceasefire. Shortly after, both sides confirmed that they had decided to de-escalate after tensions peaked. It was one of the most decisive 88-hours war where Indian aerial supremacy was well established. US position was further emboldened as Pakistani PM Shehbaz Sharif tweeted, "We thank President Trump for his leadership and proactive role for peace in the region. Pakistan appreciates the United States for facilitating this outcome, which we have accepted in the interest of regional peace and stability. We also thank Vice President JD Vance and Secretary of State Marco Rubio for their valuable contributions for peace in South Asia". It was right for Islamabad to do so or more expedient since they have been asking the Americans and the others to intervene for the ceasefire having faced utter humiliation in a short conflict which in any case primarily was against the terror groups. In fact, in their statements post Op Sindoor most of the countries in the Middle East as well as Russian President Vladimir Putin attributed and thanked President Trump for the ceasefire. Likewise, most of the Arab countries also thanked President Trump for de-escalation.

Trump has not stopped to claim the credit as he continues to believe that he averted a nuclear war between India and Pakistan by threatening to cancel all trade deals unless both sides ceased fighting. But stopping Trump is not easy since again on 15 July during a meeting with NATO Secretary-General Mark Rutte, Trump said, "We've been very successful in settling wars. You have India and Pakistan. You have Rwanda and the Congo that was going on for 30 years. India, by the way, Pakistan would have been a nuclear war within another week, the way that was going. That was going very badly, and we did that through trade".[8]

But India, which wants to handle the relations and issues with Pakistan bilaterally clearly stood its ground as Foreign Secretary Vikram Misri said, "DGMO (Director General of Military Operations) of Pakistan called up DGMO (of India) at 3.35 pm. They agreed that both sides will stop all firing and military action from land, air and sea from 5 pm onwards." India did not need any persuasion since it had made a limited objective strike only on nine terror hideouts killing over one hundred designated terrorists of groups like the LeT and JeM. It had no intention of militarily escalating unless Pakistanis retaliated which they did, and New Delhi was forced to take a pre-emptive action and forceful and decisive action decimating Pakistani airports deep inside their territory, establishing their military and air supremacy in the non-contact, perhaps the shortest, war, lasting 88 hours only. Terror cannot go unpunished that was the clear message to the terrorists and their sponsors.

Although Pakistan continued to make lame excuses on behalf of the terror groups even stating that there was no group like "The Resistance Front", New Delhi provided evidence of having raised this at the UNSC for over two years. It made renewed efforts in the wake of Pahalgam to get the TRF listed. Despite standard Chinese technical hold and Pakistan trying its delaying tactics at the UNSC and 1267 Committees, finally, as a result of India's diplomatic efforts, the US State Department on 17 July 2025 declared TRF as a Foreign Terrorist Organisation (FTO) and Specially Designated Terrorists, even referring to their role in Pahalgam and other terror attacks. It unequivocally read "TRF, a Lashkar-e-Tayyiba (LeT) front and proxy, claimed responsibility for the 22 April 2025 Pahalgam attack which killed 26 civilians. This was the deadliest attack on civilians in India since the 2008 Mumbai attacks conducted by LeT. TRF has also claimed responsibility for several attacks against Indian security forces, including most recently in 2024. These actions taken by the Department of State demonstrates the Trump Administration's commitment to protecting our national security interests, countering terrorism, and enforcing President Trump's call for justice for the Pahalgam attack".[9]

Indian External Affairs Minister Dr S Jaishankar tweeted, "A strong affirmation of India-US counter-terrorism cooperation" while conveying his appreciation to Secretary of State Marco Rubio. In any case, India maintained that the ceasefire was agreed at the request of the Pakistanis and not due to any mediation, which was also later explained during the telephonic discussions between President Trump and PM Modi. However, President Trump, who has been projecting himself as the Peace leader, continued to take credit for the ceasefire umpteen times. Since he did not get the endorsement from New Delhi on this, he started entertaining the Pakistanis a bit more conspicuously including hosting General Asim Munir at lunch and two months later meeting for the military-to-military consultations, knowing too well the real role the deep state and the Pak military play in cross-border terrorism against India and others. Rawalpindi is basking in that glory since they also laid out the red carpet for the US ambitions and wish list including nominating Trump for the Nobel Peace Prize. Trump's unmanaged anger against India was also evident in his sudden unilateral and unreasonable imposition of 50% tariff on Indian exports for manufactured reasons. A global comprehensive strategic partnership has been compromised for the sake of convenience. Crass Transnationalism has become a currency at the highest level in the US Administration.

Russia

Russia is India's special and privileged, and strategic and a trusted partner and the relationship is based on mutual trust and respect which serves the geo-strategic interests of both countries. Moscow has often stood with and for India since the Cold war days. The more than two decades old strategic partnership is further underscored by excellent inter-personal relationship with President Vladimir Putin and Prime Minister Narendra Modi. Despite its entanglement in the war with Ukraine, Kremlin has assured fullest support to India in securing itself, occasionally even against China and Pakistan. Op Sindoor was no exception.

Condemning the Pahalgam terror attacks, President Putin was quick to send his condolence message to Indian President and Prime Minister stating, "Please, accept my deep condolences in connection with the tragic consequences of the terrorist attack near the town of Pahalgam, which claimed the lives of peaceful people, citizens of various countries. This brutal crime cannot be justified. We trust that its organizers and perpetrators will receive the punishment they deserve. I would like to reiterate our readiness to further step up interaction with our Indian partners in the fight against all forms and manifestations of terrorism".[10]

On the other hand, Foreign Minister Sergey Lavrov called his Indian counterpart Dr S Jaishankar on 2 May urging restraint. Their read-out stated that Sergey Lavrov called to settle the differences between New Delhi and Islamabad by political and diplomatic means on a bilateral basis in conformity with the 1972 Simla Agreement and the 1999 Lahore Declaration. The ministers also discussed the timetable of the upcoming contacts at the top and high levels. He also called his Pakistani counterpart Ishaq Dar on same lines. This comment was not taken kindly by the Indian establishment especially in the public discourse as one has become used to far more robust and unifocal support from Moscow.

Public disappointment and criticism in India, since Moscow's support fell well below expectations, perhaps led President Putin to call PM Modi, assuring full support to India's action and response to terror attacks even as Russia preferred cooling down of tempers. The Kremlin read-out reemphasized, "The President of Russia has once again expressed sincere condolences over the death of Indian citizens as a result of a barbaric terrorist attack committed on April 22 in Pahalgam, Jammu and Kashmir. Both leaders emphasized the need for an uncompromising fight against terrorism in all its forms. During the conversation, the strategic nature of the specially privileged partnership between Russia and India was highlighted. Impervious to outside influence, this relationship continues to develop rapidly across all areas".[11]

India was in no mood to allow the world to create an equivalence between the terror perpetrators and the victims. The hypocrisy needed to be called out. Moreover, efforts to re-hyphenate India and Pakistan were dismissed outright. This was one of the key reasons that neither India wanted to let Pakistan internationalise the Kashmir issue once again nor was it prepared to let it get away with impunity.

China

Although Beijing condemned the terror attacks in J&K, its strategic support to Pakistan, which is its iron-clad friend and ally, was unquestionable and consistent with its geo-political priorities in South Asia. Pakistan has in reality become a state of China. However, in the wake of Op Sindoor, while it continued to support Pakistan's demand for investigations into the Pahalgam terror attacks according to its diplomatic support to Islamabad, China's Foreign Ministry Spokesperson Guo Jiakun, said, "China hopes that India and Pakistan will exercise restraint, work in the same direction, handle relevant differences properly through dialogue and consultation, and jointly uphold peace and stability in the region".[12]

During Operation Sindoor, Beijing reportedly provided significant air defence and satellite support, helping Pakistan reorganise its radar and air defence systems to detect Indian troop deployments. This level of logistical and intelligence support, as assessed by a research group under India's Ministry of Defence, goes beyond mere arms sales and actively contributes to India's "two-front situation".[13] This, even though well-known, was further averred by Lieutenant General Rahul Singh, Deputy Chief of Army Staff (Capability Development & Sustenance), who underscored that India dealt with three adversaries at the border, including Türkiye also in the category. "Pakistan was at the front. China was providing all possible support ... Turkey also played an important role in providing the type of support it did", Singh said during his address at an event organised by the Federation of Indian Chambers of Commerce & Industry (FICCI) in Delhi.[14]

Neighbours

Neighbours are a gift of geography but can be pains of history. Precisely that is what is being seen as most of the neighbours with the sole exception of Bhutan have become the participants in China's Belt and Road Initiative (BRI) project of which Pakistan, with China–Pakistan Economic Corridor (CPEC), happens to be the biggest beneficiary. Most neighbours see India from the prism of "Big Brother Syndrome" and hence try to leverage through China against India despite New Delhi's continued "Neighbourhood First Policy" which is totally non-reciprocal. This impinges on their responses to India's deep security concerns, including terrorism. Relations with Pakistan and Bangladesh, and to some extent with Nepal and Sri Lanka as well as Maldives, have seen this sea–saw trajectory between India and China. Even though now as a result of their fundamental debt-related issues and economic downturn Sri Lanka and Maldives have become more pragmatic, Bangladesh and Nepal follow somewhat dubious tracks. They also fear the Indian economic and military might. Hence, in the wake of Pahalgam attacks and the Op Sindoor, their reactions were guarded and cautious. Interestingly, Taliban-led Afghanistan, with which India has just begun to open up, was categorical in condemning the terror attacks. India's immediate South Asian neighbours—Afghanistan, Bangladesh, Bhutan, Nepal, and Sri Lanka—were among the first to issue strong condemnations. Bhutan stressed its "solidarity and friendship" with India, while Sri Lanka reaffirmed its commitment to countering terrorism. Pakistan also condemned the attack, though it firmly denied any involvement and rejected India's allegations of cross-border support for terrorism. Maldives, which despite the current pro-China leadership, condemned Pahalgam terror attacks and reiterated fullest support to India and sought greater security cooperation as they hosted PM Modi (25–26 July 2025) as the Guest of Honour on the 60th anniversary of their independence.

European Union

The European Union High Representative for Foreign Affairs and Security Policy Kaja Kallas put out a series of statements condemning the terrorist attack as well as acknowledging "every state's" duty and right to "lawfully protect its citizens from acts of terror". Nonetheless, as tensions mounted in the subcontinent, and an Indian response seemed imminent, the EU's statement urged both countries to "exercise restraint, to de-escalate tensions and desist from further attacks", remarks that were poorly received in New Delhi.

India perceived them as drawing an unfair equivalence between itself, the aggrieved party and the aggressor. Prominent commentators opined that the statement is likely to undermine the EU's relations with India, at an "avoidable" time. In a public engagement soon after, Dr S Jaishankar stated that India is looking for "partners, not preachers", a statement widely considered to have been directed at Europe. Even if in line with precedent, the EU's position has disappointed New Delhi, considering the years of closer engagement since Balakot in 2019, the last major Indo-Pak conflict. The move has largely been viewed through the lens of reciprocity, a like-for-like response for India's position on Ukraine.[15] This has reinforced a perception that India's Western partners remain primarily transactional in their approach, interested in India's defence and large market rather than real strategic partnership. France and some others were a little more vocal but all wanted restraint and de-escalation even if they acknowledged India's right to respond and protect itself. As EAM Jaishankar articulated in the Lok Sabha that the German Foreign Minister not only condemned the terror attacks but supported India's right to defend. This was also evident during the interactions that the MPs delegation had in several European capitals later.

West Asia

West Asia is our extended neighbourhood with a civilisational and maritime connect. In many ways, it has an existential characteristic for India due to our dependencies including energy security; welfare and security of expatriates who account for over 9.5 million and remit over $ 60 billion annually to India; extensive economic engagement; and finally the ease of maritime connectivity and trade of over 80% through choke points of Strait of Hormuz, Bandar Abbas, Red Sea, and the Suez Canal, as India is deeply engaged in the International North South Transport Corridor (INSTC) with Iran's Chabahar Port as the focal point for its access to Afghanistan and Central Asia. And more recently it has embarked on the India–Middle–East Europe Economic Corridor (IMEEC), which has been somewhat stunted by the ongoing Israel–Hamas–Palestine conflict. But over the years convergences and mutual importance has been refocused and the relationship has moved from transactional to truly strategic partnership with most major countries, especially in the Gulf Cooperation Council (GCC). The relationship with them for decades was predicated on the Pakistan factor due to predominance of Islamic narrative and affinity. But as a result of the strategic engagement and deeper realisation of the truth about Pakistani regimes, using cross-border terrorism as a tool of their foreign policy, the intensity of their engagement with Islamabad was vastly tempered, which has been evident in their reactions on Pulwama, Art 370 abrogation, and now Pahalgam. However, like most countries and our partners, the regional majors preferred non-escalation between the two nuclear powers since Pakistan continues to project its nuclear bomb as an Islamic bomb. But several of them were very clear about the fact that terrorism must be dealt with sternly. They all expressed condolences on the Pahalgam terror attacks calling these barbaric and even un-Islamic.

PM Modi was on a state visit to Saudi Arabia and had to cut short the visit to take stock of these horrific developments. Crown Prince Mohammed bin Salman, PM of Saudi Arabia, was the first one to condemn the terror attacks in no uncertain terms and expressed solidarity with India. Retaliation and escalation, and focused and targeted elimination of threats, became an imperative as the Indian Prime Minister Narendra Modi vowed to identify, track, and punish every terrorist, and their backers. We will pursue them to the ends of the earth. At his *Mann ki Baat* he reiterated, "I once again assure the victim families that they will get justice. Justice will definitely be served. The perpetrators and conspirators of this attack will face the harshest response". Escalate to deescalate through diplomatic and military strikes became the Indian strategy.

The US Vice President JD Vance was also in India. Ironically, and not coincidentally, terror attacks also took place during the visit of President Clinton to convey the message that normalcy in Kashmir propounded by India was not there. But such acts have not deterred India from holistically working for the welfare and the development of the Kashmiris. This is not acceptable to Pakistan. Hence, India's resolve to give a decisive response to the terrorists—who will be hunted and justice served, and their sponsors will be punished—has caused a deep concern among the regional countries who would prefer and try to contain the military escalation. PM Modi clearly warned Pakistan that they cannot hide behind the terrorists and non-state actors as mere proxies and will be held accountable.

Adversity often becomes a litmus test for friends. It is also not untrue of diplomacy. For decades, India's relationship with most West Asian countries has been transactional, and only during the last decade or so it has turned truly strategic. It is also due to strategic and increasing importance of India and the realisation by the regional majors of the futility of continuation of support, directly and through OIC partnership, to Pakistan, which uses terrorism as a tool of foreign policy against India and others, that it has become a reality in action. Parroting the Islamic brotherhood has run its course. Pakistan used to be a factor, and their relationship with India was often predicated on their Islamic connect with Islamabad.

Several countries, especially the regional majors like Saudi Arabia, UAE, Egypt, Iraq, Jordan, Israel, and the Gulf Cooperation Council (GCC), etc. were the first ones to condemn the heinous, dastardly, and cowardly attacks in Pahalgam by the Pakistan-based terror group TRF which initially claimed responsibility and then tried to backtrack. But footprints of Rawalpindi and LeT are unmistakable. An exceptional diplomatic response has been given by way of punitive measures against the terror sponsor and the perpetrating state, of which the most important and far-reaching is holding the Indus Waters Treaty in abeyance, which will define the contours of relationship with Pakistan. India has once again taken up for listing and designating TRF and LeT terrorists at the UNSC 1267 Committee and as usual China has put a technical hold on it.

While expressing solidarity with India, most West Asian countries reaffirmed their commitment to the global fight against terrorism. Even the Taliban offered condolences and condemned the attacks against innocent Indian tourists who were targeted on account of their religion. Türkiye and Azerbaijan became the posterchild for support to Pakistan.

Several leaders called PM Modi including the Iranian President Dr Pezeshkian, who after talking to Pakistan PM Sharif also offered to mediate to de-escalate. Presidents of UAE, Egypt, Jordan, Palestine, and Israel and others called PM Modi to express their solidarity. Several Foreign Ministers also spoke to Dr Jaishankar expressing their sympathy and condolences and resolve to fight the menace of terrorism while hoping to de-escalate the imminent war between India and Pakistan. Israeli PM Benjamin Netanyahu was categorical in his unstinted support to India in her decision to deal with this menace as it deems appropriate.

Initially, even Türkiye's President Erdogan, during his press conference with PM Sharif (22–23 April) did not take the bait and avoided direct reference to Kashmir but condemned terrorism. However, their subsequent statements in favour of Pakistan and criticism of India for the strikes led to further deterioration in bilateral relations as the popular calls for "Boycott Türkiye" became vocal due to their blinded support to Islamabad. Thc shady and shadowy presence of their Naval ships and aircrafts and use of Turkish drones by Pakistani retaliatory strikes further accentuated the Indian ire against Erdogan, which is not likely to improve in the near term.

Iran and Saudi Arabia indulged in shuttle diplomacy among calls by various leaders from the region for de-escalation once India struck the terror hideouts in Pakistan. Pakistani leaders also reached out to many of these countries for intervention but India completed the task in a resolute and decisive manner. Iranian Foreign Minister Dr Araghchi, after his visit to Islamabad, dashed to Delhi and had a meeting with EAM Dr S Jaishankar along with the Joint Commission meeting during which India clearly conveyed its position with regard to "War on terror" and response to Pakistani retaliation in favour of terrorists. Iran welcomed the ceasefire agreement between India and Pakistan, viewing it as a significant step toward regional stability. Foreign Ministry Spokesperson Esmaeil Baqaei praised the decision as a demonstration of "responsible and wise statesmanship" by both nations.

Saudi Arabia, under the directives of its leadership, dispatched Minister of State for Foreign Affairs Adel Al-Jubeir to both New Delhi and Islamabad on 8 and 9 May. During these visits, Al-Jubeir engaged with top officials from both countries, advocating for restraint and emphasising the importance of resolving disputes through dialogue and diplomatic channels.

Israel's PM Netanyahu, fighting against terrorism himself, tweeted "My dear friend @narendramodi, I am deeply saddened by the barbaric terrorist attack in #Pahalgam, Jammu & Kashmir, that killed and injured dozens of innocents. Our thoughts and prayers are with the victims and their families. Israel stands with India in its fight against terrorism". He also spoke to PM Modi and supported fully in the fight against terrorism. The exchanges across the security spectrum also intensified as India prepared and launched decisive strikes in accordance with its "New Normal".

It will be recalled that President Trump's visit to the Middle East was critical for the region as it defines new contours of US re-engagement but in the context of controversial statements and role with regard to India-Pakistan conflict, most countries in the region referred to and lauded Trump's role in stopping the war from escalating between India and Pakistan. Trump repeatedly claimed credit for it. But India has maintained that further escalation was paused due to Pakistan's direct request and that it was not India's intention to escalate in any case.

PM Shehbaz Sharif was in Türkiye on 22–23 April and visited again. There were also visits of several senior Pakistani officials to Türkiye around that time. Even the arrival of Turkish Airforce planes and naval vessels to Pakistan coincided with the timelines of escalation between India and Pakistan. A statement from Türkiye's Ministry of Foreign Affairs warned that India's strikes risked "an all-out war" and condemned what it called "provocative steps" as well as "attacks targeting civilians and civilian infrastructure".

Ankara and Baku, being good friends endorsed the Turkish stance; Azerbaijan also issued a statement expressing solidarity with Pakistan and condemning Indian military strikes on civilian (terrorist) infrastructure in the region.

Pakistan is under constant vigil and watch for its behaviour going forward and how it comes clean on complicity with terror networks in its "fertile for terror" land is to be seen. In order to explain the role of Rawalpindi and India's "Zero Tolerance to Terror" policy, several official and parliamentary delegations have been sent across geographies, including to West Asia. There is a clear understanding and appreciation of Indian position as per reports emanating from the region and beyond. But Pakistan is also up to its tricks. The fact that economically fragile but terror-wise strong Pakistan was able to secure the $1bn IMF loan, $800 Mn from the Asian Development Bank (ADB) as well as the World Bank within the same timeline made them feel victorious despite being defeated on the battle field. No wonder they claimed victory and even promoted their General to Field Marshal Asim Munir. While the Indian government has repeatedly accused Pakistan of diverting international aid toward terror activities, Trump approved nearly $400 million to support Pakistan's F-16 fighter jets for counter-terrorism operations. And while New Delhi has long sought to de-hyphenate India from Pakistan diplomatically, Trump did the exact opposite.[16] Later Trump's invite to Munir for lunch at the White House emboldened the Pakistani deep state as it believes that their narrative has been bought by the West effortlessly and it feels rewarded. Munir's second visit to meet his US counterparts of United States Central Command (CENTCOM) and meeting of their bilateral discussions on counter-terrorism as well as eulogy thereafter are hypocritical to say the least. This would also indicate that India's core concerns will have to be defended by ourselves.

War of narratives has become the new weapon of statecraft which with the connivance of western media and deep state of Pakistan, through its advantage of "First Lie" created an unsustainable hypothesis which had to be countered with facts and firmness. Having a proactive robust communication strategy with a whole of nation approach is absolutely essential to counter fake and fraudulent narratives created by Pakistani deep state in favour of their non-state actor buddies who have been admitted by their leadership as their first or second line of defence. NSA Ajit Doval rightly confirmed that India hit the terror targets in Pakistan, precise to the point. He further questioned "Foreign Press said Pakistan did this and that. You show me one photograph, one image which shows damage to any Indian (structure), even a glass pane having been broken. They just wrote such things". We also need to carefully watch the evolution of China-Pakistan-Türkiye-Azerbaijan axis and seek pathways to neutralise its caustic impact through recharging our strategic partnerships with the regional majors and beyond.

Finally, we must also be careful and considerate about our own narratives and policy of Dialogue, Peace, and Diplomacy since the same arguments are ploughed back to us in times of crisis which was clearly evident this time. PM Modi, of course, clarified that though "This is not an era of War" but "This is also not an era of terrorism", i.e., there is a qualitative difference between war betwixt two states and war on terrorism which several countries like USA and Russia and China have undertaken when confronted with the scourge of terrorism.

Central Asia

Central Asia is also our extended neighbourhood and India has been following the "Connect Central Asia" policy for over a decade, at least since 2012. Bilateral relationship has moved apace and strengthened over time. Cooperation in multilateral fora like Shanghai Cooperation Organisation (SCO) and BRICS as well as in 5+1 formats at various levels has deepened. Collaboration against terrorism is also a defining characteristic of the relationship. The responses from these countries are also instructive.

Kazakhstan (8 May 2025)

The Ministry of Foreign Affairs of the Republic of Kazakhstan expresses its profound concern over the escalating tensions between the Republic of India and the Islamic Republic of Pakistan. We urge all parties involved to exercise maximum restraint to prevent any further escalation. Kazakhstan remains committed to the settlement of international and regional conflicts exclusively through political and diplomatic means in accordance with the norms of international law and the principles of the UN Charter.

Uzbekistan (7 May)

Uzbek President's Press Secretary Sherzod Asadov said, "The President of the Republic of Uzbekistan Shavkat Mirziyoyev expressed his condolences to the President of the Republic of India Draupadi Murmu and Prime Minister Narendra Modi for the loss of many lives and serious injuries as a result of the terrorist act committed in the territory of Kashmir. The head of our state expressed his sincere condolences to the families and relatives of the victims, to the people of India, and wished for the speedy recovery of the injured". Another statement by the Ministry of Foreign Affairs of the Republic of Uzbekistan stated that Uzbekistan is closely monitoring with concern the development of the situation related to the rising tensions between India and Pakistan. "We call on both parties to exercise restraint, act in the interests of peace and stability, and prioritise diplomatic dialogue to prevent further deterioration of the situation. Uzbekistan is ready to support any international or regional efforts aimed at de-escalation and the peaceful resolution of the situation".

Kyrgyzstan

On 7 May, Kyrgyz President wrote on his twitter handle, "We, our friendly member countries of the Shanghai Cooperation Organisation, express our deep concern over the escalating tensions between India and Pakistan. We call on both sides to exercise maximum restraint, prevent further escalation of the conflict, and return to negotiations for a peaceful resolution. The Kyrgyz Republic has always advocated stability, security, and respect for international law".

Turkmenistan

The President of Turkmenistan Serdar Berdimuhamedow has sent condolences to Indian President Draupadi Murmu and Prime Minister Narendra Modi following the terrorist attack in the town of Pahalgam, Jammu and Kashmir, that claimed human casualties and injuries, according to Turkmenistan's state media. In his message, Berdimuhamedow strongly condemned all forms of terrorism and extremism, reaffirming Turkmenistan's full support for the international community's efforts to combat and eradicate these threats. On behalf of the people and government of Turkmenistan, as well as personally, Turkmen President expressed heartfelt sympathies to the families of the victims and wished a speedy recovery to those injured.

Later the Indian External Affairs Minister hosted his Central Asian counterparts in New Delhi (on 6 June) when he conveyed appreciation that their countries stood by India and condemned the heinous terrorist attack that took place in April in Pahalgam. Later, Defence Minister Rajnath Singh, during the SCO meeting in China, held bilateral talks with Tajikistan, Belarus, and Kazakhstan, emphasising defence cooperation and India's self-reliance in defence production. He briefed them on the Pahalgam terror attack and Operation Sindoor, aimed at dismantling terrorist networks in Pakistan. India declined to sign the joint declaration due to the omission of the Pahalgam attack.[17]

QUAD countries

At a recent meeting, in Washington DC, of the QUAD Foreign Ministers, comprising India, USA, Australia and Japan, Dr S Jaishankar clearly articulated and underscored that India expected QUAD—a strategic grouping of leading maritime nations committed to a free and open Indo-Pacific—to understand and appreciate India's right to defend its citizens from cross-border terrorism. Subsequently QUAD issued a statement, which sounded more generic, but addressed the concerns and condemned the terror attacks in strong unequivocal language stating "We condemn in the strongest terms the terrorist attack in Pahalgam, Jammu and Kashmir, on April 22, 2025, which claimed the lives of 25 Indian nationals and one Nepali citizen, while injuring several others, ... We call for the perpetrators, organizers, and financiers of this reprehensible act to be brought to justice without any delay and urge all UN Member States, in accordance with their obligations under international law and relevant UNSCRs, to cooperate actively with all relevant authorities in this regard". Like the UNSC statement it also failed to mention Pakistan by name. But EAM Jaishankar clarified in the Parliament "QUAD unequivocally condemns all acts of terrorism and violent extremism in all its forms and manifestations including cross-border terrorism. We condemn in strongest terms the terrorist attacks in Pahalgam on 22 April, and call for perpetrators, organizers and financers of this reprehensible act to be brought to justice without any delay".

Hopefully, in the upcoming QUAD Summit in New Delhi, the leaders will truly address this global concern and challenge.

BRICS member countries

Prime Minister Narendra Modi, speaking at the Rio BRICS Summit 2025 (6–7 July) was categorical in calling out the global hypocrisy and double standards with regard to selective and convenient response to terrorism especially in the context of dastardly Pahalgam attacks. He reiterated that "Terrorism has become the most serious challenge for humanity today. Recently India faced an inhuman and cowardly terrorist attack. On 22 April, the terrorist attack in Pahalgam was a direct attack on the soul, identity, and dignity of India. This attack was a blow not only to India but to the entire humanity. In this hour of grief, I express my heartfelt gratitude to the friendly countries who stood with us, who expressed support and condolences, further adding that condemning terrorism should be our 'principle', not just a 'convenience'. If we first see in which country the attack took place and against whom, then it would be a betrayal against humanity". No wonder the Joint Statement of BRICS Summit was quite categorical even if did not directly mention Pakistan, which India would have preferred but was an anathema to China and some others. But reference to cross-border terrorism gives it away in any case. The statement is the clearest support to India's fight against terror.

India's consistent position and efforts yielded an unequivocal condemnation of terrorist attacks as well as reference to cross-border terrorism while fixing the responsibility of states to prevent such occurrences. Para 34 of the Joint Statement clearly articulated "We express strong condemnation of any acts of terrorism as criminal and unjustifiable, regardless of their motivation, whenever, wherever and by whomsoever committed. We condemn in the strongest terms the terrorist attack in Jammu and Kashmir on 22 April 2025, during which 26 people were killed and many more injured. We reaffirm our commitment to combating terrorism in all its forms and manifestations, including the cross-border movement of terrorists, terrorism financing and safe havens. We reiterate that terrorism should not be associated with any religion, nationality, civilization or ethnic group and that all those involved in terrorist activities and their support must be held accountable and brought to justice in accordance with relevant national and international law. We urge to ensure zero tolerance for terrorism and reject double standards in countering terrorism. We emphasize the primary responsibility of States in combating terrorism and global efforts to prevent and counter terrorist threats". It further talked about the BRICS efforts and institutional mechanisms to counter extremism, terrorism and radicalisation in which India had played a significant role as the Head of the Working Group. BRICS Counter-Terrorism Working Group (CTWG) and its five subgroups based upon the BRICS Counter-Terrorism Strategy, the BRICS Counter-Terrorism Action Plan, and the CTWG position paper, reiterated, "We look forward to further deepening counter-terrorism cooperation. We call for an expeditious finalization and adoption of the Comprehensive Convention on International Terrorism in the UN framework. We call for concerted actions against all UN designated terrorists and terrorist entities". It referred to this Indian draft of Comprehensive Convention on International Terrorism (CCIT), which has been gathering dust in the sacred corridors of the UN, driven by "My terrorist vs yours" paradigm, for decades.[18]

Even though India would have preferred clear reference to Pakistan as a terror-sponsoring state, even this was definitely a cut above the rest as far condemnation and support to Indian position on terrorism is concerned.

G7 countries

India has been a consistent invitee for the G7 Summits. This time despite the lukewarm relations with Canada, the host, Prime Minister Modi was invited to attend the Summit. They also condemned the terror attacks but did not call out Pakistan.

The statement reads "We, the G7 Foreign Ministers of Canada, France, Germany, Italy, Japan, the United Kingdom and the United States of America and the High Representative of the European Union, strongly condemn the egregious terrorist attack in Pahalgam on April 22 and urge maximum restraint from both

India and Pakistan. Further military escalation poses a serious threat to regional stability. We are deeply concerned for the safety of civilians on both sides. We call for immediate de-escalation and encourage both countries to engage in direct dialogue towards a peaceful outcome. We continue to monitor events closely and express our support for a swift and lasting diplomatic resolution".[19]

United Nations Security Council (UNSC)

Pakistan is currently the non-permanent member of the UNSC for the years 2025–26. This provides it a strategic advantage in the Council since it would be easier for them to lobby with other members. Hence with the help of China and some other friends, it tried to water down the UNSC statement and made it into a generic one absolving itself of the direct responsibility and reference despite being the master sponsor of terrorism. This is the irony and irrelevance of the United Nations.

On 25 April, the UN Security Council strongly condemned the Pahalgam terrorist attack and said that those responsible for this heinous act should be held responsible. It further added, "The members of the Security Council underlined the need to hold perpetrators, organizers, financiers, and sponsors of this reprehensible act of terrorism accountable and bring them to justice". They of course reiterated the need for de-escalation stating, "we again urge both the Government of India and the Government of Pakistan to exercise maximum restraint to ensure the situation does not deteriorate further". While Pakistan took credit and boasted of watering it down and removing reference to TRF, being the surrogate, Indian External Affairs Minister Dr Jaishankar considered it as the mandate to execute "Operation Sindoor". The Council statement on 25 April "demanded that its perpetrators be held accountable and brought to justice ... We have since seen that happen",[20] Jaishankar said while speaking at the inaugural of an exhibition "The Human Cost of Terrorism" at the UN headquarters. He further added that it is imperative to call out terrorism publicly when it is supported by a state against a neighbour and is fuelled by the bigotry of extremism.[21]

This was further substantiated on 7 May by Foreign Secretary Vikram Misri, informing about India's surgical strikes on nine terror hideouts in Pakistan, "it was deemed essential that the perpetrators and planners of the 22 April attack be brought to justice. Despite a fortnight having passed since the attacks, there has been no demonstrable step from Pakistan to take action against the terrorist infrastructure on its territory or on territory under its control. Instead, all it has indulged in are denials and allegations. Our intelligence monitoring of Pakistan-based terrorist modules indicated that further attacks against India were impending. There was thus a compulsion both to deter and to pre-empt".[22] India exercised its right to respond. Equally important is India's shift from "strategic ambiguity" to "conditional clarity". The message is simple and direct: any cross-border terror attack will be treated as an act of war. No more grey zones. The consequences will be calibrated but unavoidable. This clarity is crucial to reimposing deterrence, making Pakistan's traditional playbook of low-cost proxy warfare far less viable.[23]

Assessing the responses, overall, we see that even though naming and shaming of Pakistan and direct and overt support to India's Op Sindoor may have been somewhat lukewarm and may not be that accentuated, EAM Dr Jaishankar countered that narrative speaking at the Lok Sabha when he reiterated "I would like the members of this House to understand, if India is attacked, if there is a terrorist attack on India, and a country says we condemn cross-border terrorism, I think it is obvious to everybody what that cross-border terrorism is". He further underlined the global support saying "that there are 193 members of the United Nations. Only three, apart from Pakistan, opposed Operation Sindoor, only three. If you look through this period, and I would be very happy to share with the House the exact positions of various governments. Overwhelmingly, the world's recognition that terrorism is unacceptable, that the country which has been attacked has a right to defend itself, and that India was doing exactly that".[24]

In the light of the Security Council's press statement, India's actions are justified under international law. Under Article 51, India has the right to self-defence when faced with an armed attack. Given the repeated cross-border terrorist incidents, India's military response aligns with established legal principles of necessity and proportionality. Since Pakistan failed to prevent the actions of terrorist groups based in Pakistan and PoK, India could invoke state responsibility principles to justify counterterrorism operations. The unwilling or unable doctrine further supports India's stance, allowing action when a host state fails to curb terrorist activities.[25]

"Ekla Chalo Re" and the new Normal Doctrine

Over the decades that India has suffered from cross-border terrorism from Pakistan-sponsored terrorists, the global response has ranged from sheer indifference to verbose condemnation. Period. New Delhi also graduated from its policy of giving Pakistani State a benefit of doubt, and naively believing that it could control the deep state therein, whose sole existence and exalted status is dependent on continuing with the bogey of Indian threat by projecting Kashmir as "The Issue". India's concerns were not even acknowledged until 9/11 happened in the USA and threats of Al Qaeda and ISIS and a large number of Pak-based groups like the LeT and JeM directly responsible for scores of terror attacks against India became real for the world. New Delhi vainly hoped that the world will pay more heed to this threat against humanity. But that was not to be, especially as pockets of terrorists and groups were being used by many a powers and countries to serve their geo-political ends. In recent years, this has been clearly evident in the legitimisation and transfer of power to hitherto designated terrorist groups, especially in Afghanistan and Syria and holding Pakistan with kid gloves, be it an invitation to Democracy Summit, non-NATO ally status or huge multimillion-dollar grants for maintenance of their F-16 fleet, supposedly to fight terrorism. Ludicrous as it may sound, such precedents and implicit and explicit support, to such state and non-state actors justifies their cause and demeanour, while emboldening their resolve to continue as they are rewarded.

Türkiye has had its iron-clad relationship with Pakistan for a very long time and has been overtly partisan for Pakistan and against India even in a highly rabid manner. They have been supporting Islamabad diplomatically and militarily and even condemned India's surgical strikes on terror, while sympathising with Pakistan whole-heartedly. This led to public outrage against Türkiye and reactions were rampant against normalising relationship with Ankara. Hence, New Delhi is spreading its convergence with Armenia, Greece, and Cyprus quietly. All three countries carry their complex histories, with Türkiye, which, from "Dost" turned to "Drones" against India. PM Modi's recent visit to Cyprus was also seen in this context. While India's presence in West Asia has historically been shaped by energy needs and diaspora connections, this new equation reflects something deeper: a response to Turkish assertiveness that now crosses diplomatic boundaries.[26]

Speaking for the first time after Operation Sindoor was launched, the Prime Minister said, "Operation Sindoor is now India's new policy against terrorism, a new line has been drawn". He also asserted that India will not tolerate any "nuclear blackmail", and said that operations against Pakistan have only been kept in abeyance and the future will depend on their behaviour. PM Modi also stressed that this is not an era of war but also not an era of terrorism. Hence, I am repeating again, we have just suspended our retaliatory action against Pakistan's terror and military camps. In the coming days we will measure every step of Pakistan on the criterion that what sort of attitude Pakistan will adopt ahead", he added. He was also categorical in the direction ahead, "we will not differentiate between the government sponsoring terrorism and the masterminds of terrorism. During Operation Sindoor the world has again seen the ugly face of Pakistan, when top Pakistani army officers came to bid farewell to the slain terrorists. This is strong evidence of state-sponsored terrorism. We will continue to take decisive steps to protect India and our citizens from any threat".[27]

But all said and done, India could feel comforted by the battlefield successes even though several controversies continued not to be extinguished. One of them was the loss of aircrafts by India. Lack of clarity gave wind to speculation with Trump adding fuel to fire even as it is not abnormal to lose some assets in war. But it could have been handled better. John Spencer, US Military Expert and Chairman of Urban Warfare Studies was categorical in his tweet claiming that "Operation Sindoor was not about seizing ground. It was about shaping the future balance of power. It was not just a military operation. It was a statement of national capability and will. And that statement may define the next fifty years of deterrence more than any movement since 1971".

Blood and Water Cannot Flow Together

The Indian Water Diplomacy provided a new dimension to the Indo-Pak rivalry as the Indus Waters Treaty was held in abeyance for the first time, as India maintained that blood and water cannot flow together, especially in the wake of Pahalgam attacks. Since 1948 through 1960 when the Indus Waters Treaty was signed and considered highly benevolent by India to Pakistan the bi-national Indus Waters Commission played a constructive role and the Treaty was often touted as the model for the sub-continent and beyond.

In effect, the six Indus system rivers still flow through both India and Pakistan; the water flows of three rivers apiece are assigned to each country. According to the provisions of the Treaty, all the water of the "Eastern Rivers" of the Indus system—Sutlej, Beas and Ravi—shall be available for the "unrestricted use" of India. Pakistan shall receive water from the "Western Rivers"—Indus, Jhelum, and Chenab.

The Indus Waters Treaty 1960, as has been argued and admitted by experts, is the most benevolent and generous Treaty where the upper riparian state (India) not only agreed to get only 18% of the water but even for that it paid out Pound Sterling 62.06 million to Pakistan. This could be more than $4bn today. But an ungrateful Pakistan has only continued to accuse India and abuse the Treaty provisions with alacrity by trying to stop the development in Kashmir itself by objecting to every project. Pakistani hypocrisy with regard to its shouting from the rooftops becomes evident from its obstructions over the decades with respect to the Indian developmental projects in J&K. The same also applied when it indulged in terror attacks at Pahalgam, trying to scare away tourists, who are the bread and butter for the Kashmiri people. Hopefully, common people of Kashmir by now have fully understood the Pakistani hack and ulterior motives which seems to have been displayed during protests post Pahalgam in Kashmir, itself.

Pakistan literally takes its water from the Western rivers, while India draws from the Eastern streams. This arrangement enables each state's engineering service to operate its irrigation and hydropower systems with the minimum possible cross-border coordination. A 2005 study by strategic Foresights Group claimed that water wars might be looming large on the Indus and the noted expert Sundeep Waslekar maintained that the existing treaty did not represent true cooperation. At that time India was not building damns on the upstream; however, Pakistan's recent international arbitration battles against India's genuine requirement of Baglihar dam and Kishanganga diversion scheme demonstrates this fact adequately. India has been seeking consultations with Pakistan over decades which have not fructified or even acknowledged while the material circumstances as provided for in the Treaty have been highlighted by New Delhi. More importantly, Islamabad and the Pakistani deep state at Rawalpindi have continued to use cross-border terrorism as an instrument of their foreign policy against India. Pahalgam was the last straw.

Hence, the decision was taken that the Indus Waters Treaty of 1960 will be held in abeyance with immediate effect until Pakistan credibly and irrevocably abjures its support for cross-border terrorism. In a letter addressed to the Pakistani officials, India's Water Resources Secretary Debashree Mukherjee said that sustained cross-border terrorism by Pakistan targeting Jammu and Kashmir impedes India's rights under the Indus Waters Treaty. The obligation to honour a treaty in good faith is fundamental to a treaty. However, what we have seen instead is sustained cross-border terrorism by Pakistan targeting the Indian Union Territory of Jammu and Kashmir, it said.[28]

Implications of Holding the Treaty in Abeyance

Data Sharing Halted: India will cease sharing hydrological data with Pakistan, which is vital for managing water resources. This includes information on river flows, flood forecasts, and drought risks.

Increased Water Usage: The suspension allows India to potentially manage its usage of water from the western rivers (Indus, Jhelum, Chenab) better, without the binding aspects of the treaty's restrictions. There were outdated provisions in the treaty that made it difficult for India to harness even the permissible water allocations under the original treaty, which will no longer apply till replaced by a fresh treaty in the future.

Legal and Diplomatic Challenges: The treaty does not explicitly provide for unilateral suspension or termination, leading to a complex legal situation. Article XII of the treaty states that modifications or terminations require mutual agreement, leaving the status of the treaty in a legal grey area.

Regional Tensions: The suspension has escalated tensions between India and Pakistan, with Pakistan's National Security Committee warning that any diversion of water would be treated as an act of war. This situation raises concerns about potential conflict over water resources, which are critical for both nations.

Addressing Parliament during the debate on Operation Sindoor, Modi described the treaty as a "blunder" committed by India's first Prime Minister Jawaharlal Nehru. Hence, New Delhi is unlikely to yield on this, despite China raising a red flag on Brahmaputra system of rivers being the upper riparian state. The bluff is to beef up Pakistani claims.

India is moving forward with its biggest hydroelectric power project yet—an 1856-megawatt plant to be built on the Chenab River in Jammu and Kashmir. This major project, named the Sawalkote Hydroelectric Project, comes just weeks after India suspended key provisions of the Indus Waters Treaty with Pakistan.[29] India is pushing ahead decisively. The Sawalkote project will be built in two phases and will cost an estimated Rs 22,704 crore. It is seen as both a strategic and developmental milestone, aimed at boosting energy generation in the region and reducing dependence on fossil fuels. India is evidently serious to use its legitimate share of water rather than being magnanimous to an ever-ungrateful terror sponsoring state of Pakistan.

General Asim Munir on his second trip in two months to Washington DC (10 August) threatened India not only with the nuclear jibe that if "We think we are going down we will take half the world down with us" but also said that let India build the dam and we will use ten missiles to blow it up. The fact that he is able to get away with these kinds of irresponsible statements tantamount to the extent Pakistan seems to have become emboldened by the US support this time.

Castigating General Munir's threats and remarks, the Ministry of External Affairs on 11 August condemned it stating "nuclear sabre-rattling is Pakistan's stock-in-trade". The MEA said that the international community can draw its own conclusions over the irresponsible remark made by Asim Munir during his visit to the United States. India said that Munir's statement raises doubts about the integrity of nuclear weapons and their control and stated that "the military is hand-in-glove with terrorist groups" in Pakistan.

Prime Minister Narendra Modi, speaking from the ramparts of Red Fort for the 12th time on the 79th Independence Day warned Pakistan with regard to Indus Waters Treaty being held in abeyance and clearly underscored the Indian position "that blood and water cannot flow together. The decades-old pact with Pakistan caused major harm to agriculture in India". The people have come to realise that the Indus Waters Treaty is unjust. Water from the Indus River system has been irrigating the lands of the enemy, while our farmers have suffered. Amid repeated warnings from Pakistan PM Shehbaz Sharif and Army Chief Asim Munir over the Indus Waters Treaty, the PM said, "India has decided that it will not tolerate nuclear threats anymore; we won't fall for any blackmail".

Calling out the Global Hypocrisy and Double Standards

Even as India suffered from cross-border terrorism for over four decades it was only after 9/11 and twin tower attacks in New York that the western world took realistic cognizance of this menace. US in the beginning was also ready to work with the global community against the faceless enemy. It acted more responsibly but that did not last much longer since as soon as it became clear that it would be able to decisively defeat the Al Qaeda and Taliban, it began to internationally behave like the arrogant superpower. Therefore, the big powers were suspicious of US designs, and the geo-politics came into play that has also dented the fight against terrorism. USA had to stay on for another two decades to leave Afghanistan, handing the power back to the same Taliban. However, after the first round of victory in Afghanistan, USA did not dispel fears that its choice of terrorists was determined by political convenience. It created the unmistakable impression that it could use the charge of terrorism to target all its adversaries. This obviously caused a major blow to international efforts to contain the terrorist groups since most countries began to discriminate between and among the terror groups, through their narrowly defined contours, and myopic political lenses. Ad hocism and exclusivity became the norm, and lip sympathy the mannerism, to fight against the menace, as the terror and extremist groups thrived across regions and consolidated their gains and spaces, making the fight against them even more sketchy and difficult.

The problem is that till now we do not have a clear definition of terrorism which was so well articulated by PM Modi at the UN in 2015 during his visit to USA after 25 years. Prime Minister Narendra Modi said the world should stop differentiating between "good terrorism and bad terrorism". "The UN is celebrating its 70th anniversary but till now it has not been able to arrive at a definition for terrorism. If defining it takes so much time, how many years will it take to tackle terrorism. Humanist forces in the world will have to put pressure so that it is decided in black and white what is terrorism. Since there is no definition, talk about good terrorism and bad terrorism is going on. We cannot protect humanity with this good and bad terrorism," Modi said, adding that "terrorism is terrorism". Unfortunately, political convenience has been exercised by many countries including the USA when it started differentiating between the "Good Taliban" and "Bad Taliban" even though India stuck to its principled stand and even paid a price in this context when USA cut a side deal in 2020 with the Taliban, giving Pakistan a free pass, despite knowing too well that it is harbouring all shades of terror and extremist groups, which even a FATF (Financial Action Task Force on terror financing) acknowledged while holding it in the "Grey Zone". On top of it only recently former Pakistani Prime Minister Imran Khan lamented and regretted his country's participation in the US "War on Terror" enterprise in Afghanistan, since a quid pro quo was not forthcoming. Khan said that Pakistan's decision to join America's 20-year-long war in Afghanistan was a self-inflicted wound, and one that was taken for monetary purposes, and not by considering the welfare of the general public. The considerations were the same as in 1980s when we participated in the Afghan Jihad against the Soviet Union", he said.

The global counter-terrorism strategy, even if we concede that there is one, has failed miserably despite the claims to the contrary. It was so true in the case of Daesh or ISIS /ISIL or its "Variants of Concern". It has been worse than the Pandemic.

In Hindu legends and scriptures, there is an instructive story of a demon popularly known as Bhasma Sur. The tale goes that the demon prayed to Lord Shiva for years. Shiva eventually became pleased and agreed to give him a boon and asked what he wanted. Demon said that he wished to have the power to burn anything to ashes on whoever and whatever he placed his hand on. Shiva said: *Tathastu* (so be it). The demon, not so sure, told the Lord that he wanted to try it on the Lord himself first. And then the Lord had to run for life, till eventually Lord Vishnu, another god who is part of the Indian trinity, helped him. The sum and substance of the story is for those countries who enable or support terrorism, extremism, and radicalisation are bound to suffer from it themselves. In the context of Pakistan, it is pretty obvious and so is it for many of its benefactors, current or the erstwhile. According to a list compiled by South Asia Terrorism Portal (SATP), there are at least 48 terrorist and extremist groups operating out of Pakistan, which claims that it is also suffering from terrorism. According to Pakistan's National Counter-Terrorism Authority (NACTA), terrorism attacks caused 357 deaths in Pakistan in 2020, a clear increase in the number of victims of terrorism from the previous year. No wonder PM Modi, while addressing the 76th UNGA, stressed that the danger of regressive thinking and extremism was also rising in the world. He said, "Regressive thinking *ke saath jo desh atankwad ka* political tool *ke roop me istemal kar rahe hain, unhe ye samajhna hoga ki atankwad un ke liye bhi utna hi bada khatra hai.* (With regressive thinking, the countries that use terrorism as a political tool will have to understand that terrorism is an equally big danger for them too.) In these circumstances, the whole world has to make science-based, rational, and progressive thinking the base of their development programmes" and in a veiled warning to Pakistan, he said the current delicate situation of Afghanistan be not exploited, saying that the world has to ensure that Afghanistan isn't used to "spread terrorism or launch terror attacks".

Despite Pakistan agreeing through "Lahore Declaration" not to allow its territory for cross-border terrorism against India, it has continued with much greater vigour with its fullest support to various groups like Hizbul Mujahideen, Jamaat-ud-Dawa (JuD), Lashkar-e-Taiba (LeT) and scores of others to indulge in terror acts against India especially in J&K, in addition to its political rant at the UN or OIC. India, therefore, changed its strategy of dealing with terror groups through direct action. This was clearly evident in its responses on the Uri and Pulwama terror incidents as the 26/11 or the 2016 Pathankot and Uri incidents were avenged in a different and "go to the source" strategy. In my conversations, Ambassador TCA Raghavan, former High Commissioner to Pakistan referred to the vigorous countermeasures taken by India. He maintained that the Uri attack was responded to by a cross-LC military operation by the Indian Army; this entered the military lexicon and popular imagination in India as the "surgical strike" response to Pakistan's provocation. (Even a Bollywood movie was made on this operation that became a roaring success.) He added that the Pulwama terrorist attack saw an even more robust response, confined not to a cross-LC operation but an air strike deep inside Pakistan (Balakot). Similarly, CDS General Anil Chauhan, addressing an event in Gorakhpur, said that both India and Pakistan learned lessons after Balakot. He said that India focused on long-range precision strikes, while Pakistan likely focused on air defence. He added, "During the surgical strikes after the Uri terror attack, we entered Pakistan by land and destroyed terrorist camps. After Pulwama, we opted for air strikes in Khyber Pakhtunkhwa. When the Pahalgam terror attack happened, we had already enhanced our precision strike capabilities".[30] This indeed shows a change in Indian strategy but "is it adequate" only time will tell. A 24×7 vigilance at all levels and a robust international cooperation is a primary condition for conclusively defeating the extremist tendencies and terrorist entities as their reintegration and rehabilitation would take the front seat as well. Even as New Delhi has combined the military deterrent strategy in dealing with cross-border terrorism, it has worked consistently in the bilateral, plurilateral, and multilateral fora to institutionalise the response mechanisms. Most recently this approach was evident under her Presidency of the BRICS in 2021, when it was instrumental in developing an effective CT-strategy for the BRICS and accepted by all members. Likewise, this was clearly evident in the strongest condemnation of Pahalgam attacks at the BRICS RIO Summit 2025. PM Modi declared that "Condemning terrorism must be a principle, not a matter of convenience".

Grey Zone Warfare: A Sino-Pak Axis Advantage

While India excelled in the military campaign and political resolve to fight terror and sponsors of terrorism, most observers believed that Pakistan was able to, at least initially, score better in the game of narratives. Its "first lie" advantage and spreading of canards were lapped up by the western media where for years it has assiduously planted its assets and think tanks who rose to the occasion in supporting and widening the fake narratives. It completely denied the very existence of TRF, which had initially claimed responsibility for the Pahalgam attacks, but under the advice of its masters in Rawalpindi and LeT it backtracked. Eventually, they were exposed and the Americans also listed them as terror entity and so did China. Pakistani ISPR also based its arguments that India had made baseless accusations without any evidence or investigations into the attacks playing innocent. It completely dismissed its historic role as a proven terror-supporting and funding state. But it all became clear when Pakistani leaders like Khwaja Asif and Ishaq Dar and scores of others started lamenting the fact that they had become a crucible and haven of terrorism, extremism, and radicalisation, and surrogate of terrorists for the Western countries, especially the USA, basically to play the victim card to garner sympathy and support. This worked to some extent but exposed them beyond any doubt and question as a state sponsor of cross-border terrorism.

USA is a country run by lobbies. Pakistan has been quite adept at it. I recall even in 1990s they had employed several PR firms to work on the Kashmir issue and create mis-perception on the Capitol and the media as well as think tanks. The strategic trend continues. This time round also, as soon as President Trump was declared victorious the second time in the US Presidential elections, a spree of hiring PR firms continued that were supposedly closer to Trump. Jason Miller was hired by India in the wake of Pahalgam attacks;[31] later two other PR and lobbying firms were hired. Miller was hired to provide "strategic counsel, tactical planning", traditional lobbying services, and perception management.[32] Pakistan was a step ahead as two other former Trump aides signed an agreement with the Pakistani government. Keith Schiller, Trump's former bodyguard, and Georges Sorel, former compliance chief at the Trump Organisation, registered through their firm Javelin Advisors to help Pakistan build "long-term economic partnerships" in the US by strengthening ties with the American government, the report added. On 6 May, there was a dramatic surge and hashtag volume reached the highest level in the observed period. The increase in social chatter coincided with India's retaliatory strike on Pakistan and the viral amplification of false flag claims by high-profile influencers like Jackson Hinkle.[33]

We have seen the result of India's consistent diplomatic efforts when the US State Department designated the Pak-based terror group responsible for Pahalgam—TRF—as a Foreign Terrorist Organisation, and a Specially Designated Global Terrorist. This indeed is a diplomatic victory. Even Pakistan accepted it after the US designation of TRF, and China too removed its technical hold at the UNSC. All this happened even as Pakistan remains not only the non-permanent member of the UNSC or Chair or Vice Chair of the counter terrorism committees but also was its Chair of UNSC for the month. Indian diplomatic outreach placed limitations on Pakistani designs to a great extent even as it continued to benefit from the Trumpian affection.

Post Operation Sindoor

Indian government decided to send multi-party and multi-faith parliamentary delegations to nearly three dozen important countries to convey the correct message to the target audience. They did a good job of effectively projecting India's cause and concerns in a united and distinguished manner to the leaders, parliamentarians, think tank groups, opinion makers and the Indian diaspora. In several cases they were able to correct the skewed perspectives created due to geo-politics or fake narratives by Pakistan and Sino-Pak axis. A government Press release mentioned the objectives as "In the context of Operation Sindoor and India's continued fight against cross-border terrorism, seven All-Party Delegations are set to visit key partner countries, including members of the UN Security Council later this month (May and June). The All-Party Delegations will project India's national consensus and resolute approach to combating terrorism in all forms and manifestations. They would carry forth to the world the country's strong message of zero-tolerance against terrorism".[34]

Comprising MPs across party lines, renowned diplomats, and former ministers, each delegation was tasked with reinforcing India's diplomatic stance globally. Of the 51 political leaders, 31 were part of the NDA and 20 from the opposition parties. While tweeting about the details of the delegation, Parliamentary Affairs Minister claimed, "One Message, One Mission, One Bharat" as the motto of India expressing unique solidarity in adversity. That is what precisely the delegates did across geographies and with important partners and a majority of current members of the UNSC, with the exception of Pakistan and Somalia whose stance and complicity were evident.

Congress MP Baijayant Panda led Group 1 visiting Saudi Arabia, Kuwait, Bahrain, and Algeria. The members who accompanied him were Nishikant Dubey (BJP), Phangnon Konyak (BJP), Rekha Sharma (BJP), Asaduddin Owaisi (AIMIM), Satnam Singh Sandhu, Ghulam Nabi Azad and Ambassador Harsh Vardhan Shringla.

Ravi Shankar Prasad headed the Group 2 to the UK, France, Germany, the EU, Italy, and Denmark. This group included Dr Daggubati Purandeswari (TDP), Priyanka Chaturvedi (Shiv Sena, UBT), Ghulam Ali Khatana, Dr Amar Singh (INC), Samik Bhattacharya (BJP), M.J. Akbar, and Ambassador Pankaj Saran.

Group 3 was led by JDU's Sanjay Kumar Jha to Indonesia, Malaysia, Republic of Korea, Japan, and Singapore. The members of this group were Aparajita Sarangi (BJP), Yusuf Pathan (AITC), Brij Lal (BJP), Dr John Brittas (CPI M), Pradhan Baruah (BJP), Dr Hemang Joshi (BJP), Salman Khurshid and Ambassador Mohan Kumar.

Shrikant Shinde led Group 4 to UAE, Liberia, Democratic Republic of Congo, and Sierra Leone. The members were

Bansuri Swaraj (BJP), E.T. Mohammed Basheer (IUML), Atul Garg (BJP), Dr Sasmit Patra (BJD), Manan Kumar Mishra (BJP), S.S. Ahluwalia, and Ambassador Sujan Chinoy.

Shashi Tharoor steered Group 5 to the United States, Panama, Guyana, Colombia, and Brazil. The members of this group were Shambhavi Choudhary (LJP Ram Vilas), Dr Sarfaraz Ahmad (JMM), GM Harish Balayogi (TDP), Shashank Mani Tripathi (BJP), Bhubaneswar Kalita (BJP), Milind Murli Deora (Shiv Sena), Ambassador Taranjit Singh Sandhu, and Tejasvi Surya (BJP).

DMK's Kanimozhi was the head of Group 6 to Spain, Greece, Russia, Slovenia, and Latvia. The members were Rajeev Rai (SP), Mian Altaf Ahmad (NC), Capt. Brijesh Chowta (BJP), Prem Chand Gupta (RJD), Dr Ashok Kumar Mittal (AAP), Ambassador Manjeev S. Puri, and Ambassador Jawed Ashraf.

NCP MP Supriya Sule led Group 7 visiting Egypt, Qatar, Ethiopia, and South Africa. The members were Rajiv Pratap Rudy (BJP), Vikramjeet Singh Sahney (AAP), Manish Tewari (INC), Anurag Singh Thakur (BJP), Lavu Sri Krishna Devarayalu (TDP), Anand Sharma, V Muraleedharan, and Ambassador Syed Akbaruddin.

Prior to their departure, they were briefed by Lt Gen Rajiv Ghai (DGMO, Army), Air Marshal A.K. Bharti (DGAO, Air Force), Vice Admiral A.N. Pramod (DGNO, Navy), Maj Gen S.S. Sharda (Army), Foreign Secretary MEA Vikram Misri, and Commodore Raghu R Nair, Colonel Sofiya Qureshi, and Wing Commander Vyomika Singh.

Shashi Tharoor, Chairman of the External Affairs Committee of the Parliament, led the delegation to several Latin American and Caribbean countries as well as to the USA which had become a unique challenge in the wake of Pahalgam and Operation Sindoor, with President Donald Trump continuing to claim the credit for the ceasefire much against the Indian stance that the ceasefire happened at the level of DGMOs and on the request of the Pakistani side. In fact, the re-hyphenation of India and Pakistan and internationalisation of the Kashmir issue, let alone the claimed mediation are an anathema to the Indian diplomacy. Hence, the task in the USA was indeed not easy. Besides, the Sino-Pak axis and lobbies worked overtime against India, let alone their own leaders and Parliamentary delegations virtually chasing the Indian Parliamentary delegations to reinforce their fake narrative. Tharoor on return mentioned, "In my private conversations in Washington, when I asked people bluntly why USA was still allowing Pakistan to get away with providing a safe haven to terrorist organisations, I was pointed to Pakistan's alleged cooperation with the US on counter-terrorism operations, notably the recent surrender of the individual allegedly responsible for the Abbey gate bombing that had killed 23 US marines at Kabul airport". He, however, added while briefing the US media on 6 June, that "We got tremendous amount of support and sympathy, some more in private than in public, some also openly expressed".

This unprecedented outreach demonstrated bipartisan resolve and India's commitment to global anti-terror cooperation after Operation Sindoor. However, some observers felt whether it would not have been better to dispatch the special envoys and parliamentary groups in the aftermath of the Pahalgam Attacks rather than after Op Sindoor as this provided the Sino-Pak axis an advantage, not only to prepare militarily but also to prepare and pedal its own narratives across major countries garnering support and blunting the legitimacy of Indian military response. In the end, the winner takes it all and India won convincingly even if Pakistanis claimed on paper to have won by promoting General Asim Munir to the rank of Field Marshal. Army Chief General Upendra Dwivedi (COAS) concluded, "It is important that how a small name Operation Sindoor connects the whole nation... That is something which galvanised the whole nation... That is the reason the whole nation was saying why have you stopped? That question was being asked and it has been amply answered".[35]

EAM Dr Jaishankar laid down the contours of Indian policy going forward in his statement at the Lok Sabha. The challenge of cross-border terrorism continues but Operation Sindoor marks a new phase. There is now a new normal. The new normal has five points:

- One, terrorists will not be treated as proxies.
- Two, cross-border terrorism will get an appropriate response.
- Three, terror and talks are not possible together. There will only be talks on terror.
- Four, not yielding to nuclear blackmail.
- And finally, terror and good neighbourliness cannot coexist. Blood and water cannot flow together.

The Battle in the Information Domain: Strategic Communication

Lt Gen Shokin Chauhan has constructed a quick analysis of the Pakistan disinformation campaign and Indian reticence which is worth a read and consideration for ameliorating the gaps and shortcomings in Indian strategic communication networks. From terming Pahalgam as a false-flag operation, he underscores that "within hours of the Pahalgam massacre, even before India had formulated its response, Pakistan's strategic communication machinery was already in motion. This wasn't reactive damage control, it was pre-emptive narrative warfare executed with military precision". He further adds that within 48 hours of the Pahalgam attack, three Pakistani cabinet ministers, Ishaq Dar, Khawaja Asif, and Attaullah Tarar, along with PPP chief Bilawal Bhutto, had conducted over 25 interviews across major Western outlets including BBC, CNN, and *Al Jazeera*. Their message was carefully crafted and relentlessly consistent: "The root cause is

Kashmir, not terrorism". In the wake of Operation Sindoor on 7 May, Pakistan's Inter-Services Public Relations (ISPR) was ready with what can only be described as an information blitzkrieg. Their five-phase disinformation campaign unfolded with the precision of a military operation, each phase designed to dominate different aspects of the information landscape with their fake narratives, be it the downing of Indian fighter aircraft, emotional manipulation through fake videos on humanitarian impact, using western powerful think tanks like the Atlantic Council or RUSI and media, with well entrenched Pakistani or pro-Pakistan western commentators and the fullest use of the AI and thousands of chatbots to create narratives and hashtags like #India lies. It also played the underdog advantage to the hilt.

Gen Chauhan also calls out the Indian strategic silence during the sixteen days which would have cost us greatly in the fight against Pakistani fake narratives, as India's global communication strategy was virtually non-existent. During this critical period, 75% of Indian embassies in G20 nations, including the United States, the United Kingdom, and Germany, issued no statements or held media briefings about the terrorist attack or the mounting evidence of Pakistani involvement. The Ministry of External Affairs' social media presence during this time was almost surreal in its disconnection from reality.[36]

Despite these observations one will have to concede that for the first time India's factual and powerful presentation of facts with evidence of damages during the Op Sindoor was quite convincing and revealing. Selection of Foreign Secretary Vikram Misri as the Chief Spokesperson along with two female military officers Col Sofiya Qureshi and Wg Cdr Vyomika Singh was indeed a brilliant move given the causal connection and meaning of Operation Sindoor (vermilion that Hindu married women adorn in their hair parting as a symbol). Subsequently, the initial perceptional gains by Pakistan in the information warfare were neutralised. It may also be necessary to understand that countries' positions are driven by their own geo-political and geo-economic considerations. In India's case it is also a fact that a large number of major players prefer to stunt India's exceptional growth and story of growing influence by any means. Hence smart and agile diplomacy is the answer with our strategic and multi-alignment policies.

But this cannot be a one-off event and exercise since working on the constituency abroad and expanding it through novel communication and credible strategies and content is an ongoing process. We also need to identify, and accordingly strategise, whether we are targeting the domestic audience or the international clientele or both? It appeared that this time round we were more focused on domestic audience which had the desired result of the whole nation standing united except some opposition politicians and parties, while we could not achieve the same effect in the international fora.

It is an imperative that we craft a proactive strategic communication strategy and institution or Directorate with military-diplomacy at its core. Time has come to combine and synergise the strengths of Ministry of External Affairs. Ministry of Defence, and Indian Military organisations tasked to communicate in a focused and proactive manner even as often it becomes necessary to react to situations in the diplomatic an information domain. This domain of warfare cannot be left to chance with a committee-cum-coordination approach; it needs specialists, an institutional framework, mandates for implementation, and a suitable budget, none of which has been put in place today. Social and new age media requires strategic manipulation and outreach. It is already too late to dispense with the silo-driven approach. Information is knowledge and should be used in a razor sharp and consistent manner deploying all available means. Going forward, India, as it grows in economic and diplomatic international stature, will face increasing challenges and headwinds not only from enemies and adversaries but also from friends and frenemies.

Indian diplomatic missions must be geared up to create local constituencies in the influential media, think tanks, universities, parliamentarians, military communities, and the youth in general. It would be good to study the Chinese and US models, in this art of Gey Zone Warfare, which they have mastered.

Speaking in Lok Sabha (Lower House) of the Indian Parliament, during the debate on Operation Sindoor on 28 July, Indian External Affairs Minister Dr S Jaishankar clearly outlined the diplomatic outreach and objectives stating that the focus for our diplomacy was understandably the UN Security Council, and "Hon'ble Speaker Sir, the challenge for us was that at this particular point, Pakistan is a member of the Security Council, we are not. So we had to achieve our objectives in a Security Council where Pakistan is a member. Now, our goals in the Security Council were two: one, to get an endorsement from the Security Council on the need of accountability; and two, to bring to justice, those who perpetrated this attack. And I am glad to say, Speaker Sir, and I hope that this is appreciated and recognised by the House, if you look at the Security Council statement of 25 April, the members of the Security Council condemned in the strongest terms the terrorist attack, they affirmed terrorism in all its forms and manifestations constitutes one of the most serious threats on international peace and security, and most important, the Council underlined the need to hold the perpetrators, organisers, financers and sponsors of this reprehensible act of terrorism accountable and bring them to justice". This provided India the international support for the action it took. He further underscored "when many Hon'ble members asked today 'where was the world on Pahalgam', I think the answer is there. The answer is there in a Security Council statement, which says 'hold them accountable, bring them to justice', and that is exactly what we did through Operation Sindoor".[37]

Military Diplomacy is the Need of the Hour

Military Diplomacy or Defence Diplomacy may sound like an oxymoron to many but it is intrinsically embedded in the comprehensive power strategy of any country that wishes to be a regional or a global player. Peacekeeping and deterrence, and Humanitarian and Disaster Relief (HADR) are some of the reflections of the soft power along with hard power projection and that too for a cause especially for rendering humanitarian assistance and help achieve peace. All these activities have been successfully conducted by Indian military and diplomatic establishment for over seven decades since the times of the Korean crisis in 1953. HADR operations and ensuring security of the maritime lanes and fight against piracy apart from being part of the largest peacekeeping operations across major conflict zones have garnered India with a distinct honour and prestige.

Humanitarian and Disaster Relief (HADR) has been a real forte for India's military diplomacy as it has emerged as a saviour and net security provider for a large number of countries through the policy of "Vasudhaiv Kutumbakam" (The world is one family). The role of Indian forces is critical, be it the evacuations from conflict or pandemic-ridden zones of Indians and foreigners alike or for that matter providing maritime security for the commercial shipping against the piracy, terrorism, and interventions by non-state actors. The most recent example has been the way Indian Navy has kept the Sea Lanes of Communications (SLOCS) open under the unremitting Houthi attacks in the Red Sea and even the Indian Ocean trying to disrupt the maritime trade and navigation. Likewise, providing humanitarian assistance in the wake of man-made or natural disasters in time has become the Indian foreign and security diplomacy, and consequently military diplomacy's hallmark in recent decades, from Nepal to Türkiye from our neighbourhood to Africa and Latin America.

India has excelled in peacekeeping operations being part of the largest number of UN deployments in several peacekeeping missions across geographies and conflict zones. It has acquitted itself honourably. I recall meeting President Ellen Johnson Sirleaf of Liberia who was so full of praise for the Indian female contingent and their role in her country. Eventually this dimension of our diplomacy has become one of the key arguments substantiating India's claims for a permanent seat of the reformed UNSC, an Organisation whose founding member was India among few others and has remained committed to its centrality and UN Charter in conflict resolution but urges for reforms lest it is consigned to irrelevance. Hence, here again one witnesses the congruences of military diplomacy. The positive impact of these contributions needs to be capitalised upon, in an institutional manner, that correctly harmonises military diplomacy with the nations' objectives in International Relations.

One of the most successful examples of military-diplomacy has been the firm dealing with China after the Galwan 2020. While stationing our forces in an eyeball to eyeball position with continued building of the commensurate infrastructure on the border in the last five years may have deterred the Chinese from further escalation, the real success lay in diplomatic and military consultations through the established mechanisms of the Working Mechanism for Consultation & Coordination on India-China Border Affairs (WMCC) and Commander-level talks. Incidentally the 34th meeting of WMCC was held on 23 July 2025, a few days before PM Modi's visit to China to attend the 25th SCO Summit in Tianjin. Dialogue and diplomacy and deterrence remained the key tools for achieving the desired objectives as the political leadership from PM to EAM to Raksha Mantri (RM) to NSA remained engaged with their Chinese counterparts confirming that cooperation and competition can be pursued firmly without conflict. No doubt China will remain a major challenge for us in all geographies; hence it is important to upgrade the mechanisms to counter any eventuality while securing peace for development of the country.

I was posted in Bangladesh in the mid-1980s during an anti-India regime of General Ershad and witnessed something unique. On one fine day we started getting the news of state-managed riots against Hindus and that the famous Dhakeshwari temple in Dhaka was vandalised and defiled by the miscreants. Frantic calls kept coming in and many of the Hindu leaders also rushed for help. While the High Commission was mulling over the responses, the news arrived that the Indian Forces (IPKF) had landed in Jafna, Sri Lanka. This news in itself had a deterring and salutary impact as the government machinery doubled up to contain the riots in less than two hours. Fear crept in and served the purpose. President Ershad also sent his special envoy to the then Prime Minister assuring India. While the story of the success of IPKF in Sri Lanka has a lot of commentary, the unintended consequences in a third country were seminal.

More importantly, a robust communication strategy with military diplomacy and techno-economic inputs will have to be devised to counter the Grey Zone Warfare tactics and cyber threats of our adversaries and friends alike, which should be possible with new technologies like AI and quantum computing and analysis becoming available. A constant review is needed to create timely and profound and credible narratives in national and international discourse. Perhaps the Government may consider regular briefings of the largely retired diplomats and defence personnel jointly by Defence Ministry and External Affairs who can be good and reliable interlocutors if they have the line and facts at their disposal.

It is imperative to not only do a SWOT analysis of the structural elements of military diplomacy but also improve the coordination among various branches and forces to create an integrated strategy of congruences and synergies. For the military it should be easier with the institution of the Chief of Defence

Staff (CDS). Fortunately, in developing strategic partnerships with various countries, defence, security, and technological cooperation have become important drivers and must be specifically and vigorously pursued. "Make in India" in defence sector and exports have become a priority for which military diplomacy can play an important role. India has instituted 2+2 dialogue at the level of RM and EAM with various important countries. This should percolate down to the grassroots level to cut through the siloes between defence forces, bureaucracy, and diplomats to effectively execute the defence or military diplomacy for national security and country's interests in a fast-changing and often disorderly world where conflicts and hotspots are aplenty impacting on our own wellbeing. A whole of government approach will be a force multiplier.[38]

India's Proactive Re-Assertion Post Operation Sindoor

The most significant outcome of Operation Sindoor may be that deterrence is no longer episodic in India's strategic playbook—it is institutionalised. Each major Indian operation since 2016 has built upon the credibility of the previous one, creating a trajectory that few can ignore. This layered deterrence is difficult to dismantle. It rests not only on the military's demonstrated capability to strike, but also on political will, diplomatic acumen, and economic leverage. Unlike in earlier decades, India is no longer content to absorb the costs of terrorism quietly. It has created a system of consequences that can be activated and scaled at will.[39]

One of the biggest force multipliers that India has, compared to any other country, is its highly successful over 35 million diaspora which is politically savvy and economically robust. Although PM Modi has recharged the "Diaspora Diplomacy", Indian strategy must factor their strength at all times and not sporadically to harness the advantage for building bridges and dispelling the fake narratives among the elites and the common people alike while harnessing their expertise in other areas of economy and polity.

But going forward, as the "New Normal" and "Op Sindoor" remain in force, several factors and trends in our policies and actions will have to be analysed and calibrated for maximum impact. Using Indus Waters Treaty as a leverage is no doubt a diplomatic master stroke but its implementation will have to contend with the humanitarian crisis angle that Pakistan will project to the international community and Arbitration bodies, especially the one supplemental award (27 June) by the Court of Arbitration, which India does not recognise and has dismissed. Ignoring and dispensing those judgments away will require an increased diplomatic heft and engagement which might militate against the broader brush of our "Vasudhaiv Kutumbakam" policy. Moreover, Sino-Pak axis has already begun to play as Beijing has made a veiled threat stating that India is also a lower riparian state with regard to China especially with regard to Brahmaputra River. Already the Chinese PM Li Quiang announced the start of the construction of the largest hydropower project on the lower reaches of the Yarlung Zangbo (Brahmaputra) river (CGTN 19/21 July) with an investment of over $168 bn. This would bring a new dynamic and twist into the water bomb or hydro-diplomacy even if for India it may not be the most decisive and impactful development.

While domestic constituency is extremely important and our foreign policy is also a reflection of the domestic situation and policies, the international actors and audiences are also equally important for which a reliant, responsible, and resilient Public Diplomacy will have to be charted. For this, it is compulsory that a comprehensive robust communication strategy and network be established, deployed, and harnessed forthwith with sufficient funding and with a vertical driving structure and horizontal and three-dimensional outreach. Think tanks, media, opinion makers, right kind of lobbies, and the Indian diaspora with all available digital tools and communication mediums will have to be integrated in it. Track 1.5 and Track 2.0 diplomacy with important partners has to be a regular affair rather than sporadic happenings. We also need to be clear about what we are aiming at and what kind of credible facts and evidences are being presented to beef up support for our stance.

Time has come for the military-diplomacy to be fused properly and appropriately not only to complement the targets of comprehensive power but for meeting the exigencies of narrative building on almost daily and 24×7 basis. It will be extremely useful to create a standing group of former diplomats and defence attaches in a regional and sub-regional matrix to assist the government throughout. Likewise, for the narrative building it is essential that a monthly briefing of various experts, mostly former diplomats and retired military officers frequently seen on the TV channels, is done. Other media organs that are often seen, by the ordinary people, as representing the government view could be also be jointly briefed on a monthly basis by the Ministry of External Affairs and the Ministry of Defence at a reasonably higher level, on key issues, concerns, and government responses and policies on those issues. This will help create a consistent narrative both domestically and internationally.

Another area that government could give serious attention to is to appoint special envoys with domain expertise and extensive contacts in designated geographies and countries. Their job would be to carry the messages from the Indian leadership and indulge in shuttle diplomacy and bridge-building in an agile and credible manner in close concert with respective Indian Ambassadors, and keep the Government apprised and warned of the developments and potential developments well in time in a proactive manner. The Government will also have to be open-minded and ready to use their expertise and inputs in a constructive manner. Course correction in diplomacy can be a game changer at times.

Since creating constituencies across geographies is a prerequisite, it is important that our ambassadors remain in constant touch with the local influential people with an India connect and not only on

National or Indian Technical and Economic Cooperation (ITEC) days. The political officer in the mission should be the designated officer and entrusted with the task to keep it going. We annually train thousands of foreigners in government and across their social spectrum from over 160 developing countries from Asia, Africa, Latin America, and Europe under the Indian Technical and Economic Cooperation (ITEC) Programme of the Ministry of External Affairs, and other programmes for capacity building and infrastructural development; many of them even rise to become leaders and Heads of State of their countries; their affection for India could provide a significant advantage in our diplomatic engagement, even better than certain lobby groups and PR agencies we hire in certain countries where that is a standard practice and requirement, like in the USA and various western countries.

The same should apply to our defence cooperation. Understandably, our Military Attaches and officers are forbidden to maintain contacts with their counterparts or friends during the course of their duty abroad or their training in Indian military institutions, thereby losing a significant leverage. It is imperative that an institutionalised architecture with sufficient firewalls be created to remain in regular contact with the alumni and frequent exchanges and modalities can be devised.

Often in foreign policy, the strategic and comprehensive strategic partnerships are expected to work for mutual advantages and deliver a clear message of solidarity during the crisis situations. However, even though most countries condemned the terror attacks on Pahalgam, most of them wanted the two sides to exercise restraint and not escalate the situation. On the other hand, Pakistani friends like China, Türkiye, and Azerbaijan openly and covertly cast their might with Islamabad raising some questions whether strategic autonomy was the most optimal strategy in view of India's own stance of propagating dialogue, diplomacy, and respect of UN Charter and that this is not an era of war which appears to have been dished out to us by our close partners too.

This requires a deep analysis and country-specific strategic and diplomatic war gaming scenario, as we will have to face similar situations over and over again. This highlights the intricate challenges India faces in navigating foreign policy within a highly contested and fragmented information environment.

Although we have junked the nuclear bogey and blackmail of Pakistan, given the persistent threats from several nuclear fronts and to maintain requisite deterrence, perhaps time has come for India to revisit its "No First use" doctrine as many others have done.

As far as terrorism and India's decisive response are concerned, we should not be seeking any validation or approval from anyone since it is our battle but we are informing them to highlight the source of this scourge and that this is a global problem and does require global solidarity rather than selective approaches. The world may remember the words attributed to President Putin "To forgive the terrorists is up to the God but to send them to him is up to me".

How shall we convince the world that *Shathe Shathyam Samacharet* (Reciprocity of action in the Newtonian style) is the most effective weapon against the scoundrel and vicious groups and terror-sponsoring countries. Unless our power differential becomes decisive, this will remain a goalpost and a challenge. Let us not forget the old dictum, "Keep your friends close, but your adversaries closer".

Notes

1. Media Centre, Ministry of External Affairs, GOI, 24 April 2025, Decision regarding Visas of Pakistani nationals. https://www.mea.gov.in/press-releases.htm?dtl/39445/decision+regarding+visas+of+pakistani+nationals
2. *Hindustan Times*, 25 April 2025, India's 7 big decisions against Pakistan in 2 days after Pahalgam terror attack. https://www.hindustantimes.com/india-news/pahalgam-terror-attack-in-2-days-7-big-decisions-by-india-against-pakistan-101745539292065.html
3. *The Economic Times*, 25 June 2025, We are ready to talk with India on all issues ... https://economictimes.indiatimes.com/news/india/we-are-ready-to-talk-with-india-on-all-issues-pakistan-pm-shehbaz-sharif-tells-saudi-price-salman/articleshow/122066954.cms?from=mdr
4. Manoj Gupta, News18, 25 June 2025, Strategic Snub? China's Muted SCO Response Reveals Pakistan's Waning Influence, Fractured Alliances. https://www.news18.com/world/strategic-snub-chinas-muted-sco-response-reveals-pakistans-waning-influence-fractured-alliances-ws-bkl-9402761.html
5. The White House, 13 February 2025, United States-India Joint Leaders' Statement. https://www.whitehouse.gov/briefings-statements/2025/02/united-states-india-joint-leaders-statement/
6. U.S. Department of State, 8 May 2025, Secretary Rubio's Call with Pakistani Prime Minister Sharif. https://www.state.gov/releases/office-of-the-spokesperson/2025/05/secretary-rubios-call-with-pakistani-prime-minister-sharif-2/
7. U.S. Department of State, 8 May 2025, Secretary Rubio's Call with Indian External Affairs Minister Jaishankar. https://www.state.gov/secretary-rubios-call-with-indian-external-affairs-minister-jaishankar-3/
8. *First Post*, 15 July 2025, 'India, Pakistan were going to nuclear war in a week': Trump claims success in 'settling' military conflicts. https://www.firstpost.com/world/india-pakistan-were-going-to-nuclear-war-in-a-week-trump-claims-success-in-settling-military-conflicts-13906923.html

9. U.S. Department of State, 17 July 2025, Terrorist Designation of The Resistance Front. https://www.state.gov/releases/office-of-the-spokesperson/2025/07/terrorist-designation-of-the-resistance-front/?utm_source=homepage&utm_medium=hero&utm_campaign=trf
10. President of Russia, 22 April 2025, Condolences to President of India Droupadi Murmu and Prime Minister of India Narendra Modi. http://en.kremlin.ru/events/president/news/76780
11. President of Russia, 5 May 2025, Telephone conversation with Prime Minister of India Narendra Modi. http://en.kremlin.ru/events/president/news/76841
12. India's World, 1 May 2025, Global Response to the Pahalgam Attack: From Sympathy to Strategy. https://indiasworld.in/global-response-to-the-pahalgam-attack-from-sympathy-to-strategy/
13. News 18, 24 June 2025, Modi's Realpolitik in A Fragmented World Order. https://www.news18.com/opinion/modis-realpolitik-in-a-fragmented-world-order-9402067.html
14. *India Today*, 4 July 2025, China gave Pak live inputs on our vectors during Op Sindoor: Top Army general. https://www.indiatoday.in/india/story/operation-sindoor-china-pakistan-updates-important-vectors-india-dgmo-talks-deputy-chief-of-army-staff-rahul-singh-2750708-2025-07-04
15. Devika Makkat, 2025, 'Between Words and Weapons: Europe and the India–Pakistan Flashpoint', *Operation Sindoor and India's New Doctrine of Deterrence*, Lt Gen D S Hooda and Dr Happyman Jacob (eds), (New Delhi: Council for Strategic and Defence Research)
16. Rahul Singh, 14 June 2025, *The Wire*, Operation Sindoor: Realities, Rhetoric, Responses and After-Effects. https://thewire.in/diplomacy/operation-sindoor-realities-rhetorics-responses-and-after-effects
17. *The Economic Times*, 27 Jume 2025, Defence Minister Rajnath Singh briefs counterparts from ... https://economictimes.indiatimes.com/news/defence/rajnath-singh-briefs-counterparts-from-tajikistan-belarus-kazakhstan-on-pahalgam-terror-attack-op-sindoor/articleshow/122114768.cms
18. Media Center, MEA, Govt of India, 6 July 2025, Rio de Janeiro

Declaration-Strengthening Global South Cooperation for a More Inclusive and Sustainable Governance. https://www.mea.gov.in/bilateral-documents.htm?dtl/39770/

19. U.S. Department of State, 9 May 2025, G7 Foreign Ministers' Statement on India and Pakistan. https://www.state.gov/releases/office-of-the-spokesperson/2025/05/g7-foreign-ministers-statement-on-india-and-pakistan/
20. Defence.In, 1 July 2025, Operation Sindoor authorised under UNSC statement demanding action against Pahalgam terrorists: Jaishankar. https://defence.in/threads/operation-sindoor-authorised-under-unsc-statement-demanding-action-against-pahalgam-terrorists-jaishankar.14734/
21. Money Control, 30 June 2025, Imperative to call out terrorism publicly when it is supported by state: Jaishankar at inauguration of 'The Human Cost of Terrorism' exhibition at UN. https://www.moneycontrol.com/news/india/imperative-to-call-out-terrorism-publicly-when-it-is-supported-by-state-jaishankar-at-inauguration-of-the-human-cost-of-terrorism-exhibition-at-un-13207795.html
22. Media Center, MEA, Govt of India, 7 May 2025, Statement by Foreign Secretary: OPERATION SINDOOR. https://www.mea.gov.in/Speeches-Statements.htm?dtl/39473/
23. Ajay Bisaria, 2025, Will India's 'Integrated Deterrence' Stem Cross-Border Terror? *Operation Sindoor and India's New Doctrine of Deterrence*, Lt Gen D S Hooda and Dr Happyman Jacob (eds), (New Delhi: Council for Strategic and Defence Research)
24. Media Center, MEA, Govt of India, 28 July 2025, Statement by EAM Dr. S. Jaishankar on the special discussion in Lok Sabha on Operation Sindoor. https://www.mea.gov.in/Speeches-Statements.htm?dtl/39883/
25. Dr Chemmalar Patcheappan, 31 July 2025, NatStrat, Operation Sindoor – Assessing India's Doctrine of 'Terrorism as an Act of War' – Part II. https://www.natstrat.org/articledetail/publications/operation-sindoor-assessing-india-s-doctrine-of-terrorism-as-an-act-of-war-part-ii-217.html

26. Lt Gen. AB Shivane, 10 July 2025, *First Post*, India's West Asia re-alignment: Strategic partnership or message to Turkey? https://www.firstpost.com/opinion/indias-west-asia-re-alignment-strategic-partnership-or-message-to-turkey-13904841.html
27. NDTV, 12 May 2025, Read Full Text of PM Modi's First Address to Nation After Op Sindoor. https://www.ndtv.com/india-news/read-full-text-of-prime-minister-narendra-modi-first-address-to-nation-after-operation-sindoor-india-pakistan-jammu-and-kashmir-pahalgam-terror-attack-8396956
28. Himanshu Mishra, 26 April 2025, *India Today*, India forms 3-step plan on Indus water to stop flow to Pakistan. https://www.indiatoday.in/india/story/india-pakistan-indus-waters-treaty-suspension-government-3-step-plan-stop-water-increase-dam-capacity-pahalgam-attack-2715229-2025-04-25
29. Zee News, 31 July 2025, India announces mega hydro project in J&K after Indus Treat Suspension. https://zeenews.india.com/india/india-announces-mega-hydro-project-in-jk-after-indus-treaty-suspension-2939473.html
30. Ajay Kumar, 5 September 2025, *Financial Express*, India changed its strategy after Balakot, increased aerial attack system: CDS Chauhan on Op Sindoor – Video https://www.financialexpress.com/india-news/india-changed-its-strategy-after-balakot-increase-aerial-attack-system-cds-anil-chauhan-on-op-sindoor-video/3968057/
31. *First Post*, 28 May 2025, Who are the US lobbyists, close to Trump, hired by India & Pakistan amid tensions? https://www.firstpost.com/explainers/us-lobbyists-jason-miller-keith-schiller-donald-trump-aides-india-pakistan-tensions-13892425.html
32. Priyanjali Narayan, 22 May 2025, *India Today*, Who's Jason Miller, India's high-profile lobbyist in DC, and can he turn the tide? https://www.indiatoday.in/world/us-news/story/who-is-jason-miller-india-lobbyist-washington-dc-trump-campaign-pakistan-keith-schiller-pahalgam-terror-attack-war-2728779-2025-05-22
33. NCRI, 2025, https://networkcontagion.us/wp-content/uploads/Inside-a-Pakistani-network-promoting-false-flag-conspiracies-about-Pahalgam-terrorist-attack.pdf

34. Ministry of Parliamentary Affairs, 17 May 2025, All-party delegations to carry forth to the world India's strong message of zero-tolerance against terrorism. https://www.pib.gov.in/PressReleasePage.aspx?PRID=2129254

35. *Hindustan Times*, 10 August 2025, Day after Pahalgam, Rajnath said 'enough is enough', forces given free hand: Army chief on Op Sindoor.

36. Shokin Chauhan, 26 June 2025, Substack.com, Winning Hearts and Minds: How Pakistan Mastered the Art of Information Warfare During Operation Sindoor. https://substack.com/inbox/post/166891873?utm_campaign=post&showWelcomeOnShare=true

37. Media Center, MEA, Govt of India, 28 July 2025, Statement by EAM Dr. S. Jaishankar on the special discussion in Lok Sabha on Operation Sindoor. https://www.mea.gov.in/Speeches-Statements.htm?dtl/39883/

38. Anil Trigunayat, 15 January 2025, NDTV, Opinion | India-China Is Why 'Military Diplomacy' Works. https://www.ndtv.com/opinion/india-should-take-its-military-diplomacy-more-seriously-7477368

39. Ajay Bisaria, 2025, Will India's 'Integrated Deterrence' Stem Cross-Border Terror? *Operation Sindoor and India's New Doctrine of Deterrence*, Lt Gen D S Hooda and Dr Happyman Jacob (eds), (New Delhi: Council for Strategic and Defence Research)

7

Implications on India's Security Calculus

MAJOR GENERAL BIPIN BAKSHI

They have sown the wind, and so they shall reap the whirlwind.

—Air Marshal Sir Arthur Harris, 1940[1]

Op Sindoor is being closely studied by security specialists to analyse emerging trends, not only on the conduct of operations on the battlefield, but also for the nature of armed conflicts that a nation needs to prepare for, in the rapidly evolving global security environment. Conflict is as old as mankind itself, and the tectonic shifts that are envisaged in the global security order do not carry the portends of a conflict-free future in the coming decades of the 21st century. If anything is to be seen from the last five years, it is only an increasing propensity to apply trans-border kinetic force; Europe, Middle East, and the Indian subcontinent being no exception. Further, there is now an established norm of using focused kinetic force without even a declaration of war, and border violations are no longer so infrequent as before. This is seen as a viable method to achieve political objectives with minimum commitment of forces, reduced collateral damage and lesser cost. The effectiveness of multilateral mechanisms to rein in rogue elements has largely diminished, leading to an increasing number of nations resorting to the use of various kinetic options without any fear of significant international repercussions. However, none of the previous instances has seen two nuclear armed nations in a direct military conflict.

Op Sindoor was the first military exchange in history wherein both sides were in possession of nuclear weapons. This made the geostrategic nuances of escalation infinitely more complex, as all other major powers were observing the exchange with great concern. Many of them had varying perceptions of the issue and they all have a different nature of stakes in the Indian subcontinent.

India is being forced to navigate a rapidly changing geopolitical landscape as evidenced by the Trump–Munir lunch in Washington soon after Op Sindoor and just preceding the bombing of Iran by the USA. This was accompanied by deals in crypto currency and oil, and quickly followed up by another Trump Munir meet, while India has the most significant partnership for the USA as quipped earlier. It is increasingly evident that there is a complex web of divergent, but closely related interests, playing out in the Indian subcontinent and West Asia, with USA, China, and Pakistan unabashedly seeking their own advantages while ignoring India's security concerns.

In the wake of Op Sindoor, our group of authors undertook this project for analysing the myriad aspects of this conflict, looking at specific themes with a view to understand the unfolding of events, escalation dynamics, military technologies utilised, departures, if any, from previous similar operations, and the pointers for the future.

It was not too long ago when the words of our PM, addressed to Putin at Samarkand in September 2022, "this is not the era of war"[2] resonated with nations which propound democratic values and a rules-based international order. However, we must never forget that pragmatism demands that peace can only be achieved if we are simultaneously prepared for war as has been underlined by recent events. The increasing activities of transnational terror groups have altered the circumstances significantly from Samarkand 2022 to Pahalgam 2025, when our PM qualified this statement on 12 May 2025, by the important insert "this is also not the era of terrorism".[3]

"This is certainly not the era of war, but this is also not the era of terrorism. Zero tolerance against terrorism is the guarantee of a better world", PM Modi said on 12 May 2025.

The implications are clear—credibility in a stated policy of punitive deterrence can only be realised by maintaining a strong military force along with a demonstrated willingness to use it. The concept of world peace being ensured on a multilateral format and the larger goals of nuclear disarmament, conventional and nuclear deterrence, on a regional or global level, are all fading memories of the last century. As brought out in Chapter 6, Diplomacy Redefined, the better choice for India is to chart her own path. Further, India is in a neighbourhood where regional trade and regional groupings have not been successful, in contrast with other regions like South East Asia with their ASEAN countries and Europe with their EU members. India thus participates in a wider ranging minilaterals like BRICS, QUAD and RIC, where issue-based cooperation is pursued in areas of common interest, without any overall alliance imposing constraints on its strategic autonomy. This is a period of transition in the global order and India needs to hedge its bets and maintain its independent approach.

Our multiparty delegations visited 33 countries in the wake of Op Sindoor and explained India's position on terrorism in the backdrop of a lack of international action to proscribe state sponsors of terror. With the abject failure of multilateral fora like UN Security Council and Financial Action Task Force (FATF) to put substantial curbs on transnational terror networks, India seeks bilateral and minilateral efforts in this regard.

There is no sense of security being provided by the UN Security Council, when permanent members with veto powers are themselves using kinetic force, based on their own national interests; therefore, India too has a right to take action in support of her own national security. It was explained to the interlocutors whom the delegations met that Pakistan has a long history of using terror as an element of foreign policy and more stringent steps would need to be taken to reel back their terror factories. India's current policy for dealing with this menace for the future was also explained. By and large, the diplomatic outreach to all these nations met with resonance as mentioned by the delegates of our delegations on return.

There is an increasing erosion of trust in the multilateral institutions touted as the panacea to all evils and the guarantor of peace and stability in a so called "rules-based international order". These institutions, set up on the debris of the Second World War, served their purpose for a limited time, but the international environment that prevailed at that time has undergone a dramatic transformation, rendering them ineffective today. In this backdrop, India's outreach to various nations on a bilateral basis or a minilateral format signifies the direction in which its international engagements will proceed in future.

During Op Sindoor, a new range of weapons was used. It was a live demonstration of politico-military and tri-service synergy to execute kinetic, non-contact battle within the conventional domain. Multidomain, well-coordinated, precise actions were launched to inflict significant damage while keeping escalation below the nuclear threshold. We also saw the Indian military arsenal, a mix of Russian, Indian, Israeli, and French equipment, suitably integrated by indigenous innovative technology, pitted against Chinese weaponry and Turkish drones, to good effect. In the geopolitical sphere, there was clear Sino-Pak collusion and support for Pakistan by Türkiye and Azerbaijan, which India was able to counter effectively.

Op Sindoor has reshaped the security paradigm in the region and showcased a new playbook of India's strategy.[4] It forces Pakistan to tread with extreme caution in its "thousand cuts" strategy[5] to bleed India, as it faces not only increased costs for each cut, but an enhanced punishment for such acts in new domains, hitherto not exploited by India. At the same time, it demonstrates a well-calibrated response strategy that takes into account all nuances of escalation dynamics.

Escalation Dynamics and Off-Ramps

While the term "Strategic Restraint" was earlier used to indicate an indefinite elasticity of India's patience, it may be noted that this time too restraint was shown in the selection of targets, avoiding civilian casualties, unlike Pakistan's unrestrained targeting of populated areas. An escalatory matrix was evidently formulated, placing several diplomatic and military actions in between the lower rungs of Kahn's 44-step ladder,[6] explained in the Annexure to this chapter. The terms "escalatory ladder" and "Off Ramps" which were heard often in the discussions during Op Sindoor are borrowed from American writings on the subject. It may be argued that the diplomatic measures, holding the Indus Waters Treaty in abeyance and the restrained action under Op Sindoor were moving only between Level 2 and Level 5 of Kahn's ladder;[7] however, in actual fact significant changes in technology and geopolitics necessitate a newly designed ladder as India has aptly demonstrated. The highly nuanced calibration of weapons used, targets selected, and restraint in crossing the border was a masterclass in escalation control; evidently it was meticulously wargamed and each step anticipated.

It was way back in 1962 that Kahn published a 16-step escalation ladder. By 1965 he had developed this into a 44-step ladder. In terms of this matrix, and the "New Normal" set by India, the response to a terrorist attack in the next instance may begin from Step 3 (Solemn and Formal Declarations) and could very quickly escalate to Steps 9 (Dramatic Military Confrontations) and 10 (Provocative Breaking off of Diplomatic Relations) while Step 12 (Large Conventional War) would be very much on the horizon.[8] However, this formulation caters for only vertical escalation, whereas the changing nature of conflict now provides for horizontal escalation with new domains like cyber, space, and grey zone warfare.

It is a well-accepted fact that Kahn's ladder, which came into prominence in 1965 in the context of USA-USSR nuclear war, is now outdated and needs revision. However, it is still in discussion 60 years after it was enunciated, which lends credit to the scholar and the RAND Corporation for whom he wrote and strategised it. Further, there has never been a military engagement with or without declaration of war between two nuclear armed adversaries; hence, Kahn's theories written at the height of the Cold War between USA and USSR are the only ones at present that cover aspects of an all-out nuclear war with Mutually Assured Destruction.

Immediately after the cessation of hostilities, PM Modi delivered an address to the nation, which was certainly pointed at the world. Terror under nuclear blackmail will not be tolerated, he said. The conviction with which he spoke suggests that Pakistan's nuclear option had been carefully considered, and adequate steps taken to obviate its activation. While avoiding various red lines and restricting collateral damage, nuclear de-fanging of Pakistan must be a factor for the future as well, so that India can repeat the conventional operations response to deter Pakistan's decades-old proxy war, while remaining below the nuclear threshold. The ill-conceived veil of a nuclear shield for protection from conventional response to persistent sub-conventional attacks has been ripped off. There have been feeble attempts to bring back the sceptre of irrationality in their nuclear doctrine with recent pronouncements covered in Chapter 4. However, Pakistan now has to face the new reality announced by Op Sindoor and take onus for instant escalation if it continues on its previous path of proxy war.

War Stamina and Stocking Estimates

Nations across the world have made varying choices when it comes to stocking levels of weapons and ammunition depending on their threat perceptions, appreciation of the duration of military conflict that they may need to be engaged in, domestic production capabilities, and the nature of military alliances which would impact their supply chains in the event of a protracted war. In the "guns vs butter" debate, the need to allocate greater resources for overall development of the economy among multiple competing priorities has seen nations like India adopting stock levels that would suffice for approximately a month of a full-scale military conflict. During this time there would be an expectation to ramp up domestic production and bring in necessary armament from external sources wherever needed.

Did this stocking philosophy yield the desired effects in Op Sindoor? In the emerging scenario, there may be a need to review our overall stocking policy, enhancing stock levels for specific types of arms and ammunition, while improving domestic production capability. This is because the stocking levels are always decided based on statistics drawn from previous conflicts, which would yield data that may be completely irrelevant in a future conflict.

The stocking levels of ammunition for Air Defence Guns is a case in point. Based on their original use case scenario, these guns were stocked with ammunition to ward off enemy aircraft, which were expected to attack in certain limited numbers. However, in Op Sindoor, the AD guns were faced with multiple drone attacks, running up to 1000 drones on some days, representing as high as a ten-fold increase over the anticipated number of aircraft launching attacks. AD guns' ammunition would have been initially stocked for 30 days of battle, with plans made to enhance production within those 30 days in case of a long-drawn conflict. However, with a ten-fold increase in ammunition expenditure, even after readjustments, the 30 days stocks would have been practically exhausted in three to four days. This would be under review now to meet future challenges in an optimum manner, as over-stocking creates many logistic and economic challenges. A similar review will be needed for all surface-to-air missiles specially those used against drones. Besides ammunition stocking, the issue of the vintage and firing capabilities of the AD guns would also be under review. There would be a need to modernise the metallurgy and ensure the availability of spare parts for these guns which would be firing more frequently against multiple low-cost drones as compared to their original design parameters.

Moreover, the present philosophy of AD deployment is based on guarding a few critical airfields and military assets. There is barely enough AD for even guarding these critical assets. Many of our civil population centres are largely without permanent AD weapon deployment. Some enhancement was done to critical areas like Jammu and Amritsar during Op Sindoor as the threats developed. But in case we face a similar threat from the Northern Borders there will be a need for much greater AD gun coverage over a large span of area, especially for low-cost drone swarms.

Several trends are shaping the changing geopolitical landscape, as well as the way armed forces will need to formulate their doctrines, stocking levels, and force structures to meet the requirements of national security; the preceding chapters have dwelt on many of these issues. General Anil Chauhan, Chief of Defence Staff, India, speaking at the Raisina Dialogue[9] on 3 March 2023, had said that the Russia–Ukraine conflict overturned the perception of all future wars being short and swift, and nations need to look closely at their war stamina and resilience for a prolonged conflict. The emphasis was on the fact that future wars could be long drawn, or the kinetic exchanges could be very short; there is no "one size fits all" prescription. He also mentioned that Self-Reliance (Atmanirbharta) was one of the main lessons that could be drawn from the Russia–Ukraine conflict, and that fast-paced military manoeuvres sweeping through vast swathes of territory had not been seen for months in the Ukraine conflict. In fact, frontlines had largely frozen, reminiscent of trench warfare during World War I.

There is thus a huge flux in the way future conflicts will unfold, with military forces being forced to prepare for both conventional conflicts and new-age warfare, for very short intense conflicts as well as long-drawn battles.

Technology and Warfare

Technology has transformed warfighting for centuries, with armed forces adapting their doctrines to weapon development, while the basic character of armed conflict has remained largely unchanged. In earlier times, military technologies were largely developed through research supported by the state, and closely monitored by militaries, due to the prohibitively high costs of such innovation, the lack of availability of both technological know-how and materials to pursue such development, and the lack of a civilian market for military products. Absorption of technology into the armed forces was facilitated by this process as the developments were largely driven by military requirements. Civilian use of warfighting technologies, consequently, was an unintended offshoot of such technological development. Little wonder, then, that aircraft, which were developed for transforming warfare, later gave rise to a booming civil aviation industry that has metamorphosed the travel sector irreversibly. Many more such examples exist where technology developed to solve military problems later found civilian utility.

This sequencing of military to civilian technological adaptation has now changed, with the barriers to technological innovation being removed by the availability of wide-spread technological knowledge, reduced cost of materials, global inter-connectivity, and galloping digital innovation.

The shoe is now on the other foot, and military technology will need to adapt to innovations from the civilian technological landscape. The Revolution in Military Affairs (RMA), undertaken at the end of the last century, was triggered by the civilian development of computers and networked systems, transforming the way battlefield surveillance could feed higher military headquarters and shorten the sensor-shooter loop. However, in recent times, the Ukrainian Armed Forces used Starlink, satellite-based internet, and Microsoft cloud computing, designed for civilian use by private entities, to offset the breakdown of command, control, and communication systems in the face of the Russian onslaught. The era of civil use innovation by private entities impacting military technology has dawned and military forces now need rapid adaptation to changing technology that is causing paradigm shifts in both the digital and kinetic spheres. Some examples are cheap drones, robotics, artificial intelligence, exoskeletons, and changes ongoing in ship fuel systems moving away from marine diesel to greener systems. Do these developments portend another RMA? Or are they also only part of the steady evolution process that warfare undergoes. Possibly we are in the midst of this transformation of warfare from contact to non-contact warfare with fusion of the most recent technologies and precision munitions taking primacy over conventional means of warfighting. The challenge, again, is to prepare for battles embracing this emerging RMA, while retaining expertise in conventional warfighting.

As India embraces new technologies and moves towards indigenisation or Atmanirbharta, the lessons from Op Sindoor must be analysed to modify the blueprints for future security architecture, military doctrine, defence technology, and international relations. It is, therefore, proposed to consider the strategic implications of this operation before drawing conclusions and making recommendations for refining India's security posture to meet future challenges.

The Strategic Implications of Operation Sindoor for India's National Security and Future Directions

Operation Sindoor represents a pivotal moment in India's counter-terrorism doctrine and its approach to national security in a volatile geopolitical landscape. The operation marked a significant shift from India's previous policy of strategic restraint to one of assertive deterrence and cost-imposition against state-sponsored terrorism, using conventional means without the declaration of war. Here are the key implications of Op Sindoor for India:

Robust deterrence capability within the nuclear threshold

Op Sindoor showcased India's ability to expand the operational bandwidth of conventional force within a nuclear context, thereby resetting the escalatory ladder and tilting it in India's favour. India demonstrated its capacity to dictate terms of engagement and maintain escalation dominance. The precision strikes extended across Pakistan's heartland, targeting key military and terrorist infrastructure from Karachi to Rawalpindi, challenging the past nuclear blackmail that Pakistan earlier resorted to.

Institutionalising a "new normal" for counter-terrorism

Op Sindoor further institutionalised a policy of prompt and harsh military retaliation for major terrorist provocations. The targeted bombing of Jaish-e-Mohammed's headquarters in Bahawalpur and Lashkar-e-Taiba base in Muridke, along with the elimination of UN-sanctioned terrorists, reaffirmed India's zero-tolerance approach to cross-border terrorism. Pakistan's inability to deter or proportionally retaliate underscores a shifting deterrent equation. India's new policy against terrorism rests on three pillars—every terrorist attack will be met with a befitting response on India's terms, with strict action on locations where terrorism emerges; India will not tolerate any nuclear blackmail; and no distinction will be made between government-sponsored terrorism and its masterminds. This will force Pakistan and the rest of the world to take note of the new approach of India towards cross-border terrorism.

Enhanced Military Capabilities and Technologies

Some of the technologies and military capabilities that came into focus are detailed below:

Precision strike and standoff capabilities

India showcased its enhanced intelligence capabilities, surgical precision, and strategic resolve. The operation utilised advanced weaponry such as SCALP/Storm Shadow missiles, HAMMER precision-guided munitions, UAV launched PGMs (ULPGMs), SkyStriker suicide drones, BrahMos cruise missiles, Israeli Spice bomb kits, Harop loitering munitions and the Indian Navy's precision guided munitions. These allowed India to strike deep within hostile territory without deploying ground troops or engaging in aerial dogfights, minimising personnel risk and avoiding broader escalation. Further enhancements in these precision guided weapons to provide increasing lethality, accuracy, resistance to counter-measures, and greater indigenisation will be a natural fallout of the success achieved by these weapon systems in Op Sindoor. The need for enhanced control over the supply chains of all these critical weapons systems, catering for a surge capability in case of operational requirements also emerged clearly.

Potent and integrated air defence systems

India's air defence systems, including the Russian-supplied S-400 and indigenous Akash missiles, successfully intercepted Pakistani missiles and drones, largely defeating several waves of Pakistani attacks. This demonstrated India's growing capabilities in modern warfare, especially in drone defence. The significance of enhancing India's air defence systems capability, while ensuring greater indigenisation of equipment emerged clearly. Improving training levels of air defence operatives, and ensuring technological integration of tri-service sensors for comprehensive coverage of the nation's land and maritime borders are evidently important issues, which have been amply highlighted in Chapter 5, Pounding the Earth and Guarding the Sky.

India's aerospace power and precision targeting

The standoff capability of precision targeting by using an array of weapons in the armoury of the IAF gave India the upper hand in this conflict. This was an intense, short-duration conflict, that was undertaken successfully despite a shortage of fighter aircraft and force multipliers (AWACS, AARs); however, the need to build up aerospace capabilities emerged clearly. In any future conflict, air dominance will again have to be ensured so that the IAF can "see first, shoot first", and connect faster across busy battle spaces.

Maritime coercion

While the ground and air operations dominated immediate headlines, the Indian Navy played a pivotal and often understated role in Op Sindoor. Direct naval hostilities were avoided; however, the Indian Navy manoeuvred in the Western Indian Ocean to demonstrate coercive options with overwhelming force, thus achieving a *de facto* blockade of Pakistan's ports, restricting Pakistan Navy vessels to their harbour berths. The Indian Navy's capabilities were deployed and the potential of attack from the sea played a major role towards the outcome of the entire operation. The Navy's crucial role in synergised operations with the Army and Air Force, especially its precision strike capability and readiness to support joint missions was amply demonstrated in Op Sindoor, as mentioned in the previous chapters, and a continued development of the maritime elements of national security need not be re-emphasised.

Surveillance and targeting in combat

The operation saw extensive use of satellites and unmanned aerial vehicles (UAVs) for intelligence gathering, relaying data, and facilitating strikes; this highlighted the importance of real-time data links and seamless amalgamation of communications for precision targeting. The need to continue the development of these capabilities emerged clearly as they are force multipliers giving crucial inputs for ensuring informed decisions and precision strikes with minimal collateral damage.

The Cyber Battlefield

This conflict has signalled a major inflection point in South Asian cyber engagement. With cyber threats ever present and evolving, India cannot let its guard down. As evidenced in this episode, cyberspace is no longer a peripheral domain in state conflict—it is a primary battleground. India's determination to protect its digital infrastructure will shape the future of cyber-security in the region.

India has responded to growing cyber threats by hardening its cyber defence through CERT-In and NCIIPC, indigenous cyber-security solutions and collaboration between government and private sectors. However, the level of coordination is far from optimum at present, with several agencies working with overlaps in the same cyberspace. In addition, partnerships with Singapore, Japan, and the UK have enhanced threat intelligence-sharing' however, there is scope to expand this further under various multilateral formats like the QUAD. The line between government, military, and civilian operators in cyber war is blurred; however, in India these remain in independent silos. This gap needs to be bridged through futuristic policy, 24×7 preparedness, and investment in both human capital and technological infrastructure. To effectively counter Chinese cyber-attacks, Pakistani hacktivists, and other hacking groups, India must expand AI-powered threat detection and real-time incident response systems and improve cyber-security training. Increased investment in quantum-resistant encryption, cloud security, and resilient infrastructure for all vital sectors is critical.

Geopolitics, Sino-Pak Collusion, and the Two-Front Threat

Enhanced coordination

Op Sindoor highlighted the reality of increased collusion between China and Pakistan, with China providing covert and diplomatic support, military aid, and technological resources. China reportedly provided significant air defence and satellite support to Pakistan, helping reorganise its radar and air defence systems.

Two-front war scenario

This collusion raises serious concerns about a potential "two-front war" for India, necessitating a stronger deterrence and dissuasion posture. This was also highlighted by India's Deputy Chief of Army Staff when he categorically stated on 4 July 2025 that India was facing both Pakistan and China, while also alluding to a third front[10] where Türkiye was assisting Pakistan. A coordinated approach from Pakistan and China could create simultaneous pressure points along India's Northern (Ladakh) and Eastern (North-Eastern) fronts, diverting India's focus from the West in case of a future conflict with Pakistan.

Grey zone warfare

While Pakistan has been employing grey zone warfare against India for decades, it has been recently observed that China is supporting Pakistan in the non-kinetic domain. Grey-zone tactics employed by China include cyber warfare, misinformation campaigns, and increased patrol violations along the Line of Actual Control (LAC), aiming to disrupt India's critical infrastructure and exploit internal fault-lines without escalating to conventional warfare. India needs to be mindful of this expanding war zone with China Pakistan collusion, which will become more potent with the use of AI and quantum computing in the future.

Impact on Bilateral Relations and International Standing

Indus Waters Treaty (IWT)

India's decision to hold the IWT in abeyance was seen as a significant punitive measure, even as an "eco-strategic chokehold" and a new tool of leverage against Pakistan, particularly given Pakistan's heavy reliance on the Indus river system. However, this view misses the point that the treaty is outdated, and imposes several restrictions on the Indian side. It is the only instance where a lower riparian state is holding the upper riparian to ransom at every step, based on a treaty that imposes unreasonable restrictions on the upper riparian state. India's requests for a review of the treaty have been stonewalled by Pakistan, hence the decision to hold it in abeyance is widely seen to be justified. A fresh treaty that will be in-keeping with changed technology and circumstances should be negotiated in due course of time. This should not be seen as an attempt to starve the people of Pakistan of the Indus waters entirely; that scenario is a far cry from the technical realities of the Indus river system, the volumes of water in the various tributaries and the alignment of the mighty Himalayan Range.

Redefining dialogue

India has maintained a firm stance that talks with Pakistan can only focus on the return of Pakistan-occupied Jammu and Kashmir (POJK) and ending terrorism, firmly rejecting any "terror and talks" or "water and blood" flowing together.

Diplomatic efforts to isolate Pakistan

Pakistan continued its efforts to gain international legitimacy through appointments to key UN Security Council (UNSC) committees (Taliban Sanctions Committee, Counter-Terrorism Committee) and procured an IMF bailout package, even in the midst of Op Sindoor. However, it could not achieve much diplomatic leverage despite all these efforts due to India's diplomacy. India's efforts to isolate Pakistan and push it back onto the FATF grey list must continue. The multiparty delegations that visited 33 countries in the wake of Op Sindoor made significant headway in this direction, enhancing a bilateral engagement with multiple stakeholders, rather that depending on a multilateral format that has not been very effective in the past. Military diplomacy would also be beneficial in this regard as mentioned in the previous chapter.

US mediation controversy

The US, particularly President Trump, claimed credit for mediating the ceasefire, which India has firmly denied, asserting it was a bilateral DGMO-level agreement. This attempted "re-internationalization" of the Kashmir issue is anathema to India's long-standing bilateral stance. However, it must be clarified that separate telephone calls from USA to both India and Pakistan, wherein cessation of hostilities were discussed without imposing conditions, do not amount to structured mediation. In all cases of mediation, the two parties and the mediation interlocutors are brought together to a selected location for joint negotiation of terms. Statements are generally issued at the end of the mediation pertaining to the results of the discussions. No such mediation took place as India had never accepted third party involvement in a bilateral issue, a stance which remains valid before and after Op Sindoor. This approach is rooted in longstanding diplomatic principles and agreements such as the Simla Agreement of 1972 and the Lahore Declaration of 1999, which underscore bilateralism as the framework for addressing disputes. Therefore, it is clear that the United States only contributed to a back-channel diplomacy, engaging in separate engagements with both countries to ease tensions. However, the agreement to cease hostilities was negotiated and settled directly between Indian and Pakistani military officials as mentioned in the previous chapters. There was no structured mediation, no joint dialogue facilitated by a third party, and it was a purely bilateral DGMO-level agreement. Back-channel discussions are a part of diplomatic finesse that remain ongoing during, prior to, and after any crisis. However, the main utility of these talks is that they remain behind the scenes when public announcements are made. Publishing a one-sided view about a back-channel discussion on social media, even before the official statement is made by the parties involved has never been the practice in International Relations; Mr Trump does not seem to understand this basic nuance of diplomacy, which resulted in an unnecessary flutter over the issue.

Vulnerabilities and Challenges in Information Warfare

Narrative control failure

Despite military successes, India's strategic communication faltered, particularly in the initial hours and days, post-Pahalgam and Op Sindoor. Pakistan, conversely, launched a rapid, coordinated information warfare campaign, effectively reframing the terrorist attack as a "Kashmir issue" and exploiting Western media biases.

Pakistan's disinformation tactics

Pakistan utilised fabricated claims of downing Indian jets, AI-generated images of civilian casualties, credential laundering through retired Western officials, institutional reinforcement via elaborate reports, and grassroots amplification through bot accounts. This led to considerable misinformation and disinformation that continues to cloud the understanding of events. Pakistan's Information Warfare was sophisticated, rapid, and well-coordinated under a central empowered agency: ISPR. This included fabricating immediate victories (e.g., claiming to have shot down five Rafale jets using recycled images), deploying AI-generated images of alleged civilian casualties, leveraging retired Western officials for "credential laundering", releasing elaborate reports, and employing thousands of bot accounts to amplify hashtags. Pakistan effectively reframed the conflict around the "Jets Downed" and "Kashmir Issue" rather than cross-border terrorism.

Consequences of narrative loss

This led to tangible consequences, such as European Parliament members calling for "Kashmir mediation", S&P Global, an American corporation, issuing warnings about South Asia instability, and China accelerating J-31 fighter jet sales to Pakistan, explicitly citing "Indian aggression". Despite India's military success, Pakistan's narrative hijacked the perception, making its people believe in a perceived stalemate against a militarily superior India.

India's reactive stance

India's communication strategy was often reactive and technically focused, failing to resonate with broader international audiences and allowing Pakistan's false claims to gain significant initial traction. The press release[11] of 14 May 2025, four days after the cessation of hostilities, carries this text which indicates the reactive nature of the Indian Information Warfare quite clearly.

Extract from press release

Alongside military operations, a fierce information war has been ongoing online. Following the commencement of Op Sindoor, India found itself targeted by an aggressive campaign launched by Pakistan, full of lies and misinformation. The aim was to distort the truth, mislead the global public and reclaim lost narrative ground through a storm of misinformation. However, India has been proactively responding and dissipating misinformation with facts, transparency, showcasing strong digital vigilance. Rather than reacting emotionally, a composed and methodical approach to information warfare was undertaken:

- **Highlighting Operational Success:** Op Sindoor's effectiveness was communicated with precision, focusing on strategic outcomes rather than sensationalism.
- **Discrediting Sources:** Indian authorities have exposed the manipulation tactics used by Pakistan-based accounts, many of which are now under scrutiny by international social media platforms.
- **Promoting Media Literacy:** Campaigns to educate citizens on how to identify fake news have helped create a more resilient digital environment.
- **Foreign Amplification:** Pakistan's information warfare was significantly amplified by Chinese state media and information networks, giving Pakistani narratives the appearance of great power backing.
- **Extensive Use of Social Media and Cyber Tools:** Cognitive warfare, driven by AI, bots, troll factories, and deepfakes, manipulated narratives to influence large audiences, with social media acting as a powerful tool due to its extensive reach and user-driven amplification. Social media handles such as X, Facebook, Instagram, TikTok, etc. were flooded

with fake videos and images, and our nearest adversaries carried out relentless aggressive action in this field using well-funded and coordinated structures.

Lack of responsible reporting by Indian media

While print media in India still retains editorial oversight that serves to rein in jingoism and irresponsible reporting, this oversight seems to be completely absent on many of the electronic media channels. Sensationalism, brinkmanship, and even fake news was being carried with impunity due to a lack of institutional control and basic journalistic ethics in some cases. In a bid to gain TRPs, commentators even used terms like Indian Occupied Kashmir for our Union Territory and Azad Kashmir for Pakistan Occupied Kashmir. There were claims that Karachi has been struck and Lahore destroyed, leading to a social media storm, whereas only the military radar at Lahore was struck by the IAF. As the fighting escalated night after night, few Indian officials were put forward to explain what was happening, said Nirupama Rao,[12] India's former Foreign Secretary. The vacuum was filled on television newscasts by "hypernationalism" and "abnormal triumphalism", Rao said, creating what she called a "parallel reality". Evidently a mechanism needs to be set up to prevent such damage to our international image and credibility.

Interconnections between cognitive, electronic warfare, and cyber domains

Information Warfare structures need to be effective to tackle challenges of new-age warfare. Cyber and Electronic Warfare (EW) are comparatively well defined and understood, but not so psychological operations, or those capacities dealing in the cognitive domain and strategic communication. This anomaly exists within the military as well as the apex level of security structures. While cyber and EW battles can be carried out in the technical domain without much use of cognitive domain warfare, the reverse is no longer true. The Indian Army Doctrines clearly establish the interconnection between these three domains, enunciated for the last 15 years in theory, but their synchronisation has not yet been achieved in practice. The Chinese have termed it Integrated Network Electronic Warfare and some tenets of this amalgamation can be adapted to suit the Indian context. Similarly, there are multiple examples of this convergence in USA, UK, Russia, Ukraine, and Pakistan's ISPR.

Lessons from Ukraine

Even Ukraine, which is being actively supported by the US Cyber Command to handle all aspects of warfighting including Information Warfare, has set up the Center for Countering Disinformation (CCD), which functions as a working body of the National Security and Defense Council of Ukraine. The CCD is actively engaged in several efforts to develop counter-measures which include:

- **Identifying and Documenting Information Warfare attacks:** The CCD identifies, categorises, documents, and monitors "Disinformation threats".
- **Analysis and Dissemination:** The CCD produces "Analytics", including "Articles" and "Reports", which likely serve to expose and analyse disinformation campaigns.
- **Public and Digital Presence:** The Center maintains an active presence on various social media platforms, including Instagram, Viber, X-twitter, Facebook, Youtube, Telegram, and TikTok, for monitoring, disseminating information, and engaging with the public as part of their counter-disinformation strategy.
- **A handbook "Weapons of Information Warfare"** has been issued by CCD[13] on 26 July 2025, for journalists, officials

of Ukraine, information security professionals, and all citizens, providing them with a key tool for countering disinformation.

Need for a new Strategic Communications Authority

As explained to the team of authors by the Chief of Defence Staff (CDS), General Anil Chauhan, during a meeting on 24 July 2025, Headquarters of the Integrated Defence Staff (HQ IDS) will be setting up a new vertical for Perception Management and Strategic Communications after the experience of Op Sindoor. He had also announced the creation of this new vertical within his HQ during his address[14] to an international gathering at an Observer Research Foundation (ORF) event titled "India's Evolving National Security Landscape", on 8 July 2025.

While this will invigorate the military aspects of Strategic Communication, there is a clear need for integrating this new structure with an apex level institutional framework, which was also discussed in outline. During Op Sindoor, an Information War Room had been set up by the Ministry of Information and Broadcasting which was taking regular inputs from the Armed Forces. Mention of this war room has also been found in media reports. The war room was led by Information and Broadcasting (I&B) Minister Ashwini Vaishnaw,[15] drawing on social media experts from the army's Corps of Signals and the National Cyber Coordination Centre as per our discussions.

Possibly the time has come to institutionalise this arrangement of information management at the national level for which some options were discussed by the team of authors with the CDS as well as the National Security Advisory Board (NSAB) during meetings and presentations held in July 2025.

The new Strategic Communications Authority, as per the proposal presented by the author, should be set up under the direct supervision of the NSA, with amalgamation of expertise from several stakeholder agencies like the Ministry of Information and Broadcasting (MIB), MeitY, NCIIPC, Defence Cyber Agency, etc. The exact composition and components should be kept flexible and overall functioning may be with the MIB or the National Cyber Security Centre (NSCS), but this should remain fixed, not vacillating between agencies in the face of a crisis. Whichever way this is evolved for best effectiveness, Op Sindoor has given the clarion call—India cannot continue to fight the Information Warfare battle with conventional warfare structures and a silo-based approach.

Consolidation and Refinement

In conclusion, Op Sindoor has undeniably reshaped India's security paradigm, marking a strategic inflection point in its counter-terrorism doctrine. The operation's success showcased India's enhanced military capabilities and its unwavering political will to defend its sovereignty. However, it also exposed critical vulnerabilities in India's information warfare capabilities and highlighted the persistent threat of a collusive China-Pakistan axis, posing a potential two-front challenge. To consolidate its gains and navigate the complex future, India must continue to enhance its military capabilities, prioritise robust strategic communication, accelerate defence modernisation towards self-reliance, and meticulously plan for multi-domain, multi-front challenges, recognising that "narrative matters" as much as military might in this new era of contested equality. Some of these pointers for the future have been elaborated in this book and a summary of the recommendations of the authors will be outlined in the next chapter.

Annexure 7A

An Escalation Ladder

A Generalised (or Abstract) Scenario

Herman Kahn was an American physicist, regarded as one of the pre-eminent military strategists and systems theorists of the latter part of the twentieth century. He designed an escalatory ladder[16] which essentially proved that there are several steps that the escalation can take before an all-out, Earth destroying nuclear war is launched, enhancing the space for a graduated escalation that was possible and winnable for USA.

Rung	
1. Ostensible Crisis	Subcrisis Manoeuvering (Rungs 1–3)
2. Political, Economic, and Diplomatic Gestures	
3. Solemn and Formal Declarations	
4. Hardening of Positions – Confrontation of Wills	Traditional Crises (Rungs 4–9)
5. Show of Force	
6. Significant Mobilisation	
7. "Legal" Harassment – Retortions	
8. Harassing Acts of Violence	
9. Dramatic Military Confrontations	

10. Provocative Breaking-off of Diplomatic Relations
11. Super-Ready Status
12. Large Conventional War (or Actions)
13. Large Compound Escalation
14. Declaration of Limited Conventional War
15. Barely Nuclear War
16. Nuclear "Ultimatums"
17. Limited Evacuations (20%)
18. Spectacular Show or Demonstration of Force
19. "Justifiable" Counterforce Attack
20. "Peaceful" World-Wide Embargo or Blockade

Intense Crises (Rungs 10–20)

21. Local Nuclear War – Exemplary
22. Declaration of Limited Nuclear War
23. Local Nuclear War – Military
24. Unusual, Provocative, and Significant Countermeasures

Bizzare Crisis (Rungs 21–25)

25. Evacuation (70%)
26. Demonstration Attack on Zone of Interior
27. Exemplary Attacks on Military
28. Exemplary Attacks Against Property
29. Exemplary Attacks on Population
30. Complete Evacuation (95%)
31. Reciprocal Reprisals

Exemplary Central Attacks (Rungs 26–31)

32. Formal Declaration of "General" War
33. Slow-Motion Counter-"Property" War
34. Slow-Motion Counterforce War
35. Constrained Force-Reduction Salvo
36. Constrained Disarming Attack
37. Counterforce-with-Avoidance Attack
38. Unmodified Counterforce Attack

Military-Central Wars (Rungs 31–38)

Rung	Unit
39. Slow-Motion Counter-city war	Civilian-Central Wars (Rungs 39–44)
40. Countervalue Salvo	
41. Augmented Disarming Attack	
42. Civilian Devastation Attack	
43. Controlled General War	
44. Spasm/Insensate War	

The forty-four rungs of the ladder have been grouped into seven units (including varying numbers of rungs), each reflecting a different stage of escalation: Kahn's escalatory ladder assumes that the pre-escalation stage called "Disagreement" is already crossed, and the post-escalation stage called "Aftermaths" is not covered.

Notes

1. Newsletter, Juno Beach Centre Association, Canada in the Second World War. https://www.junobeach.org/canada-in-wwii/articles/air-marshal-sir-arthur-harris-2/
2. Geeta Mohan, 18 September 2022, This era not of war: PM Modi tells Vladimir Putin at SCO meet, *India Today*. https://www.indiatoday.in/india/story/this-era-not-of-war-pm-modi-tells-vladimir-putin-sco-meet-samarkand-2001161-2022-09-16
3. English rendering of PM's address to the Nation, Posted on 12 May 2025, by PIB Delhi (Release ID: 2128268) available at https://www.pib.gov.in/PressReleasePage.aspx?PRID=2128268
4. Dr Walter Ladwig, 21 May 2025, Calibrated Force: Operation Sindoor and the Future of Indian Deterrence, RUSI. https://www.rusi.org/explore-our-research/publications/commentary/calibrated-force-operation-sindoor-and-future-indian-deterrence
5. Peter Chalk and C. Christine Fair, December 2002, Lashkar-e-Tayyiba leads the Kashmiri insurgency, *Jane's Intelligence Review*, 14 (10): In the words of Hamid Gul, the former director general of the ISI: "We have gained a lot because of our offensive in Kashmir. This is a psychological and political offensive that is designed to make India bleed through a thousand cuts."
6. Paul K Davis and Peter JE Stan, May 1984, Concepts and Models of Escalation, A Report from The RAND Strategy Assessment Center. https://www.rand.org/content/dam/rand/pubs/reports/2007/R3235.pdf
7. Sajjad Ahamed, 6 May 2025, Locating the India-Pakistan Crisis on Herman Kahn's Escalation Ladder, The Diplomat. https://thediplomat.com/2025/05/locating-the-india-pakistan-crisis-on-herman-kahns-escalation-ladder/
8. Shubhajit Roy, 29 May 2025, What Operation Sindoor tells us about the nature of escalation, and India's changing approach, *The Indian Express*. https://indianexpress.com/article/explained/operation-sindoor-nature-of-escalation-10036560/

9. Amrita Nayak Dutta, 4 March 2023, India needs to have tech, weapons to fight a swift as well as a long war: CDS, *The Indian Express*. https://indianexpress.com/article/india/india-needs-to-have-tech-weapons-to-fight-a-swift-as-well-as-a-long-war-cds-8478328/
10. The Wire, 5 July 2025, *Five Key Revelations from Army's Deputy Chief on Operation Sindoor,* https://thewire.in/security/five-key-revelations-lt-gen-rahul-singh-operation-sindoor
11. Press Release by PIB, 14 May 2025, Operation SINDOOR: India's Strategic Clarity and Calculated Force, https://www.pib.gov.in/PressReleasePage.aspx?PRID=2128748
12. *The Washington Post*, 4 June 2025, How misinformation overtook Indian newsrooms amid conflict with Pakistan, https://www.washingtonpost.com/world/2025/06/04/india-news-channels-misinformation-pakistan-conflict/
13. Center for Countering Disinformation, 28 July 2025, Handbook "Weapons of Information Warfare". The Center for Countering Disinformation is a working body of the National Security and Defense Council of Ukraine; it has prepared this handbook with the support of the European Union Advisory Mission Ukraine, https://cpd.gov.ua/en/manuals/handbook-weapons-of-information-warfare/
14. *The Business Guardian,* 10 July 2025, India Won't Yield to Nuclear Threats: CDS Gen Anil Chauhan, https://www.magzter.com/es/stories/newspaper/The-Business-Guardian/INDIA-WONT-YIELD-TO-NUCLEAR-THREATS-CDS-GEN-ANIL-CHAUHAN/
15. Pradip R. Sagar, 26 May 2025 Edition, Weapons of mass dissemination: The India-Pakistan cyber frontier, *India Today*. available at https://www.indiatoday.in/india-today-insight/story/weapons-of-mass-dissemination-the-india-pakistan-cyber-frontier-2726677-2025-05-18
16. Magellan's Log, *Herman Kahn's Escalation Ladder (1965)*, 13 January 2013, https://web.archive.org/web/20130113065016/http://www.texaschapbookpress.com/magellanslog41/escalation.htm

8

Way Forward

Conclusion and Recommendations

MAJOR GENERAL BIPIN BAKSHI

Yada yada hi dharmasya glaanirbhavati bharata, abhyutthanam
Adharmasya tadatmanam srjamy aham

Whenever righteousness is on the decline, unrighteousness is in the ascendant, then I body Myself forth. For the protection of the virtuous, for the extirpation of evil-doers, and for establishing Dharma (righteousness) on a firm footing, I manifest Myself from age to age.

—Bhagvad Gita, Chapter 4, Verse 7

"Operation Sindoor is still ongoing, India needs to remain on very high alert, 24×7 and 365 days", said General Anil Chauhan, CDS, addressing a defence gathering at Subroto Park, New Delhi, on 24 July 2025. PM Modi also announced this during his address to the Parliament on 29 July 2025. This encapsulates the "No War No Peace" scenario that the Indian Security Forces have been facing for decades. An undeclared war that has now come closer to the nation's consciousness. How long will this go on? Will there be a change in Pakistan's approach to their relations with India and will there be an abatement in the proverbial thousand-year war they want to wage? Will this prove to be Pakistan's culmination point in their Eastward ambitions, as mentioned in the Preface.

These were the thoughts that set us on the quest to write this book.

India's "new normal" doctrine of assertive, cost-imposing retaliation across the length and breadth of Pakistan aims to deter future grey zone attacks. Pakistan's low-cost proxy war option, adopted for the last few decades, has hit the wall of Indian retribution. Op Sindoor has given a very clear signal of significantly increased costs for Pakistan's state-sponsored terrorism; however, it remains to be seen if Pakistan will fundamentally change its long-standing strategy. Pakistan's historical reliance on misinformation, continued support from its allies, the openly stated thousand cuts strategy to bleed India, and its persistent denial of involvement in terror attacks suggest that it may continue to pursue similar objectives through adapted means, rather than abandoning their actively hostile approach towards India altogether.

Pakistan's Approach and its Multiple Allies

Despite regular international pressure, Pakistan's structural links to state-sponsored terror remain deeply entrenched. Pakistan's use of terrorism has been, for long, a "deliberate strategy" for destabilising India, with a long track record of funding, training, arming, and providing sanctuary for groups like Lashkar-e-Taiba (LeT) and Jaish-e-Mohammed (JeM). Even after the devastation wrought by Operation Sindoor, there is little concrete indication that Pakistan's security establishment will make a credible shift away from this approach. The promotion of their Army Chief to Field Marshal is only one example to show the delusion of victory the Pakistan Army has been selling to its people for decades. "Notion of Victory", an element of misinformation perfected by their military establishment, has set a completely fictional narrative in Pakistan, one that says that they never lost a war to India, and that they are in a dominant position on the Siachen Glacier, whereas the glacier is not even visible to them from their positions! Not winning a war, for them, is not the same as losing, hence even now they are claiming victory.

The multiple allies that Pakistan subserviently bows to for support may not see significant benefits in curbing the terror factory that primarily hurts only India. As mentioned earlier, Pakistan is drawing support from both USA and China in a complex dance of geopolitics which is a masterclass in duplicity. It provides USA a land base for action against Iran, monitoring of Afghanistan, and a watchtower against China. It also has a deep-seated intelligence sharing relationship with USA from the time of the Mujahideen evicting the Soviets from Afghanistan, and the two-way game they played supporting the Global War on Terror, while providing safe sanctuaries to the Taliban. Their complicity in all this "Dirty Work" was admitted to by their Defence Minister in the interview with Yalda Hakim on 25 April 2025 (refer Endnotes in Chapter 2). Pakistan's duplicity during the Afghan War from 2001 to 2021 was famously termed as "running with the hares and hunting with the hounds". All this duplicity is open for the world to see and the major powers to exploit; however, it is fooling no-one, other than the uninformed people of Pakistan itself.

Despite a full knowledge of this background, observers were still surprised by the invite for Pakistan Army Chief to lunch by Trump, in June 2025, soon after the debacle suffered by Pakistan in Op Sindoor, and just preceding the US attack on Iran nuclear facilities. This lunch meet underlined USA's recognition of the fact that Pakistan is controlled by their Army, and the civilian government leaders can be comfortably ignored. This being followed in quick succession by another invite to Munir to visit CENTCOM at Tampa in August 2025 had raised many an eyebrow in the strategic community. What gives, the world wondered, Munir the license to go on a new tirade against India from USA's soil. This gave further cause for curiosity over what kind of relationship is being nurtured between USA and Pakistan.

At the same time there is China, who is touted as Pakistan's all-weather ally, a relationship "higher than the mountains, deeper than oceans, stronger than steel and sweeter than honey", since 2010.[1] With the heavy debt burden of the China Pakistan Economic Corridor, and decades of mismanagement of funds, Pakistan's economy is suffering from galloping inflation, lack of revenue to run the country, and dependence on IMF bailouts. Despite all this, it is trying to punch far above its weight and uses religion as a plank to get support from Saudi Arabia, Türkiye, and Azerbaijan, as the exalted possessor of the "Only Islamic Nuclear Bomb", and from USA as a staging point in the subcontinent . With the recent Saudi–Pakistan pact and another meeting of Trump with both Munir and Sharif at the White House in September 2025, this trend is evidently continuing. The support and resources that Pakistan garners from all these sources go to fuel the terror factory and ensure benefits for the Pakistan Army, neglecting the issues of development and welfare of their citizens.

This heady cocktail of divergent interests described above, mingled with the malignant hatred that the Pakistan Army has nurtured against India over decades, leaves no space for detente, peace, or reconciliation. The economic problems that Pakistan is facing, coupled with the political turmoil due to the continued popularity of Imran Khan even from jail, further forces the Pakistan Army to again climb on the anti-India plank, conjuring up external threat to unite internal forces. The real issues of economic development and good governance are given scant attention as the focus is shifted to the phantom of Indian aggression and the dream of separating Kashmir from India. The flow of the Indus into the Arabian Sea would thus continue to be turbulent until there is a desire for peace in Pakistan.

At present, their *de facto* leader, Field Marshal Munir, continues to build a strong case for hostility with India. His recent remarks at a gathering in Florida[2] on 10 August 2025 fly in the face of any optimism regarding a benign peace in the Indian subcontinent. An editorial by the *Eastern Eye*, a British newspaper covering Asian affairs,[3] mentioned the details of these remarks at a gathering attended by over 100 people, hosted by a Pakistani-origin businessman. Media persons reconstructed the contents of the speech since digital devices were not permitted at the gathering. Munir reportedly reiterated the "Kashmir is our Jugular Vein" remark and went on to say: "We are a nuclear nation. If we think we are going down, we will take half the world down with us."

The same editorial informs that the officially released Pakistani version omits the nuclear nation remark and only mentions that Munir said that:

> The (Indian) aggression has brought the region to the brink of a dangerously escalating war, where a bilateral conflict due to any miscalculation will be a grave mistake.

This needs to be viewed in the backdrop of the interview of Lieutenant General Ahmed Sharif Chaudhry, DG ISPR to *The Economist*, reported in New Age,[4] a Bangladeshi newspaper, on 8 August 2025, wherein he made the startling remark that: "This time, we'll start from the East of India. They (India) also need to understand that they can be struck everywhere."

The diabolical plan of attacking India from the East and rolling up towards the West was again reportedly mentioned by Munir in his remarks at Tampa, Florida, a few days later. These remarks from the ruling elite of Pakistan do not give the signs of a benign, peace-loving, status-quoist nation which will settle for a mature and stable relationship with India.

A pragmatic analysis, thus, points towards a protracted, high-stakes competition that will seek new ways to continue its old policies with increased deniability, rather than an immediate strategic pivot by Islamabad. It is therefore prudent for India to keep its powder dry and its security apparatus well poised to meet future challenges. The 27th Constitutional Amendment (2025) only accentuates the breakdown of democratic authority in Pakistan, with a barely disguised military dictator at the helm of affairs. With all three services and the nuclear arsenal under Munir, a peaceful environment in the Indian subcontinent seems unlikely in the near future.

As mentioned by the CDS, Gen Anil Chauhan, during the Ran Samvad discussions at Mhow on 26 August 2025, India has always stood on the side of peace, but that does not mean we should be (mute) pacifists.[5] Peace without power is utopian he said and emphasised that power ensures peace. Further, he mentioned the poem by Ramdhari Singh Dinkar, *Shakti aur Kshama* (strength and forgiveness), in this context, quoting the last stanza:

Sahansheelta, kshama, daya ko, Tabhi poojta jag hai
Bal ka darp chamakta uskey, Peechhey jab jagmag hai

This translates in English[6] as under:

Tolerance, forgiveness and clemency are respected by the world only when the pride of strength glitters behind them brilliantly.

There has been a considerable transformation in India's security structures and modernisation of the military with the appointment of a CDS in 2020 and increasing emphasis on indigenous defence industry, which needs to be taken forward vigorously. India's military doctrine has also seen an ongoing evolution since the Sundarji Doctrine, which was based on decisive deep thrusts by large mechanised formations to the Cold Start Doctrine which envisaged rapid, multiple, shallow thrusts.

Evolution of India's Military Doctrine

The Surgical Strikes 2016, Balakot air strikes 2019, and Operation Sindoor 2025 marked a change from the previous responses to terrorist attacks. Was Op Sindoor just a variation of the Cold Start with new-age weapons and a freshly designed escalation matrix? The authors analysed how the various military actions, statements of military leaders, and writings available in the open domain indicate the evolution of the military doctrine to suit the environment realities and compulsions. It is evident that the continued use of Grey Zone aggression employing hybrid elements by Pakistan has been factored into India's politico-military strategic guidance. There has been a doctrinal shift in India's Strategy against terror. The response framework against Pakistan's abetment to terrorism in J&K is based on three pillars:

- Decisive retaliation
- No distinction between terror sponsors and terrorists
- No tolerance for nuclear blackmail.

India's transition to dynamic response

Cold Start Doctrine, as explained by former Chief of Army Staff General NC Vij, in his recently released book *Alone in the Ring* would have involved multiple shallow thrusts across the Western Borders (See Chapter 5 of the book). Gen Vij mentions that the Indian Army had planned for 8 to 10 limited offensives, penetrating into Pakistan to a depth of 10 to 15 km each.[7] These objectives were to be reached within 96 hours of Cold Start, while remaining below the nuclear threshold of Pakistan.

He also elaborates about the military doctrine prior to Cold Start, without naming it. He mentions that it was initiated by Gen Krishna Rao in 1981, tested during the largest military exercise of the time, Ex Digvijay in 1983, and further refined in an even larger exercise "Brass Tacks" 1987 when General Sundarji was the Chief. This later came to be known as the Sundarji Doctrine, with emphasis on mechanisation and manoeuvre in a conventional battle involving deep thrusts by the strike corps. As mentioned by Gen Vij, Operation Parakram's massive troop mobilization (2001–2002) proved ineffective, resulting in the need for a new doctrine for three reasons. These were:

- The changed circumstances of General Zia-u- Haq's proxy war in J&K with the pronouncement of "A Thousand Cuts" to bleed India.
- The Nuclear tests of 1998.
- The inability of holding corps to launch swift offensives with integral resources, and the dependence on the large-scale mobilisation of the strike corps, with a resultant loss of strategic surprise.

It has been subsequently realised that the Cold Start Doctrine may no longer be the singular response to terrorist attacks in the emerging security scenario. India's Joint Doctrine for Indian Armed Forces 2017 (Para 19) has already stated that surgical strikes will be a part of the credible deterrence posture through punitive destruction and disruption in a nuclear environment.

From the time of the 2016 Uri Strikes, India has now adopted a "Dynamic Response Military Doctrine". Therefore, we may surmise that an evolution has occurred from the erstwhile Cold Start Doctrine to the Dynamic Response Doctrine that encompasses a wider range of actions at various stages of a redefined escalatory ladder. Escalation control is a critical element of this doctrine as a full-scale conventional war or a nuclear war will only be executed if the politico-military aims are not achieved at a lower rung of the escalation matrix.

Significantly, the new doctrine enables India to execute military operations without formal declaration of war and remaining within the nuclear threshold. The triggering of the flexible response should not be seen as automatic, at the drop of a hat. It will be a proportionate response at a time, place, and scale of choosing by the politico-military hierarchy, and should not be seen to bind India into a knee-jerk reaction. Further, the termination of conflict on favourable terms is another key element of India's new playbook. Referring to Op Sindoor, Indian Air Force Chief, Air Chief Marshal AP Singh, said that the world could learn from India how to start and terminate a conflict swiftly.[8]

Credibility of this military doctrine has already been demonstrated, with the increasing time interval between major terrorist attacks since the 2016 surgical strikes. Therefore, there are significantly better chances of deterring Pakistan's cross-border terrorism by adopting this flexible response for retribution against future proxy war attacks. India, thus, aims to achieve "Credible Deterrence" against Pakistan's proxy war doctrine by adopting the "Dynamic Response" military doctrine.

For operationalising this military doctrine and ensuring the preparedness of India's security apparatus certain lessons have been drawn from Op Sindoor, and an analysis of the same has been carried out in this volume, which is detailed below.

Recommendations for Improvement of India's Security in the Emerging Geopolitical Environment

To consolidate its gains and prepare for future challenges, India needs to focus on several key areas to improve its security posture. While we draw from the aspects covered in the previous chapters and the implications of ensuring a "Dynamic Response" to make these recommendations, we also need to keep in mind that the future battles will be fought as much in the "non-kinetic quadrant", as with "bullets and bombs". General Dwivedi, India's Chief of Army Staff,[9] speaking at a landmark event at IIT Madras on 10 August 2025, while inaugurating the Army Research Cell mentioned this, and said that this non-kinetic domain is one where technology, civil preparedness, and public engagement are just as critical as conventional military action.

Enhanced defence capabilities and self-reliance

- **Accelerated Modernisation and Indigenisation:** Defence procurement and indigenous development of cutting-edge technologies like high-power jet engines, hypersonics, long-range precision weapons, AI, and advanced air defence systems need to prioritised and expedited. Focus should be on achieving "Atmanirbharta" (self-reliance) in the defence sector at the earliest, and judiciously fielding imported hardware from trusted allies in the interim. While we count on the iCET program (US–India Initiative on Critical and Emerging Technology) with USA and the TSI (Technology and Security Initiative) with UK, to enhance our defence technologies, we must not lose sight of the fact that transfer of technology is no panacea for genuine indigenisation. We have to invest much more in terms of academic research, quality manpower, and funds towards research and development to catch up in the technology race. Moreover, there is an urgent need to shorten the innovation-induction cycle which is famously slow in India's context. Ashley Tellis, et al. have postulated in the book, *Measuring National Power in the Post-Industrial Age*, that national power can be enhanced primarily through the ability of the nation to control the innovation cycle of its technology and economy.[10] The need for focusing on innovation was emphasised by PM Modi as well in his address to the Combined Commanders Conference at Kolkata in September 2025.[11] Evidently, there is an urgent need to shorten the innovation-induction cycle which is famously slow in India's context. Several small attempts made for this acceleration are already showing good results and indigenous defence hardware was successfully battle-tested during Operation Sindoor. However, the scale remains small and the bureaucratic obstacles impeding rapid innovation remain largely unchanged, with Public Private Partnerships and joint development of technologies being an exception rather than the rule. In addition, there is a need to have complete control over the defence equipment supply chains and a guaranteed surge capability to cater for sudden increases in ammunition expenditure or attrition in operations. Among the several important technologies, such as semiconductors, supercomputers, and drones, that India needs to develop 100% indigenously and urgently, the most important is the aeronautical engine, which is critical for both military and commercial aircraft.

- **Modernising the Indian Air Force:** To ensure strategic security and future readiness, India must rapidly restore the Indian Air Force's fighter fleet to a robust capability and urgently acquire more flight refuellers and Airborne Early Warning & Control (AEW&C) aircraft. The sanctioned strength of 42.5 squadrons has been flagged in a report published on 11 August 2025,[12] wherein the compatibility of future platforms with the existing fleet has been mentioned. Commonality of the fighter fleet of the IAF with the Navy's carrier-based Rafales is also an essential consideration. Strengthening our aerospace capability also requires a robust, layered air defence network and immediate development of indigenous technologies in drone warfare, artificial intelligence, and electronic warfare. This is essential as our adversaries are vigorously pursuing swarming, manned–unmanned teaming, and interception capabilities. Accelerated, incentivised private sector defence R&D—focusing on drones, advanced targeting systems, and hypersonic weapons—paired with supply-chain autonomy, is essential for sustainable conflict preparedness. India must also address vulnerabilities in space-based navigation by expanding and modernising the Navigation with Indian Constellation (NavIC) satellite constellation urgently; its criticality was evident in Op Sindoor. Overall, India's warfighting doctrine must urgently evolve to secure dominance in air, land, sea, outer space, and the electromagnetic spectrum, with hardened cyber defences and advanced space-enabled support at its core.

- **Recommendations for Air Defence**: The detailed recommendations for consolidating our air defence capability have been elucidated in the previous chapters. However, the critical aspect of guarding our skies against the evolving threats are reiterated here, as the significance of air defence emerged clearly during Operation Sindoor, wherein hundreds of drone attacks were witnessed every night. Integration of the IACCS, Akashteer, and Trigun platforms into a single AI-powered system is essential to eliminate operational silos and achieve real-time coordination across all services. With this integration, a unified air defence structure, led by the Indian Air Force, will enable centralised management and deployment of strategic and tactical resources. Simultaneously, with ongoing engagement among defence R&D, industry, and armed forces, further upgrades and induction of advanced equipment need to be accelerated. As regards training of personnel, simulator-based training for personnel, combined with specialised anti-drone instruction for police and paramilitary units, will prepare operators to employ both conventional and electronic warfare systems for robust air defence. Indigenous technologies such as NavIC for secure communication and robust satellite or fibre connectivity have to be deployed, underpinning the effectiveness of all command posts and air defence assets. This can be only achieved with a fast-tracked push for local research, manufacturing, and technology development. By fostering public–private partnerships, India can swiftly develop automated, AI-enabled air defence, anti-drone, and electronic intelligence (ELINT) systems, ensuring a multi-layered, future-ready air defence shield for the nation.

- **Emphasis on New Age Warfare:** Capability development in cyber, space, information warfare, AI, drones, and other critical technologies, alongside conventional modernisation, must be prioritised. Improvement of capabilities to detect terrorists who are using satellite phones and encrypted messaging apps that leverage systems like the Chinese BeiDou satellite system is imperative. Cyber engagements played a consequential, independent role in shaping the trajectory and impact of the conflict during Operation Sindoor. With its asymmetric nature, rapid scalability, and ability to influence both battlefield dynamics and public perception, cyber warfare is poised to become an increasingly decisive front in future conflicts. In addition, this is an ongoing battle that is being waged with lower visibility in the pre-conflict period, with capability of being rapidly scaled up during conflict. Certain recommendations emerge from the experience of Op Sindoor and prior cyber offensives. These mainly pertain to better coordination and increased use of advanced technology to fight this battle better, which can be achieved by looking at the following aspects:
    - **A Revamped National Cyberwarfare Policy:** Creation of a single rulebook explaining how India will defend itself online—who is responsible for what, and what actions can be taken during a cyber-attack.

- **A Responsive National Cyber Nerve Centre:** Setting up of a 24×7 central command centre to coordinate defence, response, and, if needed, counter-actions against attacks, with all key agencies and industry working together.
- **Smart Technology for Early Detection:** Use of AI tools to watch over national networks, quick spotting of suspicious activity, and taking action before the damage is done.
- **Future-Proofing Cyber Protection:** Moving to new, quantum-safe encryption so that our data stays safe even from tomorrow's super-powerful computers; moving towards indigenous operating systems and applications with full control over data.
- **Keeping a Trained Cyber Army Ready:** Improving the HR Policies to nurture in-house government talent, understanding the need to create special career paths for niche capabilities, specially within the military. Also building a strong local talent pool through universities and training, and have a reserve of skilled experts ready to respond in emergencies.
- **Cyber Offensives:** While defence is essential, there needs to be a coordinated capability to inflict damage on hostile elements and deter future attacks by developing offensive capabilities. This could include disrupting the communications of adversary radar systems, and internal source code of hostile drones using advanced cyber-attacks.
- **Measuring and Reporting Progress:** Clear goals for cyber safety should be set. Results should be tracked and an annual report published so the public knows how well the country is being protected.

- **Integrated Operations:** We should continue to foster joint and integrated operations among the Army, Navy, and Air Force, building on the synergy demonstrated in Operation Sindoor, and work towards a Combined Joint All Domain Command and Control (CJADCC) network. Closer integration is a process that is under way and a lot of progress has been made, particularly since the appointment of the CDS. This process will foster tri-service synergy and enhanced effectiveness of the armed forces in the times to come. An apex level structure with a single joint war room to harmonise all elements of national power, including the NSA and the military hierarchy is an essential element of this integration.
- **Counter Bombardment and Protection of Civilian Population Centres:** While Operation Sindoor demonstrated the excellent capability to degrade terror networks, and some of the major defence capabilities of Pakistan like radars and airfields, there was still a degree of damage done by their artillery, smaller calibre weapons, and some armed drones along the border areas, particularly near the LoC. Just as we had targeted the terror bases that strike us, we must prioritise decimation of enemy artillery guns that have been inflicting casualties on our border villages for long. We have a plethora of guns, missiles, and armed drones that can be employed effectively for this purpose. We also need to ensure better availability of bomb shelters for civilians in vulnerable sectors like Uri, Poonch, Rajauri, and Naushera. Further there is a need to greatly enhance anti-drone protection for our population centres which are largely devoid of end point air defence security. During Operation Sindoor, certain critical areas like Jammu and Amritsar were given Air Defence guns but there is an overall

shortage of these guns. In case of a similar attack along our Northern Borders, there would be a plethora of population centres, civilian airfields, oil storage depots, etc. that would need air defence from low-cost swarm drones. Bolstering the air defence and counter bombardment capabilities against these kinds of threats will assist in the protection of both military and civilian assets in future military engagements.

- **Space Capabilities:** To maintain a decisive advantage in future conflicts, India must significantly accelerate and expand its domestic space capabilities. Operation Sindoor highlighted the critical reliance on space for Intelligence, Surveillance, Reconnaissance (ISR), communications, and Position, Navigation, and Timing (PNT), yet also exposed a shortage of homegrown assets. The need to obtain inputs from foreign commercial providers led to delays at times and suffers from the risk of denial in a critical situation. To mitigate the substantial space capabilities that China's advanced satellite constellations and BeiDou system provides, India needs to expedite the launch of a larger fleet of surveillance satellites. Launching satellites in Low Earth Orbit (LEO) to achieve faster revisit times, and fully integrating these assets into its national intelligence grid will be necessary. Additionally, it is crucial to evolve towards a more distributed, "Starlink-like" network architecture to provide real-time intelligence and connectivity to frontline forces. Finally, to solidify navigation sovereignty, India must urgently launch additional NavIC satellites to address existing shortfalls and build redundancies, thereby ensuring a robust and resilient indigenous PNT system. This comprehensive investment in space infrastructure is essential for India's warfighting doctrine to align with the 21st-century realities where dominance in outer space is of paramount importance

- **Development of Maritime Capabilities:** While this arena of critical activity and action did not receive much public attention during Op Sindoor, it is an important domain of conflict and military diplomacy that could see much more vigorous action in a future conflict. The continued development of maritime capabilities will be equally essential as the other capabilities mentioned. For the Indian Navy, future modernisation should focus on increasing the range, stealth, and lethality of ship-borne weapon systems and all naval surveillance assets to maintain maritime superiority and deterrence.

> Planning to be "Future Ready" is not good enough; India needs to be "Now Ready", lending a sense of urgency to reforms and transformations to fight tomorrow's war. While some of the defence capabilities will develop over time as outlined above, the voids will have to be filled up by judicious induction of imported hardware, keeping in mind that the next round may escalate today, or tomorrow, and Operation Sindoor is ongoing, underlining the need for 365 days, 24×7 readiness.

Proactive Geopolitical Strategy

- **Addressing Two Fronts:** We have to remain fully alert and prepared for a "two-front war" scenario with China and Pakistan. This requires a balanced force disposition and adequate resource availability to avoid switching fronts during a conflict, besides the use of diplomacy to keep one front dormant in case of activation of the other front.
- **Strengthening Partnerships:** There is a need to revitalise and expand frameworks like I2U2 (India, Israel, UAE, and

the USA) and leverage platforms like the G20, QUAD, and Indo-Pacific Economic Framework to highlight India's role as a stabilising force. We have to engage actively with international partners to apply pressure on China and counter the China-Pakistan-Türkiye-Azerbaijan axis. At the same time, India needs to remain nimble-footed, utilising its memberships in SCO, BRICS and SCO for specific benefits that it can get from these. Greater use of military diplomacy will be beneficial for India in furthering its interests and strengthening its partnerships; this has been elaborated in greater detail in Chapter 6.

- **Grey Zone Tactics:** India needs to explore and utilise grey zone tactics against adversaries, developing capabilities to target their vulnerabilities and apply pressure on important Sea Lines of Communication (SLOCs) to deter hostile forces involvement.
- **Defining Terrorism:** India needs to continue to pursue the adoption of the Comprehensive Convention on International Terrorism (CCIT) which is making slow progress at the UN Security Council. Multilateral counter-terrorist actions will get facilitated once this first step is taken.
- **Exposing Adversary Duplicity:** Push for the Financial Action Task Force (FATF) to re-list Pakistan on the "grey list", highlighting its ongoing support for cross-border terrorism is crucial. India must invest in global perception management through diplomatic missions and think tanks to expose Pakistan's continued duplicity on terrorism and human rights issues.

Detailed recommendations on strategic communications are outlined in the following section.

Strategic Communication and Information Warfare

There is a need to integrate rapid, decisive strategic communication into India's counterterrorism framework through a newly structured institutional mechanism. India must engage in proactive narrative building, focusing on immediate and clear messaging, replacing the ad-hoc responses seen in previous critical events. The actions that are essential in this regard are as under:

- **Government-media Harmonisation:** Regular two-way contact, through more synchronised structural mechanisms will be necessary to improve government-media coordination. This is crucial to dominate the infospace and prevent information voids being filled by conjecture, fiction, and propaganda.
- **Institutional Framework:** It is important to establish an institutional framework at the national level, such as a Strategic Communication Authority, manned by specialists, armed with due mandates, and a suitable budget to synergise communication efforts across the Ministry of External Affairs, Ministry of Defence, and military organisations. India must build up on the Information War Room that was set up for Op Sindoor by the Ministry of Information and Broadcasting. So far as the armed forces are concerned, the lessons of Op Sindoor have already indicated a need for a tri-service organisation to work in this direction, and a mention of the Defence Strategic Communication Agency being set up was made by the CISC during the Annual Trident Lecture organised by the Centre for Joint Warfare Studies at Manekshaw Auditorium on 5 August 2025.
- **Proactive Narrative Control:** India must integrate rapid, decisive strategic communication into the counter-terrorism framework, actively pre-empting and shaping narratives

in real-time, especially on social media platforms and digital news channels. Here the aspect of regular briefings to military veterans and former diplomats mentioned in Chapter 6 could be considered, as they will continue to be frequently seen on TV channels and they are considered to represent the government view at least partially by the viewers across the country and abroad.

- **International Engagement:** Indian diplomatic missions must build local constituencies in influential media, think tanks, parliamentarians, militaries, universities, and youth abroad. Use of the defence wings to strengthen this engagement with military personnel and military think tanks could be further considered, during and after the tenures in the mission. The alumni of several training institutions in India where foreign students have been trained are another significant constitucncy that could be institutionally engaged through the diplomatic missions.
- **Diaspora Leverage:** It is crucial to actively harness the strength of India's politically savvy and economically robust diaspora to build bridges and dispel fake narratives among global elites and common people.
- **Domestic Engagement:** Crafting emotionally resonant messages will help to galvanise domestic support and effectively counter international narratives. This will also need moving towards indigenous social media platforms, browsers and operating systems to ensure better control and resilience in crisis situations.
- **Enhancement of Information Warfare Capabilities:** This can be done by developing an institutional framework for career development, fostering expertise, and training senior officials to leverage social media for real-time narrative shaping.

- **Addressing the Fall of Journalistic Integrity:** It has become critical to safeguard journalistic integrity in Indian news media by condemning unprofessional and hyper-nationalist behaviour that undermine credibility. It is imperative to lay down norms of reporting on national security issues and ensuring their implementation by the National Strategic Communication Authority.

Views of Information Warfare practitioners

Some of these issues were discussed with practitioners of Information Warfare. The views expressed were supportive of the basic thrust of the above recommendations. A summary of these views emerging from these discussions are detailed below.

- **Institutionalising Information Warfare and Strategic Communication in India—A National Imperative:** In the contemporary era of hybrid threats, where conventional conflicts increasingly intertwine with cognitive and information domains, institutionalising a national level structure for Information Warfare (IW) and Strategic Communications (Strat Com) has become not just desirable but essential. The evolving nature of warfare, encompassing cyber influence, dis-information, psychological operations (PSYOPS), and narrative dominance demands a coordinated, professional, and resourced response that transcends siloed functioning across ministries and services.
- **India Faces a Complex Information Environment:** The Indian security canvas is marked by adversaries who are leveraging information tools with precision to influence perceptions, polarise societies and disrupt democratic processes. Nations like China and Russia have institutionalised Information Operations through centralised organisations, integrating capabilities across cyber, electronic, psychological, and

media domains. The capability of Pakistan-based Inter-Services Public Relations organisation (ISPR) has adequately been witnessed during the ongoing Op Sindoor. Without a similar national level architecture, India risks falling behind in this critical dimension of national security.

- **Narrative Warfare is now Central to Geopolitical Contests:** Whether during conflicts like Balakot, Galwan, Op Sindoor, or in diplomatic arenas like Kashmir or international forums, the ability to shape global and domestic narratives has a strategic impact. A coherent Strategic Communication strategy ensures alignment of messaging across stakeholders, i.e., government, military, diplomatic, media, and others thereby avoiding contradictory or reactive posturing. Strategic Communication must no longer be treated as an ancillary function but as a force multiplier in achieving national objectives.
- **Existing Indian Structures are Fragmented and Under-resourced:** Currently, the responsibility for narrative building related to armed forces is multi-tasked across agencies like the Ministry of External Affairs, the Ministry of Information & Broadcasting, and the armed forces. As was evident during Operation Sindoor, they all contributed in absolute synchronisation to have an impactful media presence. Though as of now there is no single apex body for coordinated messaging over a sustained period, coordinated info campaigns, and counter propaganda efforts, the formation of the same is believed to be at initial stages and will hopefully be established shortly. Alongside the above, the training of subject matter experts to include psychologists, linguists, tech analysts, media strategists, behavioural scientists, etc. is also being undertaken to conduct nuanced influence operations or craft persuasive messaging across diverse audiences and languages.

- **Institutionalisation has Inherent Advantages:** This is likely to enable specialised recruitment, training, and doctrinal development. Experts from academia, media, think tanks, and private sector can be brought in through a structured mechanism. A permanent institution ensures continuity of knowledge, long-term planning and doctrinal clarity in the IW/ Strat Com landscape. It would also foster a "whole of government approach", integrating civil-military capabilities and ensuring that strategic messaging reflects security interests, cultural sensitivities, and national values.
- **Allocation of Dedicated Budget Required:** Influence campaigns, content generation, technological platforms for monitoring and engagement, and rapid response mechanisms, all require sustained funding. A budget ensures that such efforts are not ad-hoc or episodic but are proactively sustained across peacetime and crisis scenarios alike.

Fighting the Info War: A Synergised National Agency

It is evident from the above analysis and recommendations that the existing systems are inadequate to fight the fast-paced Information Warfare battle that is raging in the cognitive domain on a daily basis through peace and conflict stages. As India aspires to be a regional power with global influence, it must elevate its Info Warfare and Strategic Communication to a strategic priority. Institutionalising these capabilities at the national level backed by expertise, structure, and funding will equip the nation to counter hostile narratives, assert its voice globally, and protect its cognitive sovereignty in the age of info dominance.

Some of the considerations pertaining to the new structure to be developed are:

- Synergy of organisations working separately in cyber, cognitive, and physical dimensions, working under a nominated lead agency with authority and funding for the national narratives. This organisation needs to integrate efforts at three levels:
    - Cognitive, technical, and physical dimensions
    - Protection, response, and attack elements
    - Security, academia, government, industry, media, and digital platforms
- Creating a Central Information War Room with 24×7 response, a pool of experts, dedicated helplines, and continuous monitoring capability.
- Adoption of coordinated themes for various sectors/regions. Dedicated training in Narrative Building and Information Warfare by specialists of the central agency.
- Building resilience against info warfare through regular training, workshops, and simulations for security forces, government officials, citizens, and academia to include the use of AI and countering fake news.
- Training, HR policies, and structures to be realigned to develop information warfare specialists as a new vertical with independent career progression, doing away with the present tenure-based approach.

All the above steps are considered essential to accompany the other developments in security preparedness outlined earlier. The battle in the information domain needs to be fought in a synchronised manner as most nations have already become adept at this new form of Hybrid War, which is "no holds barred" and "unrestricted warfare" in the true sense of the word. Fragmented organisations working separately in the cyber and cognitive dimensions will be quickly overwhelmed and defeated in this new form of warfare which is ongoing today. To quote from the PhD thesis on Information Warfare research by the lead author of this book:

> With a number of adversaries or competitors adopting a more integrated approach to Information Warfare, those nations which choose to ignore this critical aspect are bound to face losses and defeats in peace, conflict and war, and will remain unable to pursue their national interests. A suitable organisational structure for Information Warfare in India needs to be formulated by drawing relevant lessons from other nations described in the study. The conceptual underpinning needs to be a synchronisation between the Information-Technical and Information-Psychological dimensions of Information Warfare to influence the Cognitive Dimension.

As mentioned by the CDS to the authors on 24 July 25, and subsequently announced by the CISC on 5 August 2025 at Manekshaw Centre, there will be Strategic Communication Agency established under HQ IDS shortly. Presumably this will set the stage for a larger organisation at the national level.

Conclusion

It is heartening to note that various agencies have noted the need for significant changes in all the domains discussed in this book. Some of the necessary steps were already under way and some will receive greater impetus after Operation Sindoor. We hope the attempt made by the authors to amplify and underline some of the critical issues will be of use to planners for the future.

Operation Sindoor transcended the realm of a mere military triumph; it stood as a profound testament to India's unwavering unity, strategic foresight, and ethical strength. The successful destruction of nine terror camps, the significant military personnel and material losses imposed, while effectively countering a series of attacks launched by Pakistan, showcased India's military prowess with clarity.[13] Operation Sindoor, thus, marks a strategic inflection point for India, demonstrating its resolve and capability.

However, it also underscored the critical need to remain ready for future misadventures by hostile elements and enhance it security apparatus. As the economy expands, it will put India into competitive positions with other major powers, and exacerbate the possibilities of conflict. There is thus an urgent need to synergise all elements of national power to continue facing the ongoing No War No Peace conflict in the Grey Zone of undeclared war. Besides military modernisation with emphasis on indigenisation, and greater integration at the apex level, this would also necessitate setting up of centralised information warfare structures to secure perceptual victories alongside its military successes, ensuring that the emergence as a major global power is acknowledged with clarity. An "all of nation approach" to every element of national security will remain essential, as India navigates her path through a volatile world order to attain our Viksit Bharat 2047 goals of becoming a developed economy. It will also be essential to improve the security posture with the assistance of partners and a steely resolve based on domestic capabilities. The potential exists. India just needs to walk the talk and continue on the current path with firm, determined strides.

Notes

1. *The Nation*, 19 December 2010, Pak-China friendship is higher than mountains, deeper than ocean and sweeter than honey: PM, available at https://www.nation.com.pk/19-Dec-2010/pakchina-friendship-is-higher-than-mountains-deeper-than-ocean-and-sweeter-than-honey-pm
2. Amira El-Fekki, 11 August 2025, Pakistan Makes Nuclear Threat to India from US Soil, *Newsweek*. https://www.newsweek.com/pakistan-makes-nuclear-threat-india-us-soil-2111554
3. Vivek Mishra, 11 August 2025, India condemns Pakistan army chief's nuclear threat in US, *Eastern Eye*. https://www.easterneye.biz/india-condemns-pakistan-nuclear-threat/
4. *New Age*, Dhaka, 08 August 2025, Pakistan warns India of deep strikes, https://www.newagebd.net/post/south-asia/272431/pakistan-warns-india-of-deep-strikes
5. *The Print*, 26 August 2025, Ran Samvad. https://www.youtube.com/watch?v=0leubOkjO5g&ab_channel=ThePrint
6. https://poems2remember.blogspot.com/2007/01/shakti-aur-kshama-strength-and-mercy.html
7. General NC Vij, *Alone in the Ring: Decision-making in Critical Times* (India: Bloomsbury Publishing, 2025), p 118.
8. Amrita Nayak Dutta, 30 September 2025, World has to learn a lesson from India on how to start, terminate conflict: IAF chief, *Indian Express*, https://indianexpress.com/article/india/world-has-to-learn-a-lesson-from-india-on-how-to-start-terminate-conflict-iaf-chief-10260381/
9. ABP Live News, 10 August 2025, 'The Next War...': Army Chief Gen Dwivedi Warns of Non-Kinetic and Unified Battle. https://news.abplive.com/news/india/the-next-war-army-chief-gen-dwivedi-warns-of-non-kinetic-and-unified-battle-1793845
10. Ashley Tellis et al., 2000, *Measuring National Power in the Post-Industrial Age*, RAND Corporation, pg 39. https://www.rand.org/pubs/monograph_reports/MR1110.html

11. PIB Delhi, 15 Sep 2025, Prime Minister Shri Narendra Modi emphasises on Jointness, *Atmanirbharta* and Innovation for enhanced operational readiness of the Armed Forces during Combined Commanders' Conference in Kolkata. https://www.pib.gov.in/PressReleasePage.aspx?PRID=2166753
12. *First Post*, 11 Aug 2025, IAF in urgent need of Rafales, seeks deal with France amid falling squadron strength, says report. https://www.firstpost.com/world/operation-sindoor-effect-iaf-in-urgent-need-of-rafales-seeks-direct-deal-with-france-amid-falling-squadron-strength-says-report-13923246.html
13. War on the Rocks. 2025. "Operation Sindoor and the Evolution of India's Strategy against Pakistan." https://warontherocks.com/2025/05/operation-sindoor-and-the-evolution-of-indias-strategy-against-pakistan/

About the Authors

Maj Gen (Dr) **Bipin Bakshi**, AVSM, VSM, Retd, is a multifaceted scholar, warrior, and sportsman. Awarded the Sword of Honour and Gold Medal at IMA, and the Gold Medal in B Tech, he has done his PhD on Information Warfare. He has an illustrious background in military service, UN Peacekeeping, and a tenure as Inspector General in NSG. He is a Distinguished Fellow at a leading military think tank (CLAWS), an author of two graphic novels on war heroes, and has several publications to his credit.

Air Mshl **Rajesh Kumar** is a product of Mayo College, Ajmer and an alumnus of National Defence Academy, Khadakvasla. He was commissioned in the Flying Branch of the Indian Air Force in June 1982. He retired from the Indian Air Force after 39 years of service. He is a graduate of Air Command and Staff College at Montgomery, Alabama, as well as College of Defence Management at Secunderabad and holds a master's degree in management studies. He has held the appointment of C-in-C of the Strategic Forces Command and has published articles in various journals with an emphasis on nuclear policy.

Amb **Anil Trigunayat** has been a diplomat for over three and a half decades, serving from Asia to Africa and Europe to the Americas. He also served as India's Ambassador to Jordan, Libya, and Malta. Presently, he is a Distinguished Fellow with prestigious think tanks like Vivekananda International Foundation and United Services Institute of India, among others. He is a regular contributor to major media outlets and publications on geopolitics, geo-economics, and India's foreign and security policy.

Brig **Akhelesh Bhargava**, Retd, was commissioned in the Army AD in June 1983. He served for over 37 years and is an achiever in both academics and sports. He has done B Tech (Electronics), MBA Finance, MSc in Defence Studies, MSc in Weapon Systems & EW, DSSC, LGSC(O), and missile technology course.

He has been an instructor at Army AD College, commanded AD Unit in Western Theatre and Eastern Command AD Brigade, Director Coordination at Army AD Directorate, and Head of Arm in Northern Command.

He is a prolific writer and has made chapter contributions for three books. His articles have been published in CLAWS, IDSA, *The Financial Express*, and *The Print*.